THE
HOLOCAUST

THE HOLOCAUST: AN ANNOTATED BIBLIOGRAPHY

Second Edition

HARRY JAMES CARGAS

American Library Association

CHICAGO AND LONDON, 1985

Cover design by Natalie Wargin

Text composed by Jaymes Anne Rohrer
in Madeleine PS on a Tandy 2000
Personal Computer. Display type,
Times Roman, composed by Pearson
Typographers.

Printed on 50-pound Glatfelter,
a pH-neutral stock, and bound
in Bamberger Iris linen cloth
by Edwards Brothers, Inc.

Library of Congress Cataloging-in-Publication Data

Cargas, Harry J.
  The Holocaust.

  Includes indexes.
  1. Holocaust, Jewish (1939-1945)--Bibliography.
I. Title.
Z6374.H6C37   1985   016.94053'15'03924   85-20069
[D810.J4]
ISBN 0-8389-0433-5

This book is dedicated to my children

> Martin de Porres
> Joachim James
> Siena Catherine
> Manon Theresa
> Jacinta Teilhard
> Sarita Jo

and to the memory of the one million Jewish children whose lives were annulled in the Holocaust, as a reminder of the responsibility of the living to the dead--and to the yet unborn.

CONTENTS

PREFACE

The Holocaust is an obsession with me; I do not approach it dispassionately. I call myself a "post-Auschwitz Catholic" and regard the killing of millions of people in the death camps of Europe as one of the greatest Christian tragedies in history. I am particularly horrified by the murder of millions of Jewish people, victimized solely because they were Jews, and I am haunted by the fact that one million were children not yet in their teens. Thus, this bibliography is for me more than a research exercise. It is an attempt to create a tool for college students, the general public, and even upper-level high school students to use in studying the Holocaust. These students, along with seminarians and teachers, must not fail to study this enormous crime against humanity, must not ignore what happened, or society will not be able to create a better world for future generations. Hence, a sense of responsibility and urgency is in these pages.

Several factors about this book should, I think, be mentioned here. One is the use of the term "anti-Semitism." It is used here in the commonly accepted hyphenated form. This usage is incorrect for two reasons. First, the phrase generally denotes anti-Judaism, rather than something so broad as to encompass all Semitic peoples. Second, since there is no hyphenated term with an opposite meaning ("pro-Semitism"), the hyphen in common usage is not correct.

I should also mention here the rather awkward situation brought about by the need to describe several of my own books in this compilation; I have restrained myself from over-emphasizing them, as they are included here from necessity. Awkward, too, is the experience of analyzing books written by friends. The world of Holocaust scholarship is not large, and many who work in this area know and respect each other. Let me simply say that I have tried to be as fair as possible in all instances. In reviewing thousands of books over the years, in print and on the radio, I have, where I found it necessary, panned books written by my friends. That same independence, I hope, permeates these pages.

The annotations describe the books they accompany, of course. But, if sections of this volume are read through, they might themselves be seen as descriptions of the Holocaust, as well as chapters about books on the Holocaust. Hence, a few more editorial comments are found in these pages than usually appear in such volumes.

As mentioned, these titles, roughly 500 of them, have been selected for college and university libraries, for good public libraries, and for more sophisticated high school collections. Holocaust centers around the nation may benefit from the recommendations here, as well. Only books written in English and published in the United States are listed. Some titles are out of print, but most are available in larger libraries. Furthermore, a number of Holocaust books have been reissued, and so it is plausible to think that a number of those now out of print will eventually be reprinted.

I appreciate the cooperation of Judith Herschlag Muffs of the Anti-Defamation League of B'nai B'rith and of a group of people who have given me assistance on many projects throughout the years, the library staff at Webster University. They are Karen Luebbert and her staff, including Ann Moedritzer, Marilyn Berra, Mahala Cox, Betty Brookes, Eunice Hayes, Elaine Harvey, Maya Grach, Mary Baldas, and Sharon Newsom. These women have not only aided me--some for a decade and a half, always cheerfully and expertly-- but they also set a standard for librarians.

Margret Brown and Karen Cooper helped prepare the manuscript. Each proved once again to be wonderfully dependable and remarkably adept at reading unexemplary handwriting.

ANTI-SEMITISM AND THE RISE OF NAZISM

The materials in this chapter discuss the roots of Nazism and its rise in a cultured and educated part of modern Europe. Centuries of Western anti-Semitism and the German romanticism and idealism of the nineteenth century combined with the ethnic nationalism common in central Europe to produce the racial vision at the heart of Nazism. Analyses of politics and society clearly indicate that the defeat of Germany in World War I, combined with the national humiliation at Versailles and the ensuing depression, created a climate in which Nazi politics of fear and hate seized and expanded upon xenophobia and anti-Semitism as matters of policy. The books discussed here range from histories of anti-Semitism by Flannery and by Isaac to discussions of intellectual problems and ideology, as in the works of Lane and Mosse, to political histories and socio-logical studies of the Nazi party and of Germany in the early twen-tieth century. Also included is Pool and Pool's book on how Hitler's rise to power was financed by non-German Nazi supporters, Henry Ford among them.

Bracher, Karl Dietrich. The German Dictatorship. New York: Praeger, 1970. 553p.
Subtitled "The Origins, Structure, and Effects of National Socialism," this widely respected book by Karl Bracher, a German political scientist and historian, traces the roots of National Socialism to the nineteenth century and follows the development of its growth through its downfall. In an objective effort, the author gives excellent portraits of Hitler and his associates and provides credible psychological and sociological readings on how the Fuehrer was able to achieve his power.

1

Childers, Thomas. The Nazi Voter. Chapel Hill: Univ. of North
   Carolina Pr., 1984. 367p.
   The social foundations of fascism in Germany from 1919 to 1933
form the basis for this study. The Nazi constituency is examined,
including the party's formation and the social groups that composed
it, as are the conditions, promises, and much else. The author
concludes that the Nazi party's position during this period was
shaky, despite increased popularity, partly because the basis of
the electoral alliance was unstable, due to its appeal on the pseudo-
issues of dissatisfaction, resentment, and fear. "If the party's
support was a mile wide, it was at critical points an inch deep."
But, just as the party's electoral support began to falter, a new
chancellor was installed: Adolf Hitler.

Cohn, Norman. Warrant for Genocide. New York: Harper, 1967.
   303p.
   Cohn here describes the persistent myth concerning a Jewish
conspiracy to take over the world and the forgery known as The
Protocols of the Elders of Zion, and how they appealed to Hitler's
fanaticism. Tracing these lies as far back as the French Revolution, the author shows how they provided the basis for whole-
sale destruction of Jews during the Russian Civil War, how they
appealed to so many between the two World Wars, and how they
prepared the way for the Holocaust.

Dornberg, John. Munich 1923. New York: Harper, 1982. 385p.
   Hitler's attempted power grab in the famous beer hall putsch--
a move to take over the government of Bavaria--is detailed here in
a fascinating hour-by-hour history. It begins with a meeting in
a Munich apartment, during which the conspirators organized their
abortive plan, and ends with the trial that briefly put Hitler in
jail (where he wrote Mein Kampf). The anxiety written into the
narrative of the actual beer hall events creates an engaging tension.
Hitler's dramatic move to wrest control for himself and his storm
troops is described, as is the bloody aftermath. It is interesting
to note Hitler's revulsion at the resulting bloodshed. Portraits of
Goering, Hess, Himmler, and others enhance the value of this work.

Flannery, Edward H. The Anguish of the Jews. New York: Macmillan, 1965. 332p.
   Flannery, a Catholic priest, makes a case for the existence
of Christian anti-Semitism through the Holocaust. He begins this
disturbing history of anti-Semitism in ancient Greece and Egypt.
He shows that the Church Fathers often expressed hatred for Jews:
Martin Luther, Origen, Pope Innocent III--the list is unhappily long.
Church Councils are surveyed. The Inquisition, pogroms, and the
invented charge of blood libel against Jews are also given serious
scrutiny. More secular turns of anti-Semitism in such luminaries

as Goethe, Fichte, Wagner, Schleiermacher, H. S. Chamberlain, and the Nazis also receive attention. This thoughtful analysis of twenty-three centuries of anti-Semitism is a much needed work.

Hamilton, Richard. Who Voted for Hitler? Princeton, N.J.: Princeton Univ. Pr., 1982. 664p.
Hamilton, a sociologist at McGill University, skillfully answers the question asked in the title and looks into a parallel query as well: who financed Hitler and the Nazi party? He indicates that as crisis grew in Germany, the German middle, upper-middle, and upper classes abandoned former allegiances to support Hitler and his programs. Hamilton studied the voting records of fourteen cities, including Berlin, and clearly refutes the idea that the lower classes bear the major responsibility for boosting Hitler to power.

Isaac, Jules. The Teaching of Contempt. New York: Holt, 1964. 154p.
Ostensibly Christian nations slaughtered some 6,000,000 Jews solely because they were Jewish. Isaac, a French-Jewish historian who lost a wife, daughter, and other family members in the Holocaust, explores the culpability of the churches in this act of anti-Semitism. He finds that while "all authorities are agreed that a true Christian cannot be an anti-Semite...anti-Semitism is profoundly rooted in Christianity." Historically Christian churches have propagated three lies against the Jews. First, that the dispersion of the Jews in 70 A.D. was a divine punishment; second, that at the time of Jesus, Judaism was in a state of degeneration; and third, that the Jews are guilty of deicide. Isaac has been criticized for minor historical and theological errors, but his forceful message against Christian churches is both convincing and condemnatory.

Jarman, Thomas Leckie. Rise and Fall of Nazi Germany. New York: New York Univ. Pr., 1956. 388p.
Designed for the general reader, this history of the Third Reich reads easily. It is written with a commonsense objectivity and avoids sweeping generalizations. The author questions how a nation of some 80,000,000 intelligent inhabitants could have fallen under the spell of a dictator who would then involve most of the world in an international conflagration. Jarman traces the influence of history on German national character, the effects of the tensions between the Hohenstaufens and the papacy, the Reformation, France's centuries-long meddling in German affairs, the German problem of undefined frontiers, and the late arrival of Germany to nationhood. He shows how all of these have influenced the mind-set and spirit of twentieth-century Germans.

Lane, Barbara Miller, and Leila J. Rupp, eds. Nazi Ideology before 1933. Austin: Univ. of Texas Pr., 1978. 180p.

In their documentation, the editors conclude that while Nazi ideology was long in formation, some of it was formed on an almost hit-and-miss scale, as individuals pushed their own brands of totalitarianism, and was clearly inconsistent before Hitler became chancellor. This volume contains twenty-eight documents with helpful introductions by the editors, covering the political writings of Goebbels, Himmler, Rosenberg, Strasser, and others.

Mosse, George L.   The Crisis of German Ideology.   New York: Grosset, 1964. 373p.

Students studying the intellectual origins of the Third Reich would do well to begin with this presentation. The ideological roots of Nazism are thoroughly surveyed; the author discusses the development of what was to become Nazi thought from the early nineteenth century through World War II. One major focus is on education; another deals with the youth movement.

------.   Germans and Jews. New York: Howard Fertig, 1970. 260p.

A volume about the political right, left, and the search for a third way in pre-Nazi Germany, Mosse presents an anthology of essays on the anti-Semitism of the period, the impact of the German youth movement on young Jews, and various intellectual developments in Germany.

Patterson, Charles.   Anti-Semitism. New York: Walker, 1982. 160p.

While the author does not have an organized thesis, he effectively states his pivotal point: the Holocaust was not without its roots in history. He traces the history of the persecution of the Jews, discusses how the Nazis built on that tragic evolution, and looks at post-Holocaust evidence of continuing anti-Semitism.

Pool, James, and Suzanne Pool.   Who Financed Hitler.   New York: Doubleday, 1978. 535p.

Henry Ford was notoriously anti-Semitic and kept a photo of Hitler in his office. (He also helped to finance distribution of the phony anti-Semitic propaganda effort, The Protocols of the Elders of Zion.)   Ford, along with others such as the head of the Bank of England and the director of Royal Dutch Shell, were among Hitler's non-German financial backers. Details furnished by the authors about these contributors, as well as the German backers of the Nazi party, are documented here. Also presented is the idea that the abdication of King Edward VIII in London was due primarily to his pro-Nazi attitude, rather than to his wish to marry a divorced woman.

Schuman, Frederick Lewis.   The Nazi Dictatorship. 2nd ed. New York: Knopf, 1936. 508p.

Subtitled "A Study in Social Pathology and the Politics of Fascism," this early examination of Hitler's rise to power contains a great deal of information, although readers may be put off by the author's apparent belief not in collective German guilt but in a collective German condition of mental pathology. The author spent eight months in Germany in 1933 and writes in an exciting style, often from an eyewitness viewpoint. Some initial reviewers were critical of the author's anti-Hitler bias, but contemporary readers will appreciate Schuman's early insights that provide an unusual perspective of the budding Nazi period.

Stackelberg, Roderick. Idealism Debased. Kent, Ohio: Kent State Univ. Pr., 1981. 202p.

The connection between ethnic nationalism in Germany in the nineteenth century and the violent racism of Nazi National Socialism, with particular reference to the Jews, is expertly traced by Stackelberg. While he suggests that some of the earlier promoters of German xenophobia, such as Houston Stewart Chamberlain (British), would not have approved of the massacre of Jews, their rhetoric must cause them to share in the ultimate responsibility for the Holocaust. This is excellent background material for a study of Nazism's roots.

Vierek, Peter. Meta-politics. New York: Capricorn, 1961. 364p.

Subtitled "The Roots of the Nazi Mind," this book traces its subject through German romantic poetry, music, and social thought. Thomas Mann's important letter which closes this volume says that he (Mann) read it with "nearly complete approval and regards it as extraordinarily meritorious." The book indicts Hitler in terms of the Judaeo-Christian ethical traditions. The first edition appeared three months before Pearl Harbor (1941), and is remarkable for that fact alone. Vierek sees a constant in German history, that authority can be achieved only by employing authoritarianism. In fact, he writes: "In setting up metapolitics against politics, Germany deliberately turns her back on western civilization."

Wheaton, Eliot Barculo. Prelude to Calamity. New York: Doubleday, 1968. 523p.

Both the Weimar Republic and Hitler's rise to power are chronicled in solid detail in this very readable background work. Wheaton shows the judgmental errors of persons and groups that helped Hitler gain ascendancy; also shown are Hitler's luck and his unconscionable behavior including lies, bluffing, and Machiavellian acts to gain and retain power. Designed primarily for the general reader rather than the historian, this volume provides a good introduction to the background and beginning of the Nazi era, encompassing Hitler's first six months in command.

HISTORIES
OF THE
THIRD REICH
AND THE
HOLOCAUST

Books on the Third Reich and general histories of the Holocaust are collected in this chapter. Shirer's comprehensive history of World War II, Grunberger's social history of Nazi Germany, and Orlow's history of the Nazi party are described here. Several general histories and collected works on the Jewish Holocaust, especially those by Dawidowicz and Hilberg, appear, along with works on other groups that suffered under the Holocaust as described by Wytwytcky and by Rector. Chapter 14 contains collections of photographs, documents, and other resources that the reader will find useful in getting a broad grasp of the Jewish Holocaust.

Nazi policies for education and science are treated by Blackburn and Beyerchen, respectively, while Conway's book describes how Hitler undermined the Christian churches. Also discussed are a number of books on the Gestapo, the SS ("elite guard"), and on those industrialists in the Third Reich who made use of Jewish slave labor under the Nazis. Incredible, too, is Higham's detailing the cooperation of some U.S. industrialists with the Nazis, throughout the war. A few additional works on Third Reich culture are mentioned in chapter 12.

Titles on German resistance to Hitler, described in this chapter, complement the materials on Jewish resistance in chapter 7, and on help for Jewish victims found in chapter 8.

Baumont, Maurice, et al., eds. The Third Reich. New York: Praeger, 1955. 910p.
A study published under the auspices of the International Council for Philosophy and Humanistic Studies with the assistance of UNESCO, this anthology contains twenty-eight essays by reputable scholars from six nations on various facets of National Socialism,

its causes, and its place in history. While the book seems to lack a specific focus, each of the articles--from one 12 pages long to another that covers 109 pages--is otherwise an excellent contribution. This is the most authoritative of the relatively early works on Hitler's "Thousand Year Reich," which lasted barely a dozen years.

Beyerchen, Alan D. Scientists under Hitler. New Haven, Conn.: Yale Univ. Pr., 1977. 287p.

"The vast majority of the scientists under Hitler were neither anti-Nazi nor pro-Nazi. They were committed solely to independence in the conduct of professional affairs." While men like Einstein, Franck, Haber, Stern, and others resigned from their work to protest Hitler's policies, they in fact helped the Nazis to achieve their purpose, that of removing opponents from the scene. (At least twenty-five percent of all German academic physicists working in 1933 lost their posts under the Nazi regime.) Many of these exiles either worked on the Manhattan Project to construct the atom bomb or "participated in the British bomb project, which contributed significantly to the American effort." Aryan physics failed for two reasons: first, its adherents lacked success in obtaining backing from political sources (the highest Nazi leaders were simply unconcerned with academic physics); and second, those same adherents failed to gain the support of the professional physicists.

Blackburn, Gilmer W. Education in the Third Reich. Albany: State Univ. of New York Pr., 1984. 288p.

Perhaps the most far-reaching educational propaganda program ever undertaken was the massive effort to control the minds of the youth in Nazi Germany. The author shows how the past was manipulated to support contemporary racial theories; the organization and design of textbooks; the Nazi concept of the hero; the education of German women; Marxism and Christianity as ideological and spiritual enemies; and a great deal more. Blackburn indicates how not only the youth but their teachers as well caved in to simplified heroic legends and all-or-nothing comparisons.

Borkin, Joseph. The Crime and Punishment of I. G. Farben. New York: Pocket Bks., 1979. 322p.

Founded in 1925, I. G. Farben was a respected, huge (the largest industrial) company in Germany. It had patents for aspirin, a treatment for syphilis, and the processes to manufacture artificial rubber and petroleum. During the Nazi era, Farben enthusiastically mobilized to support the war effort. Building and operating the slave-labor camp at Auschwitz, this industrial giant contributed to the annihilation of thousands of prisoners, mostly Jews. The author emphasizes the fact that the officers at I. G. Farben were far from anti-Semitic; he provides letters that show industrial executives writing to exiled Jewish former coworkers, in the most friendly and respectful manner. Borkin also refutes the cliché that Farben's crimes against humanity were solely the responsibility of the Nazis, who eventually took over their operations.

Conway, J. S. The Nazi Persecution of the Churches, 1933-1945. New York: Basic Books, 1969. 474p.

Hitler's plan to undermine German churches was quite elaborate and clandestine, and had an enormous effect. Property was taken away from the churches; ministers were charged as criminals or sexual perverts; Christian trade organizations were abolished, as were Christian youth movements; the religious press was severely restricted; and thousands of priests and ministers were imprisoned. These actions were carried out in such a surreptitious manner that it took some five years for people to comprehend what was happening. Conway admits in his Preface that, although most of the numerous sources he used were incomplete, he searched through and was able to distill so much that "the main features of Nazi policy...are now apparent." Several books on the activities of the churches under the Third Reich are described in chapter 8.

Crankshaw, Edward. Gestapo. New York: Viking, 1956. 275p.

Subtitled "Instrument of Tyranny," this is the first major book-length study of the organization and activities of the Gestapo, the dreaded implementation arm of certain of Hitler's policies. It is more than a look at the bureaucracy, however, as the men who administered it are introduced in some detail. As the subtitle indicates, the author's approach contains an emotional element, and Crankshaw is guilty of some broad generalizations. He has also been faulted for some errors in military history, but the volume is certainly worthwhile.

Dawidowicz, Lucy S. The War against the Jews 1933-1945. New York: Bantam, 1976. 610p.

"Written with eerie restraint," as one critic noted, this volume holds that the Nazis were more concerned with destroying Jews than with winning the war against the Allies. This exhaustive history addresses itself to three major questions: (1) How was it possible for a modern state to attempt the systematic murder of a whole people? (2) How was it possible for a whole people to "allow itself to be destroyed?" (3) How was it possible for the entire world to stand by without attempting to stop the killings? Dawidowicz writes of Hitler, his background, and German anti-Semitism in general; of the failure of intellectuals, lawyers, and judges to act with honor during the period; and the mobilization of the entire police and military establishment against the Jews. The conduct of the war and the employment of concentration camps lead to an analysis of the Holocaust. In an illuminating appendix, the author indicates the fate of the Jews in Europe, country by country.

Delarue, Jacques. The Gestapo. New York: Morrow, 1964. 384p.
    In one sense this volume lives up to its subtitle: "A History
of Horror," as many of the worst acts of the Gestapo are chronicled
here, particularly the atrocities done in France (where the author
was active in the French Resistance). Delarue has, however, been
criticized for failing to go beyond the facts alone to discuss their
meaning. For instance, how could the Nazis gain power in a nation
like Germany? Nor is the question of the totalitarian nature of
this military group addressed. The book is written with detachment
and has a series of supportive photographs.

Eisenberg, Azriel, ed. Witness to the Holocaust. New York: Pilgrim
    Pr., 1981. 649p.
    Representative writings from women and men who experienced the
very beginning of Nazi atrocities are compiled here, with valuable
introductions to each of the volume's twenty-seven chapters done
by the editor. Books, journals, diaries, and letters by concentration camp inmates or sympathetic supporters of the sufferers
present a useful picture of many aspects of the Holocaust. Early
fears of Hitler's rising influence are expressed, as descriptions
of the various terrorist groups (such as the Gestapo and the SS)
appear. Death camps are depicted, as is the resistance of the
heavily outgunned Jewish partisans. Particularly painful is the
story of children and how they fared. This work also extends
beyond the war, concerning itself with the problems of Jews in
Germany in the aftermath.

Ferencz, Benjamin B. Less than Slaves. Cambridge, Mass.: Harvard
    Univ. Pr., 1979. 249p.
    The title refers to the hundreds of thousands of men and women
who were forced to work in German industries during the Second
World War; most were Jews. All were used, as one survivor accurately
stated, "like a bit of sandpaper which, rubbed a few times, becomes
useless and is thrown away to be burned with the garbage." While
the machinery in factories was well cared for, the victims, once
exhausted, were annihilated. This book clearly demonstrates the
responsibility of the industrialists for this aspect of inhumanity;
they paid the SS for the privilege of leasing the laborers. Ferencz
himself worked for years attempting to require German companies to
compensate some 14,878 surviving Jewish workers. A few paid little, some only hoping to gain certain postwar business advantages.
On the whole, however, German industrialists were barely punished
for their crimes.

Galante, Pierre, and Eugene Silianoff. Operation Valkyrie. New
    York: Harper, 1982. 255p.
    Two Frenchmen here relate stories of German opposition to Hitler,
even among highly placed military personnel, from as early as the

mid-1930s. "Operation Valkyrie" was a plot to remove the Fuehrer, based on a Hitler-approved plan indicating procedures for how the Wehrmacht would step in if he died. In the 1940s arguments ranged from whether to arrest and try Hitler to whether to assassinate him. In March, 1943, bombs placed aboard Hitler's airplane failed to explode; ten days later, explosives requiring ten minutes to detonate failed when Hitler left the area after only eight minutes. In yet another instance, explosives designed to be used against Hitler were destroyed in an Allied bombing raid. These and other such incidents are related in detail, as is the sweeping revenge taken upon the plotters not long before the war's end.

Grunberger, Richard. The 12-Year Reich. New York: Holt, 1971. 535p.
A social history of Nazi Germany from 1933 to 1945, this book provides a comprehensive view of education under Hitler as well as justice, business, press and radio, religion, art, literature, music, the civil service, the army, Nazi speech, and much else. Completely documented, filled with anecdotes, and very readable, this is an excellent introduction to the milieu of wartime Germany. The final chapter, chapter 30, discusses the Jews: the author concludes his detailed analysis by writing that "without anti-Semitism, Nazism would have been inconceivable, both as an ideology and as a catalyst of emotions." Concerning those who claimed moral innocence regarding their government's Jewish policy, Grunberger says: "Had German wartime indifference to the Jewish catastrophe merely been due to ignorance, post-war revelations would have stirred far greater shock waves."

Grunfeld, Frederic V. The Hitler File. New York: Random, 1974. 374p.
An "easy" social history of Germany from the end of the First World War to the conclusion of World War II in 1945, this is basically a pictorial account. The book contains some 800 illustrations (48 pages in color), and includes replications of art works, posters, propaganda cartoons, etc.

Higham, Charles. Trading with the Enemy. New York: Delacorte, 1983. 277p.
Dealing only tangentially with the Holocaust, this work on a sordid aspect of history is important for an understanding of the wider picture. It is an exposé of American businesses that continued to work "as usual" with the Germans during World War II. Top officials of ITT, Ford, Standard Oil of New Jersey, and the Chase Bank, as well as several ambassadors and men in cabinet posts, were guilty of such practices. The protection of Nazi criminals after the war by their U.S. business associates in high places is also discussed.

Hilberg, Raul. The Destruction of the European Jews. New York:
Watts, 1973. 790p.
Perhaps the most comprehensive of the single-volume histories,
Hilberg's deals with what he terms the third of three historical
anti-Semitic policies, annihilation (conversion and expulsion were
the others). Precedents to the Nazi terror are first considered,
followed by a tremendously detailed analysis of the destruction
process. The humiliation of Jews, their ghettoization, followed
by the deportations and killing operations are documented with pre-
cision. Hilberg's accumulation of facts about the Holocaust makes
this an outstanding book.

Hillel, Marc, and Clarissa Henry. Of Pure Blood. New York:
McGraw-Hill, 1976. 256p.
An organization in Nazi Germany called Fountain of Life (Lebens-
born) was dedicated to assisting in the plan to produce a master
race. A major part of the activities of this group included identi-
fying "racially valuable" children, then kidnapping them--whether
they lived in Germany or other parts of Europe--for breeding purposes. It is believed that nearly a quarter of a million boys and
girls were abducted from Poland alone.

Hoffman, Peter. The History of the German Resistance 1933-1945.
Boston: M.I.T. Pr., 1977. 847p.
Occasionally a book appears to be so definitive that it is immediately recognized as the work in its field; this is one such
volume. Hoffman explores nearly every aspect of resistance to Hitler and the Nazis. He presents the background of the opposition
to Hitler, the Sudeten crisis and attempted coup of 1938, and subsequent plans to overthrow the Fuehrer, including a number of attempts on his life from 1933 to 1942. This is an extremely valuable reference tool with a large bibliography, good situation maps,
command chains, diagrams of communications, and a comprehensive index. Hoffmann is objective in his analysis of both situations and
individuals; even those deeply involved with the struggle against
Hitler are criticized if the author deems it appropriate.

Hohne, Heinz. The Order of the Death's Head. New York: Coward,
1970. 690p.
Tremendous scholarship marks this somewhat overlong book, a
study of the Nazi SS organization that helped keep Hitler in power
by destroying opposition and that enforced the massacre of nearly six
million Jews and possibly a like number of Gentiles. The findings
here are based on interviews with hundreds of people closely con-
nected with SS activities, on the files of Himmler's personal staff
and the Reich Security Office, on the central archives of the National Socialist party, on the diaries of important personnel in the
state ministries and, of course, on the records of the Nuremberg

Trials. This book is a collection of a series of pieces that appeared in twenty-two issues of Der Spiegel (1966-67) on a subject that was forbidden to German historians after the war.

The Jewish Communities of Nazi-Occupied Europe. New York: Howard Fertig, 1982. 432p.

Detailed reports on the Jewish communities of seventeen nations under Nazi domination make up this book. Originally prepared for the U.S. government in 1944, the reports present a wide range of data about these social groups from prewar years through much of the Holocaust period. Here are some of the topics covered: Jewish political activities, the anti-Semitic press, concentration camps, anti-Semitic laws, medicine, births, deaths, marriages, commerce, industry, banking, trade unions, Jewish religious organizations-- in brief, a wealth of valuable material.

Koehl, Robert Lewis. The Black Corps. Madison: Univ. of Wisconsin Pr., 1983. 274p.

The structure and power struggles of the Nazi SS are traced in this book. Koehl follows the development of this destructive institution from its beginnings as watchdog of the Nazi party to one of the most powerful forces of its kind in the world. It is probably fair to conclude that without the SS, the "Final Solution" would have made little headway. With its success against the Jews as a means, the SS expanded its power into other aspects of the Third Reich.

Levin, Nora. The Holocaust. New York: Schocken, 1973. 768p.

The most readable of the one-volume histories, this well organized work is an excellent text. After an overview of the past, Hitler's career, the situation of Jews in Germany, the beginning of World War II, the ghettoization of Jews, the "Final Solution" to the "Jewish problem" and Jewish resistance to the Nazis, Levin describes the deportation and fate of European Jews, nation by nation. The tragedy of Romania, as well as the heroism in Denmark, are contrasted, as are the courage of Bulgaria's Metropolitan Stefan and the hypocrisy of Romania's Ion Antonescu. Generous, moving quotes from appropriate documents are neatly interwoven into the body of this admirable history.

Merkl, Peter H. The Making of a Stormtrooper. Princeton, N.J.: Princeton Univ. Pr., 1980. 328p.

According to the highly respected political scientist Peter Merkl, had it not been for the riotous youth who became the SA (storm troopers), Hitler would never have come to power. Hence, the study of this group is quite important. Among the approximately three dozen Fascist movements in twenty-one European countries between the two world wars, all were somehow affected by World

War I, the Russian Revolution, and the Great Depression, but the Nazi movement followed its own particular course. Those who joined the SA were quite young and many had been members of religious youth groups. Many were unemployed, abandoned by their fathers, of low education and initially not strongly anti-Semitic. The storm troopers were only one of several militant groups in Germany during Hitler's rise; they were eventually edged out in prestige by the SS.

Mosse, George L., ed. Nazi Culture. New York: Schocken, 1981. 432p.
   This illustrated anthology gives a reasonable overview of the intellectual, cultural, and social life in the Third Reich. Much material about the Gestapo is included, as is a wide variety of pieces ranging from a Nazi child's prayer to an excerpt from Joseph Goebbels's novel. The totality and scope of this work make it worthwhile.

Neumann, Peter (pseud.). Black March. New York: Sloan, 1959. 312p.
   Written in journal style, this is the personal story of an SS man. He tells of his indoctrination in the Hitler youth program, of his training as an SS officer, and of his experiences in the war until captured by the Russians. The description of violent combat scenes appear to be authentic, although the authenticity has been questioned by critics who suggest that such a diary could not have survived the author's Russian experiences. Others believe the work to have been composed, or at least reconstructed, after the events described. A valuable appendix outlines the hierarchies of the Nazi Youth Organization and the SS.

Orlow, Dietrich. The History of the Nazi Party. vol. 1, 1919-1933 (1969, 388p.); vol. 2, 1933-1945 (1973, 538p.). Pittsburgh: Univ. of Pittsburgh Pr.
   Orlow provides the most comprehensive history of the Nazi party available in English. The first volume treats the organization of the party, its administrative history, and rise to power. The author expertly analyzes how the party developed its totalitarian policies in the midst of a pluralistic society. The longer, second volume concentrates on how Nazi policies were implemented, how power was gained and held, and how the party met the challenges of new vicissitudes, such as the need to administer new conquered territories.

Rector, Frank. The Nazi Extermination of Homosexuals. New York: Stein & Day, 1981. 189p.
   The Nazi persecution of homosexuals is one aspect of the Holocaust that is rarely discussed. For instance, the fact that a significant number of early members of the Nazi party were homosexuals

has seldom been mentioned. Rector's account of the program to destroy all homosexuals and transvestites tells much of the brutal story, such as the chopping off of limbs without anesthetic to determine the effects of battlefield wounds. In general the author does an adequate job with this segment of history. After the war, a homosexual life-style remained a crime in West Germany.

Reitlinger, Gerald Roberts. <u>Final Solution</u>. New York: Barnes, 1953. 622p.

Reitlinger, an English historian, here provides one of the earlier, authoritative books on the Holocaust. The evolution of events and the mechanics implementing the attempt to annihilate the Jews of Europe is described; the author does not attempt to remain objectively aloof from his subject, but is able to achieve an admirable balance between grief and detachment.

------. <u>The SS</u>. New York: Viking, 1957. 502p.

The SS began as a police group with a limited number (perhaps 200 men); within a decade it had grown to half a million and formed one of history's most notorious groups. The members of this organization were so vicious that they frequently plotted to eliminate each other. The personalities that emerge in this book include Hitler, Goering (Hitler's heir apparent), von Ribbentrop (minister for Foreign Affairs), Bormann (Hitler's private secretary), Field Marshal Wilhelm Keitel, and others. This is solid history with excellent detail.

Remak, Joachim, ed. <u>The Nazi Years</u>. Englewood Cliffs, N.J.: Prentice-Hall, 1969. 178p.

Designed as a supplementary text for college courses, this anthology of documents covers the Nazi party's beginning and growth. The emphasis is on the ideological content of Nazism and includes sections on anti-Semitism, resistance to the Nazis, eugenics, and occupation policy. The editor's narrative is helpful in integrating the various pieces. Foreign policy and World War II itself are given fleeting attention but, since most of the sources here are unavailable elsewhere in English, this is nonetheless a useful compendium.

Roper, Edith, and Clara Leiser. <u>Skeleton of Justice</u>. New York: Dutton, 1941. 346p.

The consolidation of Hitler's power was helped by the active assistance of many professional people. Sociologists supported his racial theories; doctors performed medical experiments on prisoners; teachers taught anti-Semitism. In this book, written before the outbreak of World War II, those who participated in the administration of justice in Germany are criticized for their moral corruption. Roper was one of a handful of newspaper correspondents permitted access to trials in Germany and allowed to report on them. While not a lawyer (the main drawback of an otherwise important book), Roper renders chapter and verse regarding the perversion of law in the Third Reich. Many political and religious trials, as well as those involving juvenile crimes, are noted; responsibility for what happened in the courts went to the very top of the system, the minister of Justice. The author tricked the Nazis into letting her get her data, the basis for this volume, out of the country.

Schleunes, Karl. The Twisted Road to Auschwitz. Champaign: Univ. of Illinois Pr., 1971. 280p.

Well researched, this study shows how little the Nazis actually knew about Jews before they began their persecution. There was, for instance, no set anti-Semitic policy when the Nazis came to power in 1933. Often followers of Hitler acted toward the Jews in ways that would fit their own anti-Semitic aims; sometimes such moves contradicted those of other ranking Nazis. This confusing situation lasted until 1938, when the enormous pogrom of that time dictated to the German hierarchy that a single approach to the "Jewish problem" was essential.

Shirer, William L. The Rise and Fall of the Third Reich. New York: Simon & Schuster, 1960. 1,245p.

This voluminous work is aptly titled; it deals with nearly every aspect of Hitler's Germany, from the Nazi beginnings to the last days. There appears to be a consensus that this is the one best work on this subject. From Hitler's ascension to power to the conquest of Germany by the Allies; from Versailles to destruction (the mythologically anticipated Goetterdaemmerung, as Shirer sees it); from the rape of Austria through Czechoslovakia, Denmark, Norway, the attacks on Great Britain, Russia, Africa--and so much else--the book provides authoritative, documented history. While there is no specific section dealing with the Holocaust, there is much here on Nazi persecutions of Jews, propaganda, medical experiments, the murder program, slave labor, and racial laws.

Snyder, Louis L., ed. Hitler's Third Reich. Chicago: Nelson-Hall, 1981. 640p.

Over 140 selections, ranging from 1918 to 1946, from a segment of the Versailles Treaty (imposing conditions on a defeated Germany in World War I) to a piece reporting on the executions after the Nuremberg Trials, make up this documentary history. Speeches by Hitler are recorded, as are anti-Semitic Civil Service resolutions, racial laws, and much else. But there are lapses as well; there is nothing on the Warsaw Ghetto uprising, for example. While the book is uneven, it does contain much not otherwise readily available to general readers.

Sydnor, Charles W., Jr. Soldiers of Destruction. Princeton,
     N.J.: Princeton Univ. Pr., 1977. 371p.
     The SS Death's Head Division in the years from 1933 to 1945 is
treated to a precise scrutiny in this study. It was, assuredly,
one of history's most powerful and destructive military units. The
author draws on a wide variety of SS manuscript materials as well
as captured German army documents for his analysis. Special attention
is given to the brutal training of the prewar SS camp guards as a
wartime creed was being developed. The founder of the Death's Head
Division, Theodor Eicke, is portrayed in all of his ruthless fanaticism. Sydnor finds no evidence that Eicke or any of the men whose
careers he molded "ever questioned or refused to act in accordance
with the racial and ideological principles of the SS."

Taylor, Telford. Sword and Swastika. New York: Simon & Schuster,
     1952. 431p.
     Taylor, the chief counsel for the prosecution at the Nuremberg
Trials, recounts the history of Germany from the Versailles Treaty
to that nation's invasion of Poland. How the Weimar Republic was
undermined, how the aging Hindenberg was deceived, and ultimately
how Hitler's Nazis achieved power are the major elements of this
work. Hitler, Himmler, and Goering are the main characters in a
thoroughly researched drama. The sinister plotting of business mag-
nates and the scheming of generals and Fascists make a fascinating story.

Wytwycky, Bohdan. The Other Holocaust. Washington, D.C.: Novak
     Report on the New Ethnicity, 1980. 96p.
     Without any attempt to diminish the uniqueness of the Jewish
experience, this book tells the story of some of the other victims
of Nazi aggression. Gypsies, Poles, and others--all who suffered--
have their stories told here. This little work closes with a plea
for all to work for humane ends.

BIOGRAPHIES AND MEMOIRS OF HITLER AND OTHER NAZIS

Adolf Hitler is one of the most puzzling figures in all of history, and the amount of material written on him supports that judgment. Most of the biographical and autobiographical works here are about him. Represented, too, are many of the major names of the Nazi era: Goebbels, Heydrich, Bormann, Himmler, Streicher, Hess, Goering, Speer, and others. Some of these entries are devoted to one figure, others (such as The Face of the Third Reich) deal with a number of persons. In all, these present the many facets of the leaders of the Third Reich.

COLLECTED BIOGRAPHIES

Fest, Joachim C. The Face of the Third Reich. New York: Pantheon, 1977. 402p.

Portraits of Nazi leaders are provided in this work. The most pages, naturally, are devoted to Adolf Hitler, whose path from a men's hostel to the Reich chancellery is traced. Next are sketches of the practitioners and technicians of totalitarian rule, including Hermann Goering, the second in command; Joseph Goebbels, the genius of propaganda; the apparently civilized Heinrich Himmler, whose SS power led him to assert that "it really makes no odds to us if we kill someone." Lesser figures like Hans Frank ("We must not be squeamish when we hear the figure of 17,000 shot") and Baldur von Schirach ("we simply believed"), as well as the officer corps in general and women in the Third Reich--so drastically manipulated--are also portrayed in this wide-ranging, highly intelligent synthesis.

Institut fur Zeitgeschichte, Munich. <u>Anatomy of the SS State</u>.
New York: Walker, 1968. 614p.

In the well publicized Frankfurt trials of the major SS officers who were assigned to Auschwitz, held from 1963 to 1965, many
details of that death camp were elicited through the testimony.
Much of the information here sheds light on how the Jews were actually treated, how the camp was operated, how the SS went about
their duties, and much else. The slaughter of Russian prisoners
is another frightful topic in this solid history.

Speer, Albert. <u>Spandau</u>. New York: Macmillan, 1976. 463p.

The armaments minister and second-ranking man in the Third Reich
kept a secret diary while imprisoned by the Allies for twenty years.
This book is an edited (and somewhat rearranged) version of that
record. Much of it deals with the tediousness of prison life, but
it is important for the human portraits of the seven (and only)
former Nazi inmates in the entire institution. Grand Admiral Karl
Doenitz believed that he was still the legal head of the German government; Deputy Fuehrer Rudolf Hess hoarded other prisoners' socks
and moaned, often entire nights, that the guards had poisoned his
milk; others quarreled interminably over petty protocol. Perhaps
most intriguing is Speer's insistence that historians misunderstand
Hitler if they consider only the raging dictator: "This seems to
me a false and dangerous course. If the human features are going
to be missing from the portrait of Hitler, if his persuasiveness,
his engaging characteristics and even the Austrian charm he could
trot out are left out of the reckoning, no picture of him will be
achieved." Speer's apparently unresolved problem of his own responsibility for his cooperation with Hitler is not satisfying.

KLAUS BARBIE

Bower, Tom. <u>Klaus Barbie</u>. New York: Pantheon, 1984. 255p.

Barbie's name became familiar in 1983 when it was revealed that,
after his escape from prosecution for war crimes, he became a paid
informer for U.S. secret operatives. Charged with numerous atrocities, Barbie is shown as a member of an SS team, the head of the
Gestapo in occupied Lyons; as a fugitive, a spy for the United States
(at $1,700 a month); and as a recently captured man finally located
in Bolivia through the efforts of Nazi hunters Beate and Serge
Klarsfeld. One of the many sad aspects of this story is the revela-
tion of the degree of cooperation Barbie, known as the "Butcher of
Lyons," received from French collaborators, who aided him in his
program of terror and murder.

Murphy, Brendan. <u>The Butcher of Lyon</u>. New York: Empire Books,
1983. 330p.

When he was Gestapo chief in Lyons, France, Klaus Barbie used his power to destroy many people. The author says of Barbie that "he was one of those who pulled the trigger and shed blood." That aspect of Barbie's life is a grim enough story, but also important is the story of how the "Butcher of Lyons" managed to escape prosecution by the Allies after the war by the complicity of French collaborators, the American Counterintelligence Corps, and Bolivian political and military leaders. Written before Barbie was to be brought to trial in Lyons, this is yet another example of many such instances in which Nazis were helped to evade prosecution in return for their assistance in fighting communism.

MARTIN BORMANN

Lang, Jochen von. The Secretary. New York: Random, 1979. 430p.
Martin Bormann was clearly Hitler's most unquestioningly loyal, high-ranking follower; he did whatever the Fuehrer asked of him. The author calls him "the indispensable assistant, the sly instigator of policy, the executor of both details and dirty work." For his participation in Nazi crimes, Bormann was tried in absentia and condemned to death. Frequent reports of his appearance in several South American nations have surfaced, but the author, through rigorous investigative procedures, has proven that his subject perished in 1945. Bormann's rise to power, from a convicted criminal (manslaughter) to a convicted mass murderer (posthumously), is further evidence of a society in which the lawless themselves were the law.

McGovern, James. Martin Bormann. New York: Morrow, 1968. 237p.
Because the writer of this biography was a Central Intelligence Agency (CIA) agent assigned to investigate the case of Bormann and his disappearance at the end of World War II, McGovern had access to information that makes this a valuable presentation. Bormann was Hitler's private secretary and, as the Third Reich declined, became the number two power in the country. A convicted murderer who rose steadily in the Nazi hierarchy, he eventually was sentenced to death in absentia at the Nuremberg Trials.

Manning, Paul. Martin Bormann. New York: Stuart, 1981. 320p.
Irrefutable evidence is available that Martin Bormann died as the Second World War came to a close. If true, this book, subtitled "Nazi in Exile," is rather meaningless. The author claims that at the time of writing, the man who held the second spot in Hitler's hierarchy lived in a luxurious estate in Argentina. Manning interviewed hosts of people who provided anonymous information and studied countless archives and documents to prove that Bormann had established an enormous financial base in South America. The book fails to convince.

JOSEPH GOEBBELS

Boelcke, Willi A., ed. The Secret Conferences of Dr. Goebbels.
New York: Dutton, 1971. 364p.
Much of Hitler's success can be traced to Joseph Goebbels's
application of exploitative propaganda techniques. Slant the truth,
use simplified points, and constantly repeat them--such was his
method. But this book holds that Goebbels never had an overall
approach to his work. He frequently contradicted his own procedures and kept far too tight a reign on the press, radio, leaflets,
rumor campaigns, etc. Nearly all of the words recorded in this
volume are those of Goebbels himself. How he attempted to manipulate people is fascinating not only to students of World War II
but to those interested in how advertising and public relations
(sometimes) work.

Bransted, Ernest. Goebbels and National Socialist Propaganda,
1925-1945. East Lansing: Michigan State Univ. Pr., 1964. 488p.
How was the image of Adolf Hitler projected to the German people? What was the plan to effectively denounce Jews in Nazi Germany? In what manner was Great Britain presented to the German
citizenry? These and other important topics are scrutinized in this
book that deals with an important aspect of Hitler's regime. The
author says that he is not attempting a biography of the Nazi propaganda minister, but "I have endeavored to throw new light on the
development of the themes and the machinery of National Socialist
Propaganda, to analyze characteristic attitudes and methods employed
by Goebbels and his subordinates in the changing circumstances of
two decades and to examine the objectives and targets of their propaganda." Bransted's success provides an important historical work.

Goebbels, Joseph. Final Entries: 1945. New York: Putnam, 1978.
368p.
Joseph Goebbels was Adolf Hitler's propaganda minister. His
media machine created the myth of Hitler the Superman, Hitler the
Savior of Germany. Goebbels would do anything to advance the Nazi
cause, from telling lies to hanging generals on meathooks and film-
ing their strangulation. This Goebbels diary contains a great deal
of information about what really went on in the German hierarchy
during the last months of World War II. Goebbels was officially
appointed the Fuehrer's minister for Propaganda and Enlightenment,
and his manipulation of news and his mob oratory helped prove Hitler's belief that the greater the lie, the better the chance it
would be believed. "The fundamental principle of all propaganda,"
he once noted, was "the repetition of effective arguments." Goebbels's contempt for human gullibility equaled that of Adolf Hitler.
His only fear was of intellectuals; propaganda must not be aimed
at converting intellectuals, he believed, since they would never be

won over. It was the average person in the street Goebbels was seeking to convince. See also the following entry for Goebbels's earlier diaries.

------. The Goebbels Diaries, 1939-1941. New York: Putnam,
   1983. 490p.
This diary opens during the first flush of Nazi victories over France, Norway, Holland, Belgium, and Denmark, and ends with the German forces in a superior position on the Russian front. The tone is very upbeat as the reader watches Goebbels grow from the insecure person found in the early pages into a man confident of his power, enjoying his skills and the favor of his beloved Fuehrer. Not written for publication, these entries show Goebbels's satanic personal efforts, as well as the competition among various Nazis for the best leadership positions in the coming Germanic world empire.

Heiber, Helmut. Goebbels. New York: Da Capo, 1983. 393p.
Well written and readable, this biography of the Nazi minister of propaganda is an excellent companion work to Goebbels's own diaries. The subject is shown to be an opportunist, one convinced by his own propaganda about the aims and invincibility of the Nazi cause.

Herzstein, Robert Edwin. The War That Hitler Won. New York:
   Putnam, 1978. 491p.
With an eye-catching, though misleading, title, this work describes how Joseph Goebbels, Nazi minister of propaganda, helped control the German populace through media management and manipulation. Goebbels wrote in his diary that "news policy is a weapon of war. Its purpose is to wage war and not to give out information." Film, too, was seen as a major tool for structuring thought. Newsreels, as well as more sentimental productions, were used by Goebbels who commissioned approximately 1300 of them. A good, brief biography of Goebbels is included; the political infighting he experienced (with von Ribbentrop, Rosenberg, Bormann, and others) is also rendered with some care. The author uses both German and American sources.

Manvell, Roger, and Heinrich Fraenkel. Dr. Goebbels. New York:
   Simon & Schuster, 1960. 306p.
The life and career of the propaganda minister for the Nazis is placed in the context of World War II and the events that led up to it. The authors do not create a chronology, but instead reconstruct the mental climate of Germany during the period under discussion. Good use is made of letters, diaries, and interviews with those who knew Goebbels. It is interesting to see how this man, so fascinated by Adolf Hitler, was himself so fascinating to others. Whether or not the relevance of the social background of the era before the Nazis is adequately presented here may, however, be questioned.

HERMANN GOERING

Mosley, Leonard. The Reich Marshal. New York: Dell, 1975. 476p.

Hermann Goering was Hitler's highest aide, the number two man in the Nazi hierarchy. He was a World War I air ace who created the German Luftwaffe; he practically designed the German economy and was a tremendous political intriguer. But he was also a dandy, gluttonous and greedy on many levels (particularly in the area of art collecting). Goering worshipped Hitler but had difficulty dealing with others in the Nazi party, especially propaganda minister Goebbels (in fact, Goebbels tapped Goering's amorous telephone conversations and reported them to Hitler). This book tells a great deal about the Nazi party and important individuals within it.

RUDOLF HOESS

Hoess, Rudolf. Commandant of Auschwitz. New York: Popular Library, 1961. 240p.

The confession of perhaps the one person in history who can honestly claim personal responsibility for more murders than anyone else forms the content of this book. The author wrote, before his execution, that he arranged for the gassing of 2,000,000 persons in a two-and-one-half-year period. He describes the life of the starving prisoners; of Russians who killed and devoured their comrades; of atrocities committed by guards; of imaginative tortures of Jews; of the attempts to psychologically destroy victims before killing them; and justified all only on the ground of following orders. To disobey? "I do not believe that of all the thousands of SS officers there could have been found a single one capable of such a thought."

REINHARD HEYDRICH

Deschner, Gunther. Reinhard Heydrich. Briarcliff Manor, N.Y.: Stein & Day, 1981. 351p.

An efficient organizer of mass destruction, Heydrich worked under Himmler to direct the secret police force. An "all-German boy," this blond physical specimen was an accomplished musician with some intellectual pretensions. He used the British practice of hiring intelligent servicemen to help him in his enforcement work. Heydrich was not politically motivated and Nazi sloganeering left him unmoved. Rather, he looked for success through jobs well done and worked to protect the German state, with which he identified very closely.

Wighton, Charles. Heydrich, Hitler's Most Evil Henchman. New
    York: Chilton, 1963. 288p.
    To compare degrees of wicked behavior, as the title of this
volume implies, is futile. Reinhard Heydrich was the chief of
the Nazi secret police and Hitler's viceroy in Czechoslovakia
when he was assassinated. In reaction, Hitler personally ordered
the total destruction of the Czech village of Lidice, including
the annihilation of the entire male population. This biography
is based on extensive research but contains a great deal of specu-
lative suggestion, which weakens the author's case considerably.

HEINRICH HIMMLER

Smith, Bradley. Heinrich Himmler. Stanford, Calif.: Hoover
    Institution Pr., 1971. 211p.
    Centering on the years 1900-26, Smith portrays a Nazi in the
making. Himmler, head of the SS, was raised in a devout Christian
household and became a cruel yet squeamish person. He took part
in the famed and unsuccessful attempt to overthrow the Bavarian
government in what has become known as the beer-hall putsch after
serving as business manager of the National Socialist party. He
was also a leading propaganda agent for the party before he was
promoted.

ADOLF HITLER

Binion, Rudolph. Hitler among the Germans. DeKalb: Northern
    Illinois Univ. Pr., 1984. 207p.
    For those who question the value of psychohistory, this book
will serve as a red flag; others will find it fascinating, at least
in its imaginativeness. The author traces Hitler's anti-Semitism
to his traumatization by poison gas in World War I. That event,
according to Binion, activated the repressed memory of an earlier
trauma, when Hitler's mother was "poisoned" by a Jewish doctor treating her for cancer. This trauma, the author claims, merged by Hitler
with Germany's national sense of trauma, led inevitably to disaster.

Bromberg, Norbert, and Verna Volz Small. Hitler's Psychotherapy.
    Edison, N.J.: International Universities Pr., 1984. 335p.
    Drawing on recent studies of narcissistic and borderline per-
sonality disorders, the authors attempt to conceptualize Hitler's
psychopathology in a comprehensive assessment of his psychological
functioning. They offer new speculations on Hitler's relationship
with a mysterious "Stefanie" as well as the intensity of his anti-
Semitism. Chapter topics include Hitler's sense of guilt and shame;
the influence of his mother; Hitler's personality development; con-

sequences of psychopathological traits for his political career; his anti-Semitism, etc.

Churchill, Allen, ed. Eyewitness: Hitler. New York: Walker, 1979. 228p.

How did contemporaries perceive Hitler at the time of his power? A number of famous people are represented in this anthology of approximately fifty articles from Liberty, a periodical that relished controversy. Soon after Hitler assumed leadership in 1933, Liberty began covering him. A variety of material is included that ranges in quality from near gossip, in an exposé by a former maid, to high journalism by John Gunther and William L. Shirer. Personal views of the Fuehrer by Gandhi, G. B. Shaw, and Neville Chamberlain make excellent reading. Others who appear in this collection include Charles de Gaulle, Anthony Eden, and Winston Churchill. Pastor Martin Niemoeller's "Conversations with Hitler" is a highlight.

Fest, Joachim C. Hitler. New York: Harcourt, 1974. 844p.

A biography of a period as well as a man, this is one of the most important works on Hitler. The analyses of German politics during the period before the Nazi era, and of the Nazi times themselves, are outstanding.

Fleming, Gerald. Hitler and the Final Solution. Berkeley: Univ. of California Pr., 1984. 219p.

In the highly controversial Hitler's War, David Irving attempts to show that the Nazi leader was not to blame for the Holocaust: rather, subordinates were at fault for the massacre of European Jews. Gerald Fleming puts that error to rest in Hitler and the Final Solution, a book based on enormous scholarship, meticulous attention to detail, and an excellent use of documents and interviews. Fleming is not the first to rebut Irving, but he is the most authoritative. He even gained access to Soviet archives in Riga, a rare coup. Hitler's statements, letters, speeches, references to his comments and those of others in documents, memoranda, letters, and recalled conversations overwhelmingly prove the author's thesis: Hitler not only knew of but initiated the attempt to annihilate European Jewry.

Goebbels, Joseph, et al. Adolf Hitler. 1931-1935. New York: Peebles Pr., 1978. 145p.

This Nazi propaganda volume was distributed throughout Germany in 1936. One hundred photographs showing the Fuehrer in formal as well as informal postures are of interest but are not nearly as fascinating as the text that simultaneously idealizes and idolizes. It is written by the "superstars" of the Third Reich. An encomium to Hitler by Hermann Goering opens the book; chapters on Hitler as statesman, orator, traveler, and his private life follow. There are also sections on Hitler and arts, his relationship to the German worker, to the army and to German youth and, of course, to the entire National Socialist movement. These are written by Joseph Goebbels, Albert Speer, Baldur von Schirach, Robert Ley, and others of note. The U.S. edition is translated by a Catholic priest, Carl Underhill Quinn, and edited by Julius Rosenthal, a rabbi.

Haffner, Sebastian. The Meaning of Hitler. New York: Macmillan, 1979. 165p.

A best seller in Germany and England, this book contains convincing insights on its subject and raises important questions as well. Haffner indicates that Hitler was often preoccupied with suicide, since his early life was so filled with lack of achievements. His "political life was . . . a life of all or nothing." The author is at his most controversial when he writes that "it required exceptional perception and far sightedness to recognize in Hitler's achievements and successes the hidden seeds of future disaster." (Some feel this was sufficiently spelled out in Mein Kampf.) But Hitler's life was an empty one, without a meaningful family life, solid friendships, etc. He could, in fact, concentrate his energies on politics and, consequently, on hatred. In the end, according to Haffner, the Fuehrer was sane, not mad, and knew he was leading his people to utter devastation; he did so to punish them for having failed him. There is much material for thought in this analysis, including questions on Hitler's major blunders: invading Russia; failing to conciliate Great Britain after France's fall; etc.

Heiden, Konrad. Der Fuehrer. Boston: Beacon, 1969. 788p.

Here is the most concentrated volume on Hitler's rise to power. Enormous in length, this work was first published in 1944. The author gives special heed to the crucial years 1933-34 and provides absorbing details. In spite of its length, the book is quite readable.

Herzstein, Robert Edwin. Adolf Hitler and the German Trauma. New York: Putnam, 1974. 294p.

Psychohistory has its dangers and critics disagree on the value of its application in Herzstein's work. He discusses Hitler's politically formative years, concluding that the Nazi leader developed his aims not only in reaction to the defeat in World War I, Germany's economic problems, and the destruction of traditional values, but also as a result of broad psychological and sociocultural aspects of the entire German people. There is little new information presented here; the volume stands or falls on the author's psychohistorical approach as he attempts to synthesize much of what has been previously published on Hitler and the Germany of his time. An interesting bibliographical essay is included.

Hitler, Adolf. Hitler's Secret Book. 2nd ed. New York: Grove, 1983. 230p.

The Nazi leader's major plans for world domination are quite baldly stated here. Hitler tells why he believed that war was a justified means to his ends. He also believed that his goals could be reached through a series of political maneuverings that seem incredible to historians today: friendship with Great Britain, ongoing alliance with Italy, Lebensraum (living space for Germany's crowded population) in Russia. France, he insisted, was Germany's natural enemy. Hitler's hatred of Jews is clearly as evident here as in Mein Kampf. One of the most interesting aspects of this book is seen in Hitler's consistently serious errors of judgment. His misreading of America is particularly fascinating (as a nation that "felt itself to be a Nordic-German state" and later, after Pearl Harbor, as a decayed country, "half Judaised and the other half Negrified"). Telford Taylor's introduction to this edition is very useful.

------. Mein Kampf. New York: Houghton, 1943. 694p.

Mein Kampf is the real bible of Hitlerism. It is all spelled out here: the hatred of others; the praise of self. The author makes it appear as if he alone founded the National Socialist movement, with little or no mention given to Ernst Roehm, Julius Streicher, Gregor Strasser, Hermann Esser, or others. On race and the state he makes wild allegations without any attempt at proof. (As Germany was said to have "the largest reading public of any country in the world," it is interesting to speculate on why this book became a best seller, second only to the Bible, and made its author a wealthy man.) Hitler could turn a phrase ("one blood demands one Reich") but his hatred and lack of proof appear on nearly every page. His anti-Semitic paranoia is hardly to be believed: he notes that European Jews had taken on a human look, that they were a protest against God's image, that no Jew could be a German, that it is the Lord's wish to defend oneself against Jews, etc. Some critics have written that Hitler really didn't comprehend the severity of the actual persecution of the Jews; obviously they simply do not understand the message of this book.

Hitler's Secret Conversations. New York: Octagon, 1972. 597p.

Translators Norman Cameron and R. H. Stevens have reissued their 1953 edition of this work, with an additional essay by Hugh Trevor-Roper on "The Mind of Adolf Hitler." This is a collection of the Fuehrer's meandering table talk during the war and as such offers glimpses of what he was really like when his guard was down.

Irving, David. Hitler's War. New York: Viking, 1977. 926p.

Hitler's War claims to be a work of scholarship, but in actuality it is an attempt to exonerate Adolf Hitler from blame for much that occurred during World War II, particularly the Holocaust. Ordinarily such a title by a "revisionist historian" would not be included in this kind of bibliography. For instance, Irving blames Great Britain for many of the ills of the conflict, suggesting that Churchill's vanity, combined with the egos of members of his cabinet, was greatly responsible for averting peace. All historians are selective; that is part of the process. But to list Red Army atrocities while almost ignoring those of the Gestapo and SS is ridiculous. Omitting the Anschluss, the attack on the Sudetanland, and much other factual material falsifies the actual story. Hitler's subordinates were responsible for the war's loss; he was actually a courageous leader, Irving writes, who went wrong because he was reclusive and too trusting of incapable followers.

Jackel, Eberhard. Hitler's Weltanschauung. Middletown, Conn.: Wesleyan Univ. Pr., 1972. 140p.

Adolf Hitler is surely one of the world's most enigmatic figures. Was he simply a madman who, through a series of historical coincidences, gained an ascendancy in Germany, or is the picture so complex that we will perhaps never really be able to comprehend it? Subtitled "A Blueprint for Power," Jackel's brief study tries to indicate the Nazi leader's consistent view of history that led him to a pair of goals which, to his mind at least, were somehow intimately related: territorial expansion for Germany, and annihilation of the Jews. The author presents Hitler as a principled person (though not morally principled, as this term is commonly understood), and so his policies had an internal consistency based on long-range ends. Jackel requires a more dispassionate analysis of Hitler and his work, rather than using subjective judgments by victims, near victims, and others. While not an overwhelmingly convincing presentation, this book does make a contribution to the Hitler corpus.

Jones, J. Sydney. Hitler in Vienna, 1907-1913. Briarcliff Manor, N.Y.: Stein & Day, 1983. 350p.

In a work that could be subtitled "How Hitler Developed His Anti-Semitism" (the actual subtitle is "Clues to the Future"), the author shows how, at age eighteen, after leaving his birthplace of Linz and going to Vienna, Hitler failed repeatedly in almost every venture and developed such hostility, in a monumental defense mechanism over his universal lack of successes, that clearly someone was eventually going to be made to suffer. Vienna at the turn of the century, well re-created here, was a good place for a "provincial dandy on the make" to test himself. It was a kind of renaissance period in Austria's capital city. Refused matriculation in the Academy of Fine Arts and eventually reduced to begging for his keep, Hitler had experiences which were inevitably transformed into his hatred of Jews.

Langer, Walter C. The Mind of Adolf Hitler. New York: New Amer. Lib., 1973. 286p.

In 1943, the Allies asked an American psychiatrist, Walter Langer, to prepare a psychological analysis of Hitler. What he produced, therefore, is not so much a biography as a psychohistory of the Nazi leader. It was top secret material for twenty-nine years. There are chapters on Hitler as he thought of himself (destined to become immortal); as the German people knew him (some insisted that "Hitler's word is God's law"); as his associates saw him (flawed, but worthy of loyalty); etc. Langer's picture is absolutely fascinating and his predictions in the final chapter, entitled "His Probable Behavior in the Future," are impressive. An afterword by Robert G. L. Waite gives valuable balance in praising and faulting Langer's report where Waite deems it necessary.

Maser, Werner. Hitler. New York: Harper, 1973. 433p.

Subtitled "Legend, Myth and Reality," this is a solid report on Hitler's life by a contemporary German historian. There is much detail here, a firm achievement. Maser is a justifiably recognized authority on Hitler and the Nazi period.

------, ed. Hitler's Letters and Notes. New York: Bantam, 1976. 393p.

A curious, complex figure emerges from this compilation of documents (including some pages from the diary of Hitler's mistress, Eva Braun): Hitler the schoolboy, the art student and, startlingly, the conscientious objector (dodging conscription in the Austrian army--by which he was found unfit anyway). But there is much more, of course, including the development of his anti-Semitism, his military strategies, his plans for world conquest and destruction. Memos urging his followers to fight to the death, when the end of the war approached, are here, as is Hitler's dismissal of Goering and Himmler as he pathetically tried to cling to power even from beyond the grave.

O'Donnell, James P. The Bunker. New York: Houghton, 1979. 339p.

Adolf Hitler's suicide followed a series of attempted assassinations. Because he lived longer than those who tried to eliminate him would have liked, his policies of death and destruction continued to be implemented. From one point of view, at least, it is important that Hitler destroyed himself, showing his weakness; thus his memory could not be hallowed, as though he had been some kind of super being. The author interviewed many of the survivors of the huge staff that served Hitler's bunker and they revealed much of interest and value about the Fuehrer.

Pauley, Bruce F. Hitler and the Forgotten Nazis. Chapel Hill: Univ. of North Carolina Pr., 1981. 292p.

The first book to trace the history of Austrian National Socialism from its beginnings in the 1880s to the German takeover of that nation in 1938, this study portrays the leadership problems encountered, the causes of the party's relatively slow growth following World War I, and the effects of the Great Depression on the party. Shown also is the extent of the Nazi terror in implementing policy and gaining ascendance. The structure of the SS and SA, the party's propaganda, and the reasons why German Nazis could not control their Austrian counterparts are also discussed at length. One of the author's conclusions that breaks new ground is that "the significance of the Austrian Nazis in bringing about the Anschluss (the move for the political unification of Germany and Austria) has heretofore either been ignored or underestimated. They refused merely to await their 'liberation.' Yet it is doubtful whether they could have seized power, even for the few hours that they did, without the intimidating presence of German troops on the Austrian frontier." Later, the German Nazis took sole credit for the Anschluss.

Rubin, Arnold. Hitler and the Nazis. New York: Bantam, 1983. 168p.

From Crystal Night, which marked the beginning of overt, programmed physical attacks upon Jews and their property in Germany, until the fall of Adolf Hitler, this volume deals with the circumstances leading up to the Holocaust, the victims (both Jews and non-Jews), the concentration camps, the death camps, and how they both were managed and endured. Interesting, too, is the author's treatment of reactions of people from around the world, who basically refused to believe what was going on in spite of the eye-witness accounts then available.

Stone, Norman. Hitler. Boston: Little, 1981. 181p.

Stone tries, in this volume, to comprehend Hitler's enormous success. Just how did he mesmerize the German people, uniting them behind his personality to build so strong a cult of "Der Fuehrer"? There is a lot of good material here on Hitler, but some of the author's conclusions are to be questioned. He believes, for example, that since there are no records before October, 1943, showing that Hitler knew of the manner and depth of the "Final Solution" to the "Jewish problem," he therefore really didn't realize until then the extent of the project. Stone also says that the only way the German people got any information on the atrocities was from troops returning from the eastern front.

Toland, John. Adolf Hitler. New York: Doubleday, 1976. 1,035p.

Complete with 157 photos, maps, tables, and a huge list of sources, this is a highly respected biographical work. Using previously unavailable materials and conducting 250 interviews with people who knew Hitler, Toland has corrected previous historical errors. A fascinating portrait emerges: Some of Hitler's methods for annihilating Jews were inspired by the United States' treatment of Indians; Hitler knew a number of Wagnerian operas by heart; he was a vegetarian; he feared that one of his grandparents may have been Jewish; at least three women committed suicide over him; he had a photographic memory. Toland shows Hitler's successes as well as his madness. He notes that many Germans loved Hitler: "They needed no whip to follow a Siegfried who was bringing them out of economic depression and wiping out the dishonor of Versailles." He was the first head of state to promote modern urban planning and antipollution devices for cities. But, of course, the full picture that emerges is one of a driven man, complex and mad.

Trevor-Roper, Hugh. Last Days of Hitler. New York: Macmillan, 1947. 254p.

When, in 1983, Hugh Trevor-Roper quickly "authenticated" what soon proved to be the fraudulent diaries of Adolf Hitler, he lost considerable standing as a historian. Nevertheless, much of his earlier work is first rate and this book is part of that body. Five months after Hitler's death, the author was given the chance to investigate the Nazi leader's final hours. He had documents and eyewitnesses at his disposal. The result is interesting and well written. The probable events leading up to and including the suicides of Hitler and Goebbels, as well as the Fuehrer's final emotional collapse, are convincingly rendered. This narrative reads like a novel in the best sense.

Waite, Robert G. L. The Psychopathic God: Adolf Hitler. New York: Basic Books, 1977. 482p.

Psychohistory is suspect by some, and this investigation falls into that category. The historic background to the Nazi era is presented, as are Hitler's childhood and youth, the development of his political ideas, and his artistic interests. Waite classifies his subject as a borderline personality in whom a tension exploded--one built up between a private neurosis and public policy. This eruption resulted in a fatal desire to destroy what he had himself created. Some of the jargon used by the author may seem too pat, some of the conclusions unwarranted. But the disclaimers here to absolute correctness are well taken and the author is quite thorough in his approach.

ERNST KALTENBRUNNER

Black, Peter. Ernst Kaltenbrunner. Princeton, N.J.: Princeton
Univ. Pr., 1983. 352p.
The subject of this biography served as the head of the Reich
Main Office for Security succeeding the assassinated Heydrich. At
the Nuremberg Trials, where some of the worst of Nazi officialdom
were brought to justice, Kaltenbrunner proved to be one of the most
reprehensible. The author makes important points in this book--
against the idea of a "demonic" Nazi leader, against Arendt's concept of the "banality of evil," and against the idea that "chance"
propelled Kaltenbrunner to his high post (initiative and political
skills got him there, according to Black). He was a murderer on
many levels (ordering all French prostitutes to be executed, for
example) and was hanged by the Allies in 1946.

KRUPP FAMILY

Manchester, William. The Arms of Krupp. Boston: Little, 1964.
976p.
Gustav Krupp was strongly opposed to the rise of Hitler. Within a month after Hitler was appointed chancellor, however, Krupp
changed his stance and became a strong supporter. Krupp worked
closely with the Fuehrer to align German industry with Nazi arms.
His son Alfred ran the family firm during Word War II and the Krupp
works produced tanks and ammunition for the war effort. Because
they used concentration camp prisoners as slave laborers, the Krupps
were to be brought to trial by the Allies. The old man was excused
because of senility; his son was convicted and sentenced to twelve
years, of which he spent just over three in prison.

BENITO MUSSOLINI

Mussolini, Rachele. Mussolini. New York: Pocket Bks., 1977.
308p.
The widow of the Fascist dictator has written this biography
of her husband. She writes of their courtship (she knew him well
from childhood), their children, Mussolini's rise to power, his
penchant for plump women, his superstitions, his relationship with
both the Vatican and Hitler, and more. Much about Mussolini the
private man is presented here, details only his wife could know.
She presents him as being greatly maligned, enormously misunderstood. He was a convenient scapegoat, she writes, and she is consistent in her approach. It is difficult to feel sorry for the
dramatic fall of "Il Duce," but Rachele Mussolini tries to elicit
sympathy, which casts doubt over the entire biography.

ERWIN ROMMEL

Irving, David. The Trail of the Fox. New York: Dutton, 1977.
496p.
Field Marshal Erwin Rommel is featured in this interesting revisionist biography. Here is Hitler's greatest military commander
who, at least tacitly, took part in a plot to kill the Fuehrer.
Here, too, is the tank commander who led his troops from the front,
providing an inspiring example of physical courage, but who weak-
ened his effectiveness at operations control in the rear. For Irving, as noted in his deplorable book on Hitler (see previous entry),
the subject of his book is a man betrayed by colleagues--a thesis
that holds up somewhat better in this volume, though not necessarily convincingly. Rommel seemed invincible, but once defeats began, he apparently lost confidence in his own infallibility; he had,
perhaps, bought the image of himself as indestructible and began to
pay for it. The author manages to present a personage here who
is rather unattractive as a human being, but never uninteresting.

ALBERT SPEER

Schmidt, Matthias. Albert Speer: The End of a Myth. New York:
St. Martin's, 1984. 276p.
The subject of this biography was the minister of Armaments
and War Production for the Third Reich. When Speer was released
from prison, after serving twenty years as a war criminal, he wrote
three books detailing personalities and events in the Nazi milieu.
While Speer accepted moral culpability for Nazi atrocities ("guilt
through ignorance"), he denied knowledge of actual crimes against
Jews and others. Matthias Schmidt here proves this thesis invalid.
He shows that Speer not only knew of certain anti-Semitic acts but
also participated in some. He domonstrates how cleverly edited
and doctored materials were used to improve Speer's self-image.
Schmidt's book gives readers a valuable corrective, although in
the U.S. edition it suffers from sloppy misprints.

Speer, Albert. Infiltration. New York: Macmillan, 1981. 384p.
After completing a twenty-one year sentence for war crimes,
former Nazi Albert Speer wrote several books about the Third Reich
and its leaders. Although most critics agree that he has attempted
to soften the harsh judgment of history regarding his role, his
volumes contain details that could not otherwise be learned. This
work centers on the SS leader Heinrich Himmler, who planned to infiltrate the war economy with his own personnel and create an industrial empire controlled by his SS, independent of the nation and
the Nazi party. Infiltration is the only volume on the SS written
by a high-ranking Nazi official and gives a strong account of what

the ruthless Himmler was like. Speer himself was an intended target of Himmler's plot.

------. Inside the Third Reich. New York: Avon, 1971. 734p.
    In this memoir, the Nazi war criminal writes of how the tragic scene of a Jewish family going to its destruction has proven more devastating to him than the twenty-one years he spent in prison for his crimes. Speer takes the reader through his schooling and marriage, professional life, attraction to Hitler, architectural jobs, the war, and the pettiness and daily double-crossing by the powerful. He describes the personalities of Hitler, Goering, Himmler, Goebbels, Bormann, Doenitz, and others (though nothing of Eichmann). Speer on the Nuremberg Trials is interesting, but on the degree of his own guilt he is suspect. Regarding the lessening of his culpability concerning the persecution of Jews because he was so isolated in Hitler's hierarchy, the author writes: "Those who ask me are fundamentally expecting me to offer justifications. But I have none. No apologies are possible." This seems clearly to be an attempt at disarming the reader with clever rhetoric--yet the book does contain important information.

FRANZ STANGL

Sereny, Gitta. Into That Darkness. New York: McGraw-Hill,
    1975. 380p.
    Based on a series of long interviews with Franz Stangl, the commander of the concentration camp at Treblinka, Sereny's work is nearly impeccable in its honest approach. So careful is the author to show how Stangl became increasingly involved in the net of human degradation that she even manages to elicit a hint of compassion for her subject. She proves to us that the Nazi crimes, with their brutality, terrorism, torture, and murders, were done by ordinary people who fell in with their orders, rather than by extraordinary monsters who behaved like most of us think we never would. Sereny also discusses the "Vatican Escape Route," which helped Nazis to flee from Allied armies and allowed them to find haven in distant countries.

JULIUS STREICHER

Bytwerk, Randall L. Julius Streicher. Briarcliff Manor, N.Y.:
    Stein & Day, 1983. 236p.
    The subject of this excellent biography was the founder of the infamous anti-Semitic periodical Der Sturmer, which printed vicious hatred weekly aimed at millions of Germans. Streicher (a hero to contemporary neo-Nazis) is portrayed as the mainstay

of Jew baiting, who not only practiced what he preached but who encouraged countless others to regard Jews as subhuman.

Showalter, Dennis. Little Man, What Now? Hamden, Conn.: Shoestring, 1982. 288p.

Julius Streicher's notorious magazine Der Sturmer is given the attention it deserves in a scholarly analysis valuable for those in Holocaust studies; it is also important for people interested in issues of freedom of the press. For some fifty years Der Sturmer published hatred of classes of people, particularly Jews, hatred that reached millions of readers. The indecencies written in the periodical are described for what they are in this needed investigation.

JURGEN STROOP

Moczarski, Kazimierz. Conversations with an Executioner. Englewood Cliffs, N.J.: Prentice-Hall, 1981. 282p.

The writer of this book spent 255 days in a prison cell with the commanding officer of the Nazis who destroyed the Jews in the epic Warsaw Ghetto uprising: SS General Jurgen Stroop. The book thus contains the author's description of Stroop's own recollections of what happened during the battle. Much material rings true and is undoubtedly reasonably accurate, but the writer's style, which includes some speculation on events, on Stroop's thoughts, and a less-than-objective tone that hurts rather than helps his presentation, is at times intrusive. Some historians have portrayed the Nazis as bunglers in their handling of the Warsaw battle, but this view is only partly true. Even Stroop, who truly despised Jews, clearly recognized their heroism and brilliance in resistance. Also apparent, however clouded, is the mind of an ordinary man doing his duty as he understands it, proud to be implementing his Fuehrer's will, disregarding the monstrous nature of his work.

GHETTO
AND REGIONAL
HISTORIES

The subjects of the books in this chapter include the Lodz, Warsaw, Vilna, and Riga ghettos, areas of Hungary, the Katyn Forest, Vichy France, Holland, and many others. Several titles might seem appropriate in the "Memoirs" chapter but are included here because they are really more about the places they discuss than the individual discussing them (a subjective choice of titles, but useful for our purposes). Readers will find a great deal of regional and local information in books discussed in the chapters on memoirs (chapter 6), resistance (chapter 7), assistance and betrayal (chapter 8), and even among the fiction and art described in chapter 13. See especially the diary of Adam Czerniakow, chairman of the Warsaw Judenrat, discussed in chapter 6.

Allen, William Sheridan. The Nazi Seizure of Power. New York: Quadrangle, 1965. 345p.
Subtitled "The Experience of a Single German Town," this book contains the story of how the Nazis divided and conquered Thalburg in the former province of Hanover, and how they solidified their position after they achieved ascendancy. The period 1930-35 is covered by the author as he uses Thalburg as a model of how a thousand towns in Germany may have been subverted. Allen did his research using local newspapers contemporary to the events studied as well as nineteen informants; citizens who were businessmen, teachers, civil servants, laborers, professionals, housewives, Christians of several denominations, and a Jew--even an atheist. The author indicates the ineffectiveness of the middle class to combat the lies of the Nazis. Various forced pressures contributed to what happened, including those of economics, conformity, and the temptation of

superficial achievement as well as the threat, real or imagined, of Nazi terror.

Arad, Yitzhak. Ghetto in Flames. New York: Ktav, 1981. 500p.
The story of the destruction of Vilna, known as the "Jerusalem of Lithuania," is chronicled here by Arad, a Holocaust survivor who was to become the chairman of the Board of Directors of Yad Vashem, the Israeli National Authority of the Commemoration of the Holocaust. This account covers Vilna from 1941 to 1944 and the liquidation of the ghetto there. It describes the expropriation of property, deportation, massacres, robbery, annihilation. What occurred in Vilna might well serve as a microcosm of what happened in countless other Jewish communities. Most perished; of those few who survived, nearly all went to Palestine "to find personal resurrection alongside national revival in the State of Israel."

Berg, Mary. Warsaw Ghetto, A Diary. New York: Fischer, 1945. 253p.
A Polish girl who, along with her family, endured several years under the Nazis and survived tells her story here. She describes her life in the constricted occupied territory: the heavy oppression, the psychological terror, the day-to-day misery--all is in evidence. The daughter of an American mother, Berg was somewhat shielded from some of the worst of the atrocities. Nevertheless, she saw a great deal and has filtered it well in this work.

Braham, Randolph. The Politics of Genocide. New York: Columbia
     Univ. Pr., 1980. 2v., 1,269p.
The definitive study of the Holocaust in Hungary is presented in this work. The conflict in Europe was nearly over when the Nazis began their massacre of almost a million Hungarian Jews. Because the means of murder were by then highly perfected, the slaughter proceeded rapidly. Many Hungarians were eager to cooperate with the Germans in the liquidation of the Jews. Results of these attitudes are chronicled in this dismal but necessary investigation.

Brand, Joel. Desperate Mission. New York: Criterion, 1958. 310p.
One of the most haunting episodes of World War II is told here, a story of bargaining in human lives. In 1944 Adolf Eichmann offered an influential Hungarian Jew the chance to purchase one million Jews in exchange for much needed war materials from the Allies. Joel Brand, relating his story, believed in the sincerity of Eichmann's words. The Allies, the British in particular, would have nothing to do with such an agreement and the possibility came to naught. This book suffers from a writing style inadequate to the drama of its topic, and all of the conversations are rendered as if recalled with absolute accuracy. Nevertheless, the enormity of the event, even though some of the historical data have been questioned, gives the volume significance.

Chary, Frederich B. The Bulgarian Jews and the Final Solution, 1940-1944. Pittsburgh: Univ. of Pittsburgh Pr., 1972. 246p.

Bulgarian Jews fared relatively well in World War II, even though their nation was allied with Hitler. Bulgaria did not participate strongly in deporting her Jews to the death camps. Nevertheless, Jews who lived in other areas occupied by Bulgarian troops (Yugoslav and Greek territories) were given over to a more tragic fate. Chary concludes that this apparent paradox resulted from political complexities having little to do with any special regard for the safety of Jews. Part of this was due to increasing pressure on Bulgaria by the Allies while Nazi military strength was fading.

Dobroszycki, Lucjan, ed. The Chronicle of the Lodz Ghetto, 1941-1944. New York: Yale Univ. Pr., 1984. 551p.

Lodz was the site of the second largest Jewish ghetto established by the Nazis. It originally contained 163,000 people with deportees continually added from elsewhere, including Germany, Austria, Czechoslovakia, and Luxembourg. When the war ended, 877 Jews were left. Written by a team of trapped authors from various backgrounds (a journalist, historian, librarian, biblical scholar, an ethnographer, and a writer), 1296 days are chronicled in what is the most complete document of its kind. Edited by a man incarcerated in the Lodz Ghetto when he was fourteen, the text has been abridged to approximately one-quarter its original size. The systematic way in which the writers went about keeping this archive makes it among the most valuable of all Holocaust primary documents. Births and deaths, the weather, gossip, suicides (attempts and "successes"), passenger service on the train, news of the day, arrests, diseases, rumors, thefts, new uses for "useless" foods (radish greens and young carrots), security forces--in brief everything of consequence and interest appears in this enormously important work. Dobroszycki has done a significant work of scholarly editing.

Ehrenburg, Ilya, and Vasily Grossman, eds. The Black Book. New York: Holocaust Library, 1981. 595p.

How the Soviet Jews were massacred by the Nazis is the subject of this volume. It is filled with detail and documentation, forming a convincing account. Equally important, perhaps, is the history of the book's publication. It was ready for publication in 1946. Many prominent Russians, Jews and non-Jews, collaborated in the gathering of the materials, but publication was prohibited by Stalin and the printing plates destroyed. A manuscript copy was preserved and smuggled out of the nation into Israel, where it was published in 1980.

Fisher, Julius. Transnistria. South Brunswick, N.J.: T. Yoseloff, 1969. 161p.

Not much has been written on the Holocaust in Romania; this is one of the few books in English that covers it. Transnistria was a province the Romanians had carved out of the Ukraine; it was also where more than 200,000 Jews were executed by the Germans and their Romanian collaborators.

Grossman, Mendel; Zvi Szner; and Alexander Sened; eds. With a Camera in the Ghetto. New York: Schocken, 1977.   107p.
Mendel Grossman was a man with a mission. In the Lodz Ghetto (Poland) he hid a camera under his coat and took thousands of photos to record the life of the Jews and their Nazi-inflicted suffering. At age thirty-two Grossman, who had a serious heart ailment, died on a forced march. The 10,000 negatives he had hidden were rescued and taken to Israel where most were destroyed during a war with the Arabs. Less than a hundred photos are in this book but they serve as an effective record of his achievement.

Gutman, Yisrael. The Jews of Warsaw, 1939-1943. Bloomington: Indiana Univ. Pr., 1982.   487p.
Chronicling the struggle of Warsaw Jews from the start of World War II through the tragic events of the Warsaw Ghetto uprising, this volume presents the rapid annihilation of the largest Jewish community in Europe. Only a small remnant of Jews now remains in Warsaw. This is a story of deportations and resistance, of killers and those they murdered, but most of all of the movement of history. It is a work that perhaps could only have been written by a historian who was a participant in the terrifying drama.

Handler, Andrew. The Holocaust in Hungary. University, Ala.: Univ. of Alabama Pr., 1982.   159p.
Hungarian Jews were generally isolated from mainstream European Jewry because of a language barrier (they more or less downplayed Hebrew and Yiddish to become increasingly involved in their local culture). For the same reason, the outside world has not learned a great deal about the Holocaust in Hungary. This anthology helps to bridge that gap. It is in two parts: the first, "It Could Never Happen Here," contains eleven pieces indicating the confidence, the resignation and the fears of the about-to-be-victims. The second section, "In Memoriam," has an equal number of responses to the Holocaust by survivors trying to understand the tragedy and face a problematic future.

Heller, Celia Stopnicka. On the Edge of Destruction. New York: Schocken, 1980.   384p.
A sociologist presents a scholarly report on Jewish life in Poland (where more Jews lived than anywhere in the world) between the two World Wars, from 1918 to 1939. The political, social and economic situations of the Polish Jews are covered, as are the fac-

tion struggles among the Jewish populace. Open and latent anti-Semitism are also discussed.

Kaplan, Chaim. Scroll of Agony. New York: Macmillan, 1964. 350p.
Later published as The Warsaw Diary of Chaim A. Kaplan (New York: Collier, 1973), this is a poignant narrative of life and death in the Warsaw Ghetto from September of 1939 to August of 1942. With incredible objectivity, given the circumstances, the diarist not only chronicles atrocity after atrocity, but reacts to them as well. Kaplan was a Hebrew school principal who lived in the Polish capitol and who died not long after mass deportations began in 1942. Despair and tragedy are here, but so is the hope of individuals and of a people.

Katz, Robert. Black Sabbath. New York: Macmillan, 1969. 398p.
On a Saturday in October, 1943, the Germans arrested more than a thousand Jews in Rome for annihilation; the title of this book refers to this event. What led up to the tragedy and what happened after it are also presented. But it is a highly disputed work. Katz finds the Jewish leadership in Rome largely responsible for what happened on Black Sabbath. He goes further, condemning world Jewry as a whole. Through a certain logic that has been challenged, Katz even states that German Jews must share the blame for the Holocaust. Some reviewers have extolled the work, while others have seen the writer as inimical to Judaism, Jews, and Zionism.

Komorowski, E.A., with Joseph Gilmore. Night Never Ending. New York: Avon, 1975. 285p.
The massacre of 15,000 Polish officers, dumped into mass graves in the Katyn Forest in Russia, took place in April, 1940. Mystery has long veiled the events there, the Soviets blaming the slaughter on the Nazis, others claiming that Stalin's secret police were to blame. Eugenjusz Andrei Komorowski, a survivor, writes of what actually happened. He fled Europe for a life in hiding under a pseudonym, but felt compelled to relate this story of Soviet atrocity. His is a harrowing tale of survival and escape, not only from the Katyn Forest but also through Romania, Hungary, Czechoslovakia, and even Switzerland, plus psychiatric hospitals in Great Britain. Now in the United States, he lives a haunted life.

Levy, Claude, and Paul Tillard. Betrayal at the Vel d'Hiv. New York: Hill & Wang, 1969. 284p.
In 1942, the Germans rounded up 13,000 Jews in Paris and jammed them into a sports palace, where they were brutally treated for many days before transportation to death camps. The authors were both members of the French Resistance movement imprisoned by the Nazis. Paul Tillard died before the book was finished due to after-effects of his confinement; Claude Levy completed the well

documented volume in a deliberately understated style. Nevertheless, the tone is not one of impartiality. The writers blame French government leaders like Laval and Petain and the many French police who collaborated with the occupation troops. The final chapter is a valuable historical survey of French anti-Semitism.

Marrus, Michael R., and Robert O. Paxton. Vichy France and the Jews. New York: Basic Books, 1981. 432p.

The authors prove, with evidence not previously accessible, that French officials in the Vichy regime not only persecuted Jews as ordered by the Nazis but actually initiated their own anti-Semitic acts. Initially, the Vichyites banned Jews from engaging in certain professions. Next they authorized and encouraged the expropriation of Jewish property. Most tragically, the Vichy figures aided in the deportation of about 75,000 Jews to death camps. The background to these catastrophic events is filled in by Marrus and Paxton as they show the tradition of anti-Semitism in Europe in general and France specifically. It was French police who guarded Jews and locked them in freight cars; they, too, selected from census files more than 27,000 Jews to be shipped out on 16 July, 1942. The German occupation troops were very pleased with the enthusiastic cooperation of Vichy.

Michaelis, Meir. Mussolini and the Jews. New York: Oxford Univ. Pr., 1979. 472p.

The mystery of why the Italians, allied with the Germans during World War II, did not participate in the massacre of Jews is cleared up in this absorbing history. Until late in his career, Benito Mussolini was not an anti-Semite. He changed when it became politically expedient, but the Italian people did not follow him in his turnabout. Only after the Italian failure in Ethiopia, which was opposed by world Jewry, did the Fascist leader seriously attack Jews. Still, it wasn't until Italy surrendered to the Allies and was then invaded by Germany that 8,000 of the nation's 40,000 Jews were deported.

Orlow, Dietrich. The Nazis in the Balkans. Pittsburgh: Univ. of Pittsburgh Pr., 1968. 235p.

In spite of its misleading title, this is a worthwhile volume on a minor aspect of World War II. It is not about the entire Nazi campaign in the Balkans, nor is the research limited to that area of the world (Czechoslovakia is also included). Instead, the book concerns the Southeast Europe Society as an instrument of Nazi power, its creation, growth, and disbanding. The Third Reich leaders had hoped to use the organization, established in 1940; since no master plan seemed to govern the Nazis in World War II, however, the Southeast Europe Society eventually died out.

Presser, J. The Destruction of the Dutch Jews. New York: Dutton, 1969. 556p.

The Netherland State Institute for War Documentation asked the author, a Jewish Holocaust survivor and professor of modern history at the University of Amsterdam, to compile this history. The English edition is an abridgment of the original two-volume Dutch edition. Presser chronicles the plight of Dutch Jews that began with German occupation in May of 1940. He writes of the Nazis but concentrates more on the non-Jewish Dutch and their individual and collective roles in the persecution of Jews. He also has important insights regarding the behavior of certain Jews and is particularly harsh with the members of Amsterdam's Jewish Council, although he maintains a laudable tone of detachment throughout.

Pryce-Jones, David. Paris in the Third Reich. New York: Holt, 1981. 294p.

Paris is unique, and pride greatly contributes to the French city's sense of unusualness. Parisians have traditionally maintained that they were different because they were better, and one of the things Parisians knew for certain was that they would act with honor in the face of the German enemy. However, to put it simply, under the Nazis they behaved no better than citizens in most European cities, and much worse than in some (Copenhagen, for example). This study of Paris is not as great a book as it might have been because it lacks focus. There is simply too much information provided without evident organization. The author, a novelist and historian, has not yet mastered techniques of selection and abstraction. Nevertheless for a reader willing to work through the plethora of material, there is much to be learned.

Ringelblum, Emmanuel. Notes from the Warsaw Ghetto. New York: Schocken, 1974. 369p.

One of the classic works of history concerning the Holocaust, this study provides eyewitness testimony by a social historian murdered by the Nazis in 1944. He buried his notes and they were found after the war--some in 1946, the remainder four years later. This resistance leader chronicles all that might be of relevance, sifting hearsay evidence to ascertain its validity before presenting it in this journal, kept as regularly as circumstances would allow. On at least twenty-six different pages the author includes the jokes or humorous stories going around the ghetto at the expense of the persecutors; there is also a remarkably complete rendering of daily life.

------. Polish-Jewish Relations during the Second World War. New York: Howard Fertig, 1976. 330p.

Many aspects of the relationships between non-Jewish and Jewish Poles are carefully presented by the author, whose execution by the Gestapo necessarily left his work incomplete (although editors have supplemented this history). The stories of the Jews, their ghettoization, their economic dealings with non-Jews, the dangers they faced even after they had fled the ghetto, political and governmental attitudes towards the Jews in Poland--all are chronicled by a trained historian. More Jews lived in Poland than in any nation in the world, and more Jews lost their lives in Poland (both in numbers and percentages) than in any other Nazi occupied territory. What happened to them, and the reasons for this dark aspect of human history, is the focus of this volume.

Schwarberg, Gunther. The Murders of Bullenhuser Damm. Bloomington: Indiana Univ. Pr., 1984. 178p.
　　Near the end of the war, twenty Jewish children from France, Poland, Holland, Italy, and Yugoslavia were hanged by SS officers in the basement of a school. The heartbreaking story of these youngsters, aged five through twelve, makes difficult but perhaps necessary reading for those who are driven to know just how vicious humans can be to one another. These children were being used for medical experiments by the Nazis and when the war was clearly lost, it was decided that they--the evidence--had to be destroyed. Some of the perpetrators were tried and found guilty. Others, whose whereabouts are known, are still free as of the publication of this book. The children are being memorialized--this book is one such testament--and an aunt of one of them has stated that because of these efforts "the dead children are no longer quite dead."

Shulman, Abraham. The Case of the Hotel Polski. New York: Holocaust Library, 1982. 240p.
　　A terrible hoax forms the basis of this book. To flush Jews out of hiding so that they might be transported to concentration camps, a rumor was started that export visas could be obtained at the Hotel Polski located on the Aryan side of Warsaw. The story gained credence because two well known Jews helped to spread it as they bartered for their own lives. The heretofore barely frequented hotel became packed as Jews slept in hallways and paid dearly for documents they thought would grant safe passage to them and their families. All ended up at Auschwitz or Treblinka. A very few survived and their writing, along with archival evidence located at Yad Vashem, the Holocaust center in Jerusalem, form the substance of this volume.

Thalmann, Rita, and Emmanuel Feinermann. Crystal Night. New York: Coward, 1973. 192p.
　　"Crystal Night" is the name given to the November, 1938, national pogrom against the Jews in Germany, so named because of the store front windows smashed in the systematic rioting. The

actual events and the bewilderment of the Jewish victims are related. Particularly effective here are excerpts from Jewish
diaries. Perhaps the most significant chapter of the book is
titled "The Nations That Looked On." The story is lamentable
(the French National Assembly wouldn't even consider the tragedy)
and instructive. The historians who wrote this volume see the
events as forming a classical Greek tragedy including the three
unities of time, place, and action.

Trunk, Isaiah. Judenrat. New York: Macmillan, 1972. 664p.
   When the Nazis occupied territories containing a significant
number of Jews, they forced a "self-government" on them. Here
such Jewish councils in Eastern Europe are examined, including
their makeup, manner of operations, the motivations and acts of
those in charge and other members, as well as the effects of
their decisions. Many Jews have condemned those who "collaborated" with the Nazis in this way; others have praised them for
doing what they could to benefit their suffering people. Various
historians and sociologists also take opposing views. Trunk does
not praise or completely blame Judenrat members, since he finds
them to have been under enormous pressure. Particularly memorable
is the story of the leader of Warsaw's council, Adam Czerniakow,
who committed suicide over the dilemma posed by his position.

Tushnet, Leonard. The Pavement to Hell. New York: St. Martin's, 1975. 210p.
   When the Nazis forced Jews into ghettos, they also imposed an
internal government on them, and today there are still mixed feelings about the heads of these semiofficial bodies. Tushnet studied
the lives of the leaders in the Jewish communities of Warsaw,
Lodz, and Vilna. He has used a great deal of archival material,
including records and diaries, and interviewed some survivors. The
findings are, predictably, not very enlightening. Chaim Rumkowski
of Lodz, for instance, had been known for charitable work with
orphans before the war. How then could he help deliver thousands
of Jewish children to the Nazi death machine? Adam Czerniakow
in Warsaw also "cooperated" with the persecutors because he felt
that in so doing he was able to somewhat slow down Nazi slaughters.
(His suicide was welcomed by some, lamented by others who saw
him as heroic.) The dilemma seems truly unanswerable but this
volume recreates the problem in a significant way.

THE
CAMPS

The concentration camps described in these books include Terezin, ostensibly a humane camp but really a gateway to Auschwitz; Treblinka, exclusively a death camp; and Auschwitz, the largest of all. Grim and factual accounts of life and death in the camps are reported by survivors, journalists, and the liberating armies. Other material on the camps is discussed throughout this book, memoirs (chapter 6) and fictionalized accounts (chapter 13). See especially Jozef Garlinski's portrayal of resistance within Auschwitz, described in chapter 7.

Bor, Josef. The Terezin Requiem. New York: Avon, 1978. 119p.
    Verdi's "Requiem" played in the Terezin concentration camp by prisoners for the benefit of the Nazi officers--this is the subject of Bor's book. Conductor Raphael Schachter was told to assemble a high-calibre orchestra from among the excellent Jewish musicians in the camp. They succeeded against the greatest of odds: disease, death, and transportation. In the end, an apparently triumphant version of the "Requiem" was presented for Adolf Eichmann and other Nazi officials. After the performance, the camp commander's promise not to break up the orchestra was kept: "All together they ascended into the first wagons of the first transport."

Crawford, Fred R. Dachau. Atlanta: Emory Univ. Pr., 1979. 68p.
    With the exception of a one-page letter to the reader by Crawford, this document "is an exact and authentic photographic copy of Dachau printed in 1945 by men of the 7th U.S. Army." Hundreds

of American soldiers saw the death camp on liberation day. Some simply had to document what they had witnessed, at once so shocking and so unbelievable. There are descriptions, with illustrations, of the history and organization of the camp, the townspeople, and the liberation period. This is a little known but very important document.

Donat, Alexander, ed. The Death Camp Treblinka. New York: Holocaust Library, 1979. 320p.

Over a million children, women, and men were massacred at Treblinka, exclusively a death camp. There was no forced labor, only death for Jews--some fifty survived in an uprising to tell the true story. Authentic documents, statistics, biographical data, historical analysis, profiles of victims and their killers, a full list of the survivors as well as original photographs and maps are included. The author, one of the heroes of the Warsaw Ghetto, escaped transportation to Treblinka but considers himself a survivor of that camp.

Eliach, Yaffa, and Brana Gurewitsch, eds. The Liberators. Brooklyn: Center for Holocaust Studies Documentation and Research, 1981. 59p.

A valuable contribution illustrating the scope of Nazi atrocities is found in this brief, highly documented compilation of eyewitness accounts by sergeants, war correspondents, medical personnel, commanding officers (including Lt. Gen. James M. Gavin), and others. The interviews are excellent and to the point; accompanying photos and other documentation are exactly appropriate. The stories are painful, perhaps traumatic, always consistent, and well presented by the editors. Yaffa Eliach's Foreword is especially noteworthy; it is emotionally moving yet not sentimentalized because of her intellectual control over the material.

Feig, Konnilyn G. Hitler's Death Camps. New York: Holmes & Meier, 1981. 547p.

Considered here are the nineteen major collection and murder points used by the Nazis against the Jews. The author visited them all, interviewed survivors and Nazis who were on the scene in World War II, and researched previous material. What happened in those camps, situated outside of civilization, is chronicled here. So is the indifference of the Allies: Anthony Eden is cited again, as are those responsible for not allowing 907 Jewish refugees (on the ship St. Louis) to land in the United States (with almost certain death the alternative). Also discussed are actions of the Polish government-in-exile, which dropped arms to Polish partisans "with the proviso that none be given to Jewish resistance fighters or the Warsaw Ghetto defenders." This is a frightening book.

Hirshaut, Julien. Jewish Martyrs of Pawiak. New York: Holocaust Library, 1982. 256p.

In the five years of Nazi occupation of Poland the Pawiak
Prison in Warsaw was used for, among other things, incarceration
of Jews caught outside the ghetto. From here they were usually
sent to Auschwitz. Hirshaut himself spent a year and a half
in Pawiak and he details his experience, which included slave
labor, hunger, and other tortures. The author tells of watching
the murder of his brother and of other families being similarly
torn asunder.

Lengyel, Olga. Five Chimneys. Chicago: Ziff-Davis, 1947.
213p.

Lengyel contributes the first comprehensive account of Auschwitz,
the death camp that stands as the symbol of Nazi persecution of the
Jews. Lengyel, a Hungarian Christian, was married to a well known
Jewish doctor. Both were deported in 1944 by the German troops
and shipped separately to Auschwitz. Dr. Lengyel was murdered but
the author was assigned to the camp hospital and thus was able to
survive.

Maurel, Micheline. An Ordinary Camp. New York: Simon & Schuster, 1958. 141p.

Maurel recounts her two years in a concentration camp. A French
intellectual and member of the Resistance, she tells of her experiences with 22,000 other prisoners who suffered from cold, overwork,
beatings, lack of privacy, and especially hunger. The author's
style is inobtrusive; she allows the events to carry their own emotional weight. The book ends with the author's plea to those who
have not undergone enormous suffering to appreciate the freedom
they have. Francois Mauriac provides a sympathetic introduction
to this vivid account.

Michel, Jean. Dora. New York: Holt, 1980. 308p.

Written by a non-Jewish survivor of Dora, the Nazi concentration camp "where modern space technology was born and 30,000 prisoners died," this devastating personal narrative reads like a novel
with commentary. From the time of his arrest by the Gestapo to
the final obsessive slaughter of inmates at Dora by Nazis who knew
the hopelessness of their own situation, this book passionately
describes and criticizes events. The images that the author, writing in his seventies ("I have been silent for a long time"), retains
include revenge on prisoners who, when given some authority by Nazis,
abused other prisoners; the suffocation of victims on trains and
trucks as they were hauled to incarceration; the faces of sadists
("I have not forgotten a single one"); the chimneys, through which
many went up in smoke; preparations for resistance; betrayals. A
whole chapter condemns space scientist Wernher von Braun, and his

new, innocent image that does not account for his role in Hitler's rocketry program. After reading of von Braun's "sense of humanity," Michel "decided once and for all to overcome the irresistible horror that Dora still instils in me and to write this book." A key chapter of the memoir describes the plan to use Dora for the building of rockets, using slaves sealed off from the rest of the world so that the secret would be well kept.

Novitch, Miriam. Sobibor. New York: Holocaust Library, 1980. 168p.

Among the least known of the death camps was Sobibor, where a quarter of a million victims perished (compared to more than double that figure at Belzec, more than triple at Treblinka). Novitch has compiled testimonies of thirty Sobibor survivors, providing a view of the daily life of the camp, survival tactics, resistance, and the revolt of October 14, 1943. In spite of cetain repetitions, this is valuable reading. But Novitch's decision to write the book in English, rather than using a more familiar language, seems to have been a mistake. Though stylistically weak, the book is nevertheless valuable. Betrayals, tortures, rapes, gassings, shootings--such incidents make up much of the eyewitness content of the book. There is another side, too, in which acts of heroism, honor, and a high level of humanitarianism occur. One unforgettable person in this book is Erwin Lambert, a master carpenter from Stuttgart. He constructed the euthanasia gas chambers in at least four cities. Later he camouflaged the Sobibor gas chambers as showers and sealed them so that carbon monoxide could not escape: he was both a "good professional" and a "monstrous criminal."

Nyiszli, Miklos. Auschwitz. New York: Fell, 1960. 222p.

Auschwitz provides an eyewitness account, particularly of SS medical doctors, by a Jewish doctor who survived by deliberately allowing himself to be used by the Nazis. The author writes of Josef Mengele, the notorious minister of life and death and of his medical experiments--tortures really--performed on unfortunate victims. An introductory section by Bruno Bettelheim opens the book.

Rousset, David. The Other Kingdom. New York: Howard Fertig, 1982. 173p.

The author describes the concentration camp universe with an objectivity that apparently sets the tone for several later volumes. Published originally in English in 1947, Rousset tries to impress on readers that while normal persons do not know that everything is possible among human beings, camp survivors know--from personal experience. The "fetid stench of destroyed social values" will always be with camp survivors--that's one of the enduring lessons of this volume. The only way to explain the "logic" of the illogical world of "the other kingdom" is this: "Buchenwald lives under the sign of a monstrous whimsicality, a tragic buffoonery."

Selzer, Michael. Deliverance Day. Philadelphia: Lippincott, 1978. 253p.
    Dachau was Hitler's first concentration camp. When, twelve years after it was established, the gates were breached by the Allies, the moment was naturally a highly emotional one. Much of the impact of the last hours at Dachau are captured in Selzer's narrative. It spans a period from the predawn military orders to take the camp to the execution of more than a hundred SS guards by a few GIs, horrified by what they saw; he also writes of the rescue of prisoners, some especially marked for death by SS head Heinrich Himmler himself. This hour-by-hour re-creation of events is based on interviews with many former prisoners and with some of their rescuers. Contemporary portraits of certain survivors, with suggestions concerning how their experiences changed their lives, closes the volume.

Smith, Marcus J. Dachau. Albuquerque: Univ. of New Mexico Pr., 1972. 291p.
    There were 32,000 starving prisoners liberated from Dachau when the Allies reached the concentration camp on April 29, 1945. The following day a team of ten American soldiers arrived to work with French and other troops and civilians to care for these survivors. In addition to being fed, clothed, and medically treated, the "fortunate" of the victims had to be repatriated as well. Smith, the medical officer of the American team, recounts this monumental rescue exercise. Among these enormous efforts were continuing tragedies: thousands of the newly liberated died from disease and the effects of starvation very soon after the Allied arrival. But the heroic actions of the Allies and the cooperation among the victims in times of a new kind of stress make wonderful reading. Many difficulties arose (prisoners came to hate the constant delousing procedures; the French despised the cooking of others; Ukranians did not want to be classified as Russians); but most problems were admirably overcome.

Smolen, Kazimierz, et al. From the History of KL-Auschwitz. New York: Howard Fertig, 1982. 225p.
    A thoroughly documented work, first published in 1967, this is a collection of chapters on the establishment and development of the most notorious of the death camps. The structure and organization of the camp, its administration, the subcamps and much else are discussed. So is the nature of punishment for prisoners, including starvation, flogging, hanging from a stake, and several types of death penalties. How prisoners were terror-

ized after others escaped is also described, as are the horrendous medical experiments that fell into three categories: outside the living organism, inside it, and on corpses.

MEMOIRS
OF THE
VICTIMS

Books from this category are among the best known works of Holocaust literature. One only has to mention Elie Wiesel's Night, Janusz Korczak's Ghetto Diary and, of course, Anne Frank's Diary of a Young Girl. The Jews are "People of the Book" and a people of books. Many kept excellent accounts and some diaries survived a war even though their writers did not. Others who outlived their persecution have written poignant memoirs that are not only excellent primary materials but art, as well. Collectively, the works here have an enormous impact and are a significant part of the history of the twentieth century. Many of the fictionalized accounts by survivors described in chapter 13 are almost memoirs, as well; the line blurs somewhat in the literature on this subject.

Arad, Yitzhak. The Partisan. New York: Anti-Defamation League, 1979. 288p.
Arad, who was to become the director of Yad Vashem, the Holocaust memorial center in Jerusalem, here relates the autobiographical adventures of a survivor who lived through exciting exploits and remarkable experiences. His memoirs trace his movements from the grief of ghetto life through the atrocities of Nazi terror and the many dangers as a Jewish partisan, battling as a heroic freedom fighter.

Birenbaum, Halina. Hope Is the Last to Die. New York: Twayne, 1971. 246p.
Called "A Personal Documentation of Nazi Terror," this is a powerful memoir of a Jewish teen-ager who survived World War II.

From 1939 to 1945 the author was subject to confinement in the Warsaw Ghetto and incarceration in three death camps: Auschwitz, Ravensbruck, and Treblinka. Written simply, this is a moving autobiography.

Boehm, Eric H., ed. We Survived. New Haven, Conn.: Yale Univ. Pr., 1949. 308p.

Fourteen people who were hunted by and hidden from the Nazis told their stories to the editor of this volume, a compilation of tragedy and success, of deportation and hope, of betrayal and self-sacrifice. The fourteen include Jews and non-Jews, an artist, workers, a clergyman, those from the upper class, and some who were associated with the plan to kill Hitler.

Cohen, Elie A. The Abyss. New York: Norton, 1973. 111p.

Cohen labels this autobiographical work a confession; in it he tells how he survived the Nazi concentration camps. As a young Jewish doctor he lived in Holland with his wife and young son but they were betrayed into the hands of the Germans just as they were preparing to flee to Sweden. The author then tells how he parlayed his skills as a doctor into keeping his family alive. However, they were eventually sent to Auschwitz, where his wife and child immediately lost their lives. Cohen then, once again, used his "privileged" abilities to help himself stay alive.

Czerniakow, Adam. The Warsaw Diary of Adam Czerniakow. New York: Stein & Day, 1979. 420p.

Adam Czerniakow's story is an ambiguous one. For almost three years he was chairman of the Warsaw Judenrat, the Nazi-appointed committee that administered the ghetto. Some researchers call him a villain; others see him much more sympathetically. Now, with the publication of his diary, a more accurate picture can be obtained. Czerniakow had onerous duties. When the Germans required a specific number of Jews (always large, frequently in the thousands) for deportation, he often had to decide who would go to die. Some called him heartless; others claimed that he tried to save from the transports those who would best preserve Jewish culture and tradition after the war. The diary of this man, who at one point offered himself as a hostage, makes heart-searing reading. He was treated badly by Germans, Jews, and non-Jewish Poles. He records this, but never in a self-pitying way. When things became unbearable, he refused an opportunity to emigrate to the safety of Palestine. He was jailed, beaten, forced to watch the random punishments of Jews who sought only the scant necessities of human existence. Czerniakow supervised the distribution of 103,000 meals (such as they were) daily, listened to the complaints of desperate individuals, was constantly threatened by Nazi officials, and witnessed heartbreakng tragedies. (He writes of a mother who was driven to an act of cannibalism on the body of her own son.) Through it all, he attempted to keep up the spirits of those under his charge. His philosophy, he noted, was to play jazz while the ship was going down so as not to panic the passengers. Czerniakow committed suicide when he was ordered to hand over children for destruction. His diary, begun on September 6, 1939, ends abruptly on July 23, 1942, the date of his death. He became one of the ninety-nine percent of the half million Jews in the Warsaw Ghetto who perished.

Delbo, Charlotte. None of Us Will Return. Boston: Beacon, 1968. 128p.

A non-Jewish survivor of Auschwitz and other concentration camps, the author--who had been active in the French Resistance-- provides a powerful account of her life as a prisoner. In spare, harsh, poetic style (this work has been compared to Picasso's Guernica), Delbo's memoir is an understandably angry recollection. She wonders about how insensitive she became, able to look at mounds of corpses, her own mother's nakedness, the death of friends walking beside her one moment and murdered the next. How could she continue to function "normally" after watching an SS guard order his dog to tear out an old woman's throat because she had stopped in a march to eat some clean snow? The agonizing despair is evident throughout this short, extremely honest volume.

Demetz, Hana. The House on Prague Street. New York: St. Martin's, 1980. 186p.

The picture offered here, from a young Czech girl's viewpoint, without bitterness, almost without passion, is quite effective. The narrator tells of the two sides of her family, her mother's (Jewish) and her German father's (Christian). The narrator's father remained loyal to his Jewish wife (some Christians turned their Jewish spouses over to the invaders), but his ineffectualness troubled the girl. The focus of the book is on a romance between the then sixteen-year-old autobiographer and an Axis soldier. His death in the war ends this episode. The memoir concludes as World War II ends. With one act the father redeems himself from a guilty inactivity; he notes the indiscriminate massacre of German civilians by the newly freed Czechs, and rushes into the midst of the firing to urge all to desist; he is killed by firing from both sides. The loss of family, playmates, and heroes during the war cannot be forgotten. Nor can certain betrayals on deeply human levels. Countering this, however inadequately, is the quiet heroism of many in the face of evil. The sacrifices of grandparents and friends became, in a certain sense, wonderfully normal.

D'Harcourt, Pierre. The Real Enemy. New York: Scribner, 1967. 186p.

A member of a wealthy and famous French family, the author was captured by the Germans when he was a French soldier. He was betrayed, then arrested. But D'Harcourt escaped to dispose of a small, compromising list of the names of his comrades. He was shot four times and captured. Four years of imprisonment followed, including two years in solitary confinement in Fresnes prison in Paris. Next came concentration camps with all of their horrors, including the traumas caused by the disloyal and dishonest relationships prisoners formed among themselves. What kept this memoirist going during isolation, betrayals, starvation, tremendous physical and psychological pain was his Christian religious faith and strong human will.

Donat, Alexander. The Holocaust Kingdom. New York: Holocaust Library, 1978. 368p.

One of the classic memoirs, this book provides extensive details of the labor and death camps, of the Warsaw Ghetto, and Janusz Korczak's quiet heroism. There is also the anguish of self-doubt as Donat asks himself the important questions about the meaning of life and death. He looks at such subjects as the value of nonresistance, the attitude prisoners had about Germans, the Poles who helped the Nazis murder Jews, Adam Czerniakow (who headed Warsaw's ghetto government and whose suicide led to so many questions), and much else.

Eisner, Jack. The Survivor. New York: Morrow, 1980. 320p.

The fantastic elements in this book are difficult to believe. The memoirist had so many heroic adventures, so many close encounters with death, so many correct intuitive responses to dangerous situations that readers may become skeptical. Yet the incidents have the tone of authenticity throughout. The writing is not memorable, but it is honest. Thirteen-year-old Eisner, a Polish Jew, became the provider of food for his family when his father became unable, physically and psychologically, to do so. The boy organized his own smuggling ring, brought food and occasionally medicine into the Warsaw Ghetto. Although comrades died around him, Eisner escaped in several mishaps and this set a pattern for his life. He out-ran Nazi pursuers; he killed others; he was saved in close calls by Nazis who took a liking to him. Eisner was whipped to near death, saw his own family perish, watched his beloved Halina die after liberation, and yet somehow kept his sanity.

Engleman, Matylda. End of the Journey. Los Angeles: Pinnacle, 1980. 310p.

When, in the Polish ghetto of Skarzysko in 1942, the author

got word that her children were going to be taken away from the family, she decided to fight to save her tiny daughter, Gila. Engelman obtained false identity papers and escaped with her child from the ghetto posing as a Christian. For three years this Jewish woman, pretending to be Catholic, survived. She fled into Germany, later had to hide from the Russians and, of course, suffered the physical and psychological traumas that accompanied these adventures. This is a story of treachery but also of aid from others; a story of heartbreak and a story with a happier ending than Engelman might have expected in the mid-1940s.

Fenelon, Fania. Playing for Time. New York: Atheneum, 1977. 262p.

In the death camp of Birkenau, a women's orchestra was formed. The conductor was Gustav Mahler's niece and they were ordered to play for SS head Heinrich Himmler, the dreaded Josef Mengele (who had dictatorial authority over the lives of the prisoners), and others including Kommandant Josef Kramer, at whose pleasure the orchestra was sustained. Fenelon was a member of the musical group for eleven months and here chronicles that period. She and forty-one others lived separately from other prisoners, somewhat more comfortably but perhaps equally starved. The tensions, both with the enemy and among the women themselves, is riveting, from concert-giving to secretly helping at the birth of a baby (and hiding it through to liberation). The episodes are memorable.

Ferderber-Salz, Bertha. And the Sun Kept Shining . . . New York: Holocaust Library, 1980. 235p.

A tribute to the Jewish victims of Nazi terror, this essay shows pride in the fact that, while the Nazis ultimately were destroyed, their targets of oppression endured with their dignity and integrity intact. Contrary to Nazi expectations, members of Jewish families retained their loyalties to each other, and the fundamental elements of friendship were preserved. Ferderber-Salz recounts her experience in a ghetto, in hiding in Poland, in camps. Her final separation from her husband, the hiding of her daughters (with whom she was reunited on liberation)--all is protrayed.

Fischer, Marianne, with Gayle Roper. Time of the Storm. Chappaqua, N.Y.: Christian Herald Books, 1981. 139p.

The life of a Jewish-Christian woman in wartime Hungary is told in this suspenseful, true narrative. A convert to Christianity from Judaism, Marianne Fischer was nonetheless subject to Hitler's anti-Semitic laws. How she lived through the Nazi occupation, then through miseries caused by Soviet occupation and finally gained freedom in the United States is what this book, written in a somewhat sentimental mode, tells--along with the story of Fischer's religious faith.

Flinker, Moshe. Young Moshe's Diary. New York: Board of Jewish Education, 1971. 126p.

A teen-ager who died in Auschwitz, Moshe was an observant, religious Jew. This Dutch boy wrote in Hebrew and struggled painfully with the question of Jewish suffering and God's justice. His disturbing conclusion: what the Jews were experiencing was a divine punishment to arouse Jews to repentance and finally to redemption in their own homeland. These pages have Moshe reflecting very maturely on the relations between Israel and its God.

Frank, Anne. The Diary of a Young Girl. New York: Pocket Books, 1978. 241p.

Probably the most widely known of all Holocaust books, this is the actual journal of a young Jewish girl who, with her parents, hid in an attic in Holland for more than two years in crowded conditions. Her book tells of the daily frustrations, bickering, fears and living conditions of her family and friends, of her hopes, her growing into young womanhood, even a little romance with the young man hiding with them. Poignant and memorable passages fill this diary of a girl who was to perish at Bergen-Belsen. There are various editions available.

Friedlander, Saul. When Memory Comes. New York: Farrar, 1979. 186p.

An eminent Jewish historian, Saul Friedlander actually studied for the priesthood at one time. After fleeing Czechoslovakia with his family when he was seven years old, Friedlander was left by his parents in a Catholic seminary in France in order to protect him from the Nazis. He was baptized, taking the name Paul-Henri, and trained for the ministry. When the war ended, Friedlander discovered his actual identity and ran away to Marseilles to ship to Israel in 1948. This affecting memoir is skillfully written.

Gabor, Georgia. My Destiny. Arcadia, Calif.: Amen, 1982. 319p.

As a teen-ager in Budapest, Hungary, Georgia Gabor survived the Holocaust only to become a victim of Soviet occupation. At seventeen she experienced the death of her parents, a struggle to survive and, in a real way, the death of her country. Her courage, her role in helping ninety-five children to escape to displaced persons camps in Germany, and her adjustment to life in the United States are among the few uplifting portions of this chronicle.

Goldberg, Izaak. The Miracles Versus Tyranny. New York: Philosophical Library, 1978. 598p.

A New York physician writes his memoir of concentration camp
experiences in both a personal account and a kind of history
of World War II. Goldberg tells what it was like to be under
bombardment in his city of Wolhowysky, where he practiced medicine; he tells of life in the ghetto there; he renders poignant
pictures of Auschwitz and Treblinka and devotes the final two
chapters to the administration of justice by the Allies after
the war. Unnerving is the account of the trial of Alvis Frey,
the Auschwitz commander; Goldberg testified against him, but
Frey was found not guilty.

Goldberg, Michel. Namesake. New Haven, Conn.: Yale Univ.
Pr., 1982. 192p.

As fiction, this story would strain credibility; as autobiography, it is stunning. In LaPaz, Bolivia, the author had an
opportunity to avenge the deportation of his father to Auschwitz
thirty-five years earlier. He had a gun and planned to kill Klaus
Barbie, whom the Bolivian government refused to extradite to France
on charges of being the "Butcher of Lyons." Living under the name
Michel Cojot, the author's life was in chaos: he despised his
Gentile wife, was remote from his three children, and experienced
pains that caused him to lose the use of his right hand. Although
he believed that an act of revenge might give new meaning to his
life, he ultimately could not pull the trigger. The pain in his
hand, that had eased considerably as he tracked Barbie, returned.
He divorced his wife, emigrated to Israel, and suffered a new adventure: he was on the hijacked Air France plane that German ter-
rorists brought to Entebbe airport in Uganda. He there became an
important figure, successfully working for the release of the non-
Israeli passengers, whom he joined in order to provide authorities
with information about the hostages' situation. But Goldberg finally
began to doubt his real motives (was he "only" trying to save his
own skin?) and the pain in his hand remained.

Gollwitzer, Helmut, et al., eds. Dying We Live. New York:
Pantheon, 1956. 285p.

One of the most unique of all of the volumes to come out of
World War II, this anthology contains the final messages and records
of those who died resisting Hitler from 1933 to 1945. This is an
important Christian document that has been compared to the sixteenth-
century martyrology known as Foxe's Book of Martyrs. The chief
difference, of course, is that here the words of the victims themselves are preserved in a true testament to humanity's possibilities.

Gurdus, Luba Krugman. The Death Train. New York: National
Council on Art in Jewish Life, 1978. 165p.

A Polish survivor of Majdanek concentration camp dedicates her autobiographical account to her son, who perished at age four, and to the million other Jewish children who were Nazi victims. She says that she was able to keep no notes from the period, but the authenticity of her recollections can hardly be doubted. She writes of how Germans would photograph violence documenting Polish hatred of the Jews; of an informer in the house; of how help was offered to Jews who were then robbed instead of aided. The establishment of the Warsaw Ghetto is described. Also given is the account of a mother forced to decide which of her two sons shall live. There are incidents of solid assistance (one in particular by a Catholic priest), but these are relatively few.

Hahn, Lili. White Flags of Surrender. Washington, D.C.: Luce, 1974. 354p.

A young woman chronicles the disintegration of her family and friends as she grows up in Nazi Germany. The author was a music critic for a Frankfurt newspaper but, because she would not cooperate with the Nazis, she lost her post. Her mother was of Jewish origin but, as a practicing Christian, tried to raise Lili to be a good Christian. However, her father was more interested in making his daugher into a good German. Neither of the parents seemed able to face the realities of Nazism. This diary account shows ordinary people being bent to the will of Nazis, the manipulating of the weak by the strong. One of her conclusions is that people prefer illusion to truth.

Hanham, Charles. A Boy in That Situation. New York: Harper, 1978. 217p.

In this autobiography, we learn of a Jewish boy in a rich family in Essen, Germany, who has the usual troublesome attitude of many his age. Then Hitler comes to power, and the child begins to experience anti-Semitism. This disease spreads throughout the school and the nation. Meanwhile, the boy grows in petty thievery as, at age twelve, his bar mitzvah approaches. He experiences the death of his mother and a serious rise in anti-Semitism at about the same time. When Crystal Night shatters more than glass in Jewish shops, his house and tranquility are left in shambles by the SS troops. The boy is packed off to England as the war breaks out. His experiences in comparative safety close out this informative memoir.

Hart, Kitty. Return to Auschwitz. New York: Atheneum, 1981. 178p.

Kitty Hart spent two years in Auschwitz. Before she was captured and imprisoned for the "crime of being Jewish," she had run with her parents from her native Polish city of Bielsko to several other communities. During imprisonment she managed to survive typhus, a fractured skull, and other physical and psychic torments thanks to her strong physique, the aid of a remarkable mother, and a tremendous will to live--along with certain strokes of luck. (Nearly every survivor will admit to "luck"--a curious word for a concentration camp victim to use.) Young Kitty quickly learned the technique of when and how to take risks, of how to assume responsibility, and in general how to cope as best she could in a nearly hopeless situation.

Heimler, Eugene. Concentration Camp. New York: Pyramid. 1961. 190p.

Originally entitled Night of the Mist, this is the account of a Jewish survivor from Hungary who came through Auschwitz and Buchenwald but who lost his entire family in a death camp. He survived because there were "messages I had to deliver to the living from the dead." He learned that "within me, as in others, the murderer and the humanitarian exist side by side; the weak child with the voracious male. That I am not in any way superior, that I am not different from others, that I am but a link in a great chain, was among the greatest discoveries of my life." Clearly this book is not just a chronicle of experiences, but also a gathering of valuable reflections on those experiences.

Hersh, Gizelle, and Peggy Mann. Gizelle, Save the Children! New York: Everest House, 1980. 319p.

The title of this book refers to the last words of Gizelle Hersh's mother. Until 1944, Hungarian Jews were not troubled by Nazi policies. But as the German cause was clearly becoming lost, the main Nazi effort was aimed at the annihilation of all of Europe's Jews, 800,000 from Hungary among them. The eldest of five children of a Transylvanian family, Gizelle tells the nearly incredible story of how she and her three sisters survived Auschwitz and Dachau, how they avoided death quotas, how through their youth they were able to survive beatings, endure near starvation and the torture that accompanied imprisonment. The account of liberation by American soldiers is equally moving and there is a satisfying conclusion, when American relatives make a home for them in this nation.

Hillesum, Etty. An Interrupted Life. New York: Pantheon, 1984. 226p.

The life referred to in the title belongs to the author of these diary entries, a "liberated" Dutch woman who was killed by the Nazis. A Jew without strong religious affiliation, she nevertheless "qualified" for a death camp under Nazi policies. These diaries tell of life during the occupation with interesting insights. They also speak of Hillesum herself, a person readers will become glad to know. She writes about wanting to be a writer, about her passion for an older man (who seems to be merely using her), about questions regarding love, friendship, and family. She learns that "despite all the suffering and injustice I cannot hate others." She also observes that it is "rash to assert that man shapes his own destiny. All he can do is determine his inner responses."

Jackson, Livia E. Bitton. Elli. New York: Time Books, 1980. 248p.

Elli is a memoir by a woman who was an adolescent Hungarian Jew at the time that Nazi deportations took place in 1944. Written to familiarize the reader with the tiny details of day-to-day existence among the tortured prisoners, this volume is reminiscent of the spare style of a Hemingway observer. Jackson is able to portray what has been recorded in other Holocaust memoirs in a fresh and penetrating fashion. She is particularly eloquent in presenting the emotional impact of the first Sabbath that the family survivors can share after liberation; so many relatives are missing. This autobiographical work contains many sensitive, powerful images.

Joffo, Joseph. A Bag of Marbles. New York: Houghton, 1974. 292p.

When the author was a boy, he played children's games like everyone else. When one day a yellow star was sewn onto his clothing everything changed: he was now a Jew. One of his young friends was attracted to the star and traded it for a bag of marbles. But while the star was gone, the humiliation remained. Joe's father, an escapee from Russian pogroms, sent the ten-year-old, with his twelve-year-old brother Maurice, to Vichy, France, unoccupied by Germans. With but fifty francs the boys survived on their wits for three years. They hustled, worked on the black market, and blustered their way through a whole series of adventures including capture and incarceration by the Nazis in Nice. They survived, and their story is an adventure of the human spirit.

Kessel, Sim. Hanged at Auschwitz. Briarcliff Manor, N.Y.: Stein & Day, 1972. 192p.

A Jew born in Paris, Kessel was a member of the French Resistance. He had also been a boxer before the war, and this fact probably saved his life. In July of 1942, he was captured by the Gestapo and tortured in French prisons until he was moved to Auschwitz a year later. A fabulous near-escape with four Polish prisoners is among the adventures of this memoir. He describes daily life in the infamous death camp: the diet, the routines, the organization of the German personnel, the distinctions between Auschwitz and its satellite camps. The series of almost unbelievable close calls that kept Kessel alive add to the readability--in spite of the horrors depicted--of this book.

Kielar, Wieslaw. Anus Mundi. New York: Times Books, 1980. 312p.

Later a film producer, Kielar was a non-Jewish political prisoner taken by the Nazis in Poland in 1940. The eye for detail he was to use so well in his professional life perhaps got its initial training in Auschwitz, the "anus spot of the world," as the title has it. He survived four years in the hell, seeing the concentration camp develop into the mass annihilation center it became. The author experienced much in the way of savage treatment at the hands of the SS troops but through imagination, bravery, and good fortune gained a job in the camp hospital (this after a long period at hard labor and as a corpse bearer). Here also is a story of friendship based on genuine affection, realism, and shared pain.

Klein, Gerda. All but My Life. New York: Hill & Wang, 1957. 246p.

Gerda Klein was fifteen when the Nazis entered her native Poland. She lived in a small town in a happy, middle-class family--her parents and an older brother--but all of that dramatically changed. As Jews, they were persecuted to such a degree that the girl lost her entire family and nearly all of her friends in the Holocaust. Her unemotional presentation of the events that transpired is noteworthy though she seems unable to find fault with anything that any of the victims did or failed to do; this has the effect of suggesting less than total objectivity.

Koehn, Ilse. Mischling, Second Degree. New York: Bantam, 1978. 213p.

The author's father had a Jewish mother; this made her subject to the Nazi anti-Semitic crusade. But the fact was a family secret (unknown even to Ilse herself). Furthermore, her parents were opposed to Hitler--but that, too, needed to be hidden. So Ilse joined the Hitler Youth and behaved in the formulistic manner as instructed. What life was like, growing up in fear in Nazi Germany, is movingly presented in this memoir. The comparison is natural: here is Anne Frank's story told from the other side. How the girl faked enthusiasm for Nazi aims, the close calls, the forced separation of her parents (for her safety), the agonies and few joys of such a childhood make this a unique autobiography.

Kogon, Eugen. The Theory and Practice of Hell. New York: Farrar, 1950. 307p.

Kogon, a Catholic sociologist and publisher, was opposed to

the Nazis from the beginning. The Gestapo had him marked for death quite early and in 1939 he was incarcerated in Buchenwald. Nevertheless, he survived for six years and was rescued by American troops in 1945. Kogon's experiences in the death camp are here related in unemotional tones in a style free of recriminations and vengeance-seeking. This book was a pioneer effort in explaining to Germans the full details of Nazi brutality.

Korczak, Janusz. Ghetto Diary. New York: Holocaust Library, 1978. 192p.

A well known pediatrician and author in his native Warsaw, Korczak left a brilliant career to care for orphans and finally to head an orphanage in the Warsaw Ghetto. After refusing many offers of rescue for himself, Korczak volunteered to accompany 200 Jewish children to the gas chamber at Treblinka. His account of the ghetto experience ends on the day before his death. What emerges here is a picture of a man of compassion and dignity. The first seventy pages of text are introductory and help in establishing the historical setting for the diary that follows.

Kuper, Jack. Child of the Holocaust. New York: Doubleday, 1968. 278p.

This is the autobiography of Jankele Kuperblum, an abandoned Jewish child in war-ravaged Poland. At age eight, the child lost his parents to the Nazis. For a while he was cared for by a Polish woman on a farm but she became so terrified of the Nazis that she forced him to leave. The child's wanderings from farm to farm make fascinating reading, a kind of factual counterpart to Jerzy Kosinski's novel, The Painted Bird. When the war came to an end, the lad's problems did not automatically cease. Many Poles, outlaws and ordinary peasants alike, tried to kill any Jews they could find. ✓ When the boy was finally placed in an orphanage for Jewish children, he was suspected of not being a Jew and bore the wrath of those who believed that he was from the kind of people who had murdered their relatives.

Leitner, Isabella. Fragments of Isabella. New York: Crowell, 1978. 112p.

A brief, moving, sometimes angry memoir, this book is by an Auschwitz survivor who cannot easily forgive certain Germans. "I curse you, even from the distance of these many years," she writes, "for keeping me so hungry that it affected my brain and subordinated me to your evil. And my apologies to the animals for comparing you to them, because surely animals are more humane." Some of the bestiality, physical pain, and psychological suffering that Leitner experienced is communicated here as she shares incidents like the loss of a sister, or the gassing of a newborn infant. For such reasons, when she is liberated she says good-bye to Auschwitz: "I will never see you again. I will always see you." Still, the book ends on a note of hope as Leitner addresses her dead mother on the occasion of becoming pregnant. A second communication occurs after the birth of a second child: "Mama, I make this vow to you: I will teach my sons to love life, to respect man, and to hate only one thing--war."

Levi, Primo. Survival in Auschwitz. New York: Collier, 1961. 157p.

One of the best known of the Holocaust memoirs, this is the account of an Italian Jew allowed to live in a death camp because he apparently could do useful work for the Nazis. He tells of his painful journey to the camp, learning the absurd routine, what a typical day was like, how the black market worked, which moral standards did not apply in the camp, how some survived primarily through retaining their human dignity in spite of the indecency going on around them, and much more. In one chapter Levi tells of being chosen to work in a laboratory where he found relative warmth, better food, some soap, and the opportunity to steal items valuable in bartering. Levi lost his faith in God in Auschwitz yet, curiously, not his faith in humanity. (This book was previously published under the title If This Man Is a Man.)

Meltzer, Milton. Never to Forget. New York: Harper, 1976. 217p.

The experience of individual Jews during the Holocaust is related here to personalize the statistics in a meaningful way. The author gives attention to Hitler's rise to power and the Nazi death machine but uses letters, diaries, poems, and songs to re-create a lost people. The narrative is in three parts: book one deals with a history of hatred. The next, titled "Destruction of the Jews," covers Crystal Night, the "Final Solution," Zyklon gas and more. Finally, in "Spirit of Resistance" there are sections on revolt, fighting back, dying with dignity and hope.

Mermelstein, Mel. By Bread Alone. Los Angeles: Crescent, 1979. 264p.

The author is the only person in his immediate family to survive the Nazis. Raised in a Ukrainian village, he tells of his childhood, his incarceration in a ghetto, his experiences in various concentration camps, and his peripatetic life after the war. This volume has a certain authenticity of tone that is captivating. It is subtitled "The Story of A-4685" to emphasize the dehumanizing efforts of the Nazis.

Michelson, Frida. I Survived Rumboli. New York: Holocaust Library, 1982. 224p.

There were 30,000 Jews living in Riga, Latvia's capital, before World War II. In a daily massacre of thousands of women, children, and elderly only two women survived at Rumboli; the author of this work is one of them. By trade a seamstress, she tells of life under the Nazis, of how she hid from them for several years in forests protected by Latvian peasants who were Seventh-Day Adventists. These men and women risked everything to help save her.

Minco, Marga. _Bitter Herbs_. New York: Oxford Univ. Pr., 1960. 115p.

Without an angry word, no accusations or curses, Minco tells the story of the loss of her family in Holland and her own salvation from the Nazis. In 1940 her father convinced the rest of his Jewish family that there really was no reason to flee the oncoming Germans. His error of judgment, typical of many who could never envision the horrors and dimensions of the Holocaust, cost all but Marga their lives. After the liberation, she tried looking for her immediate family members in the faces of those who returned but her relatives never came back. The absurdity of the German campaign to annihilate world Jewry is made very poignant in this little tale of a single Dutch family.

Muller, Filip. _Eyewitness Auschwitz_. Briarcliff Manor, N.Y.: Stein & Day, 1979. 180p.

Inmates of concentration camps were forced to labor in the crematoria, burning victims of Nazi atrocities. Usually these workers did their grim tasks for from three to six months and then themselves became victims. The author somehow managed to survive as a Sonderkommando for three years and here tells the entire, almost unbelievable account. Detail after detail, told in a totally objective manner, makes for horrifying reading. Perhaps most astonishing is Muller's pride in his efficient work that he recounts when telling of preparing for a Nazi inspection, when stacked up bodies had to be processed in a hurry. Meeting the deadline became a source of satisfaction for this man, robotized by his activities.

Oberski, Jona. _Childhood_. New York: Doubleday, 1983. 128p.

A moving memoir of childhood pain, this book should take its place with some of the important literature of that subgenre. Oberski tells his story from the point of view of a seven-year-old boy. The lad experienced the discrimination that his family felt in Holland during the Nazi occupation; incarceration at the Bergen-Belsen camp; the death of his father during the war; his mother's demise not long after liberation; and his later adoption by another family.

Pinkus, Oscar. The House of Ashes. Cleveland, Ohio: World,
     1964. 243p.
     A personal account of survival without self-aggrandizement,
this is a tense story of how the author and a few other Jews--some
from his own family--were able to stay alive in Poland from 1939
to 1945. The writer tells how entire Jewish communities were destroyed in his home town of Losice, and also in Siedice, Biala,
and Miedzyrzec. A unique feature of Pinkus's book is his portrayal of the Polish underground that acted so treacherously against
the Jews; they surely ought to have been united against their common enemy, the Nazis. Even after liberation, Pinkus was not safe.
Two attempts were made on his life and three of the twenty Jewish
survivors of Losice were actually murdered in their sleep.

Rochman, Leyb. The Pit and the Trap. New York: Holocaust
     Library, 1983. 271p.
     A diary of the day-to-day survival in Poland by the Jewish
author and four others, this book makes for both incredible and
inspiring reading. Pain and relief, evil and good, murder and
salvation make up the story, but of course it is the tragedy that
stands out. It is all here, and memorably told.

Rubinowicz, Dawid. The Diary of Dawid Rubinowicz. Edmonds,
     Wash.: Creative Options, 1982. 104p.
     Young Dawid was twelve years old when the Nazis entered his
native Poland. The events he writes of in this diary parallel Anne
Frank's, and his work complements hers in many ways. Hers is a
journal of youthful longing; his are notes of youthful terror.
Hers is done in rather mature style; his reactions, so childlike
and honest, bear the stamp of true sentiment without the excess
of a bathetic sentimentality. Perhaps most moving is the boy's
account of the arrest of his father shortly after the man had given
his son a beating. The confusion of the child at the parting is
painfully noted.

Schneider, Gertrude. Journey into Terror. New York: Ark House,
     1980. 220p.
     Based on the diary the author kept as a youngster while in the
Riga Ghetto in Latvia, as well as on interviews with other Jewish
survivors and certain Nazi documents, this is an absorbing account
of one of the central ghettos in the Nazi system. Within three
weeks after all of the Jews of Riga were forced into the ghetto in
1941, 28,000 were killed by the Nazis--including all of the children
and women. This ghetto became a transit depot for Jews being sent
to various work and death camps. Glimpses of the Jewish attempts
at education, at cultural activities, even at romance--perhaps especially at romance--tell something about human perseverance and
the will to live.

Schwiefert, Peter. The Bird Has No Wings. New York: St. Martin's, 1976. 180p.

Peter Schwiefert's letters, mostly to his mother, are presented here. He was a young man who left Germany as World War II was beginning. Born of a "mixed" marriage and raised primarily in the Christian tradition of his father, Schwiefert proclaimed his Jewishness and demanded that it be acknowledged even when his mother married a third time in order to solidify her safety, emigrate from Germany, and enter the Orthodox Christian Church. These letters indicate the young man's agony, principles, deprivations, and joys as he traveled in exile through Italy, Greece, and Portugal, finally to enlist with the Free French Forces; he was killed just before the end of the war. Peter is uncomprehending in the face of his mother's resistance. She refuses to admit her own Jewishness or (consistently, therefore) the validity of her son's own heroic act. Isolated from his homeland, further isolated by the hostility of his entire family toward his new affirmation, Peter was in an unenviable situation. As he was not raised as a Jew, he did not even have the comfort or support of its traditions. Yet, in spite of his admirable "political" behavior, these letters do not present Schwiefert in an always admirable light. His attachment to his mother seems highly Oedipal and his vanity intrudes itself on several occasions. His belief that Jews must not have their Israel is puzzling: "They must live among other people to stay fully conscious of their identity." Several letters by Peter's mother are included. They show her to be a narcissistic, petty woman who, even upon hearing of her son's death, betrays a "look what it's done to me" attitude.

Senesh, Hannah. Hannah Senesh: Her Life and Diary. New York: Schocken, 1972. 257p.

A Hungarian who emigrated to Palestine before World War II, Senesh joined a newly formed group of paratroopers who penetrated Yugoslavia and Hungary to warn Jews of German plans against them. She was captured, tortured, and executed in 1944, at age twenty-three. The early diary entries are certainly not mature in the way the later ones are. At first a teen-ager is putting thoughts to paper; the later notes, letters, and poems, however, are important to an understanding of this young woman's courage and sense of mission.

Shapell, Nathan. Witness to the Truth. New York: McKay, 1974. 386p.

A personal narrative in two parts, this is an extremely uneven but nevertheless quite valuable book. Part I deals sensitively with the author's Holocaust experiences. He is particularly effective in revealing how the SS managed to lure so many

Jews to their deaths. The second section of the book, however, deals with the life of a displaced person after liberation. This segment is less informative and seems to contain a number of less modest passages. The book was written in English, not the writer's native language, which lends poignancy to the tale at times, but proves irritating on other occasions. This is much better seen as documentation than as art.

Szmaglewska, Seweryna. Smoke over Birkenau. New York: Holt, 1947. 386p.

Written with admirable detachment, this is the account of a Polish university student imprisoned by the Gestapo in July of 1942 because of her work with the underground resistance. She lived at Birkenau for the better part of three years, and this is the story-- not only of her experiences but also those of other suffering inmates. The author is one of those who testified at the Nuremberg Trials.

Ten Boom, Corrie. The Hiding Place. New York: Bantam, 1974. 242p.

Corrie Ten Boom was a member of a family that, out of a solid Christian faith, helped save Jewish victims during the Holocaust. Her story encompasses risk, capture, pain, hunger, devotion, and sacrifice, but most of all love. Ten Boom's life, which blossomed into a worldwide ministry of comfort and counsel after she was in her fifties--before which it was a quiet, spinsterish existence--is chronicled here with less sentimentality than in her other books. Some of the lessons to be learned from this autobiography include how to love your enemy (including the prison guards who persecute you); how to get by with fewer material comforts, even necessities; how God uses weakness; on facing death; being secure in faith in the midst of insecurity; coping with separation; etc.

------. A Prisoner and Yet. . . . New York: Jove, 1977. 176p.

The Nazis arrested Corrie Ten Boom and her family for the crime of hiding Jews in Holland from their German tormentors. Their constant references to Jesus and other manifestations of Christian faith infuriated the captors. Her father was the first to die in prison; others of the family followed. But, according to this account, none of them had their religious beliefs diminished by what occurred at the hands of the occupation troops. What did this survivor not see and feel after being thrust into that first prison cell--solitary confinement, illness, young children in prison, slave labor, the horror of Ravensbruck, whippings, typhus? And yet every page bears a sign of her total faith and spiritual commitment. For some, the writing may appear overly sentimental, but the author's Christian heroism seems hardly to be doubted.

------. Prison Letters. New York: Bantam, 1978. 85p.
Joyous religious faith may be the last thing expected of a concentration camp survivor, but Corrie Ten Boom's Christianity sustained her in hours of great darkness. Her prison letters form a collection which, along with the communications of her incarcerated sister Betsie, are the nucleus of this book. Letters from other family members are also included. Prisoners were allowed very few letters; therefore many people often shared in the writing of one. Most of these documents were smuggled out by a German soldier who hid them in the clean laundry that the prisoners washed for the troops. These are remarkable illustrations of faith in times of total duress.

Tillion, Germaine. Ravensbruck. New York: Doubleday, 1975. 256p.
Now an anthropologist, the author looks back at the women's concentration camp where she was imprisoned for helping to organize a resistance movement in France. She was sent to Ravensbruck in Germany along with her mother. She here tells how the camp was run, what motivated the administrators, and how prisoners reacted. Her sources include her own secret notes, interviews with survivors, and some of the camp documents themselves.

Trepman, Paul. Among Men and Beasts. New York: Barnes, 1978. 229p.
The adventures of a young man who had to keep on the move, ever alert, always wary of the enemy--this is the autobiographical account of a Pole who fled the invading Germans by going to the Ukraine. When the Nazis came there, Trepman returned to his native land. He existed as best he could in and around the ghettos in Warsaw and Robatyn. Later he specifies how he managed to survive six concentration camps.

Von der Grun, Max. Howl Like the Wolves. New York: Morrow, 1980. 285p.
As a child in Nazi Germany, the author was brought up by parents who were anti-Nazi. However, survival was necessary and it meant adaptation. Hence, the boy's mother taught him "to howl like the wolves so as not to be eaten by them." A great deal of attention is given to the ordeal of the Jews as the author here mingles autobiography, history, and documents quite effectively.

Vrba, Rudolf, and Alan Bestic. I Cannot Forgive. New York: Bantam, 1968. 277p.

A teen-ager sentenced to Auschwitz, from which he escaped to join partisans in western Slovakia, Vrba was motivated to survive because he was obsessed with trying to live in order to tell the world what he had experienced. And what he experienced was devastating. At Auschwitz he worked initially as a Sonder-kommando in the incinerators, then as a registrar of victims. He gathered information for his testimony from many of them. Vrba meticulously collected facts but found an uncaring world when he tried to use his evidence of atrocities committed against the Jews to persuade various influential people, including Pope Pius XII.

Wells, Leon. The Death Brigade. New York: Schocken, 1978. 307p.

First published as The Janowska Road, this is one of the most startling volumes of Holocaust history. Wells was a youth in Lvov, Poland, when the Germans put him on the Death Brigade. That group's task was to obliterate any traces of mass executions of prisoners at the Janowska concentration camp. Among many unforgettable episodes in this work are the time Wells had to dig his own grave (followed by an inexplicable escape), his suicide attempt when his mother was arrested, and the narration of the death of his entire family.

Wiesel, Elie. Night. New York: Hill & Wang, 1960. 116p.

This memoir by a death camp survivor who, at fifteen, lost his parents and younger sister in Auschwitz, is a classic. Originally published in Yiddish in approximately 800 pages, Wiesel cut the work severely. The style, which places this book under the heading "Literature of Silence," is perfect for the message. Something must be written of the Holocaust events or the dead would be betrayed, Wiesel feels, and the loss of his family, friends, even God, is told here in a profoundly moving way.

Zar, Rose. In the Mouth of the Wolf. Philadelphia: Jewish Publication Society of America, 1983. 225p.

Rose Zar's story of survival, told without self-pity, is both exciting and inspiring. Zar tells of her attempts at nineteen to flee the Nazis and maintain not only her physical existence but also her spiritual well being. She was buoyed up by her strong urge to be reunited with her family after the war. For instance, she had to overcome hatred before she could care for the camp commander's baby boy, as she was tempted to avenge herself on that innocent child.

Zassenhaus, Hiltgunt. Walls. Boston: Beacon, 1976. 248p.

"For me, the Third Reich meant windows glued over by swastikas and bonfires in which 'reverence for life' went up in flames. It meant empty facades--all that was left of a people silenced by their fear of Hitler and choked by the smoke of burning cities." This quotation indicates the theme of this book. However, more central is the paragraph that follows: "But, for me, the Third Reich also meant a family who stood together in their opposition to Hitler, a father who taught his children to live by their convictions and a mother who said, 'Only what you give, you'll have.'" This is the story of that family, and particularly of one woman who defied the Gestapo, told in reflections passionless yet charged with impact.

Ziemian, Joseph. The Cigarette Sellers of Three Crosses Square. 2nd ed. New York: Avon, 1975. 140p.
A Jewish resistance fighter and one of the few to survive the Warsaw Ghetto uprising, author Joseph Ziemian chronicles the true story of a group of amazing children who also survived that tragedy and lived precariously afterwards on their wits alone. This tiny band managed to stay alive by selling blackmarket cigarettes to the Nazi occupiers and by singing in the streets, all the while hiding the secret of their true background. Disheveled, ragged, dirty, and always hungry, the young fugitives endured through courage and devotion to each other. The author, who came upon the group by chance, became their protector and their chronicler. This edition contains new material and an epilogue that an earlier edition did not.

Zuker-Bujanowska, Liliana. Liliana's Journal. New York: Dial, 1980. 162p.
When she was relatively young, this Jewish author lived .n a family well assimilated into Polish life. But to the Nazi invaders they were Jews, and all were subject to incarceration in the Warsaw Ghetto. Her father helped Liliana to escape to the Aryan side. She married a resistance fighter, but he was killed in 1944. This memoir was written soon after the events depicted, but not translated into English until more than a generation later.

Zyskind, Sara. Stolen Years. Minneapolis: Lerner, 1981. 284p.
The title refers to the author's childhood, which was robbed by the Nazis in 1939 when they entered Lodz, Poland, her home community. She was eleven at the time, a confident, happy blond child leading a normal existence. One day, it all changed abruptly. Sara experienced the misery of ghetto life and the horrors and brutality, physical and psychological, of concentration camp living. She tells of friendship in the ghetto, of the frightful

first night in Auschwitz, of having her beautiful head of hair completely shorn, of hope, of despair, and finally, of liberation, which was not without its risks (from a drunken Russian officer, for example).

JEWISH
RESISTANCE

Over the centuries, the Jewish people have earned a reputation for adapting, rather than fighting. While this theory is often valid, such adaptation has generally been a matter of policy, rather than because the Jews lack courage or numbers. In addition, many Jews believe that killing is wrong, that there is a higher form of resistance than mere physical resistance; even during the Holocaust, some stated that they went to their deaths, to face God, in innocence: "At least we didn't become like them." Nevertheless, the charge that Jews did not physically resist the Nazis during World War II is nonsense, as the following books prove. Such an accusation may even serve as an implicit attempt to blame the victims for their condition. As Terrence Des Pres indicates in The Survivor, how could anyone tax concentration camp victims with such behavior? Although stripped of their homes and possessions, their families and friends, their names (in exchange for numbers), shorn of all hair, hungry, covered with their own filth and perhaps the excrement of those sleeping in bunk beds above them, diseased and knowing that even if they escaped from camps partisans in the woods might gun them down--the prisoners showed an enormous amount of physical resistance. Such behavior is what these books are about.

Ainsztein, Reuben. Jewish Resistance in Nazi-Occupied Eastern Europe. New York: Harper, 1975. 970p.
The false idea that the Jews did not physically resist the Nazis and their collaborators is widespread, though less so now than before books such as this one were published. Ainsztein goes beyond other authors who document fighting Jews during

World War II; he finds this myth to be an extension of one claiming passivity of Diaspora Jews in general. This writer points to Jews in history serving as soldiers, sailors, corsairs, explorers, etc. The writer also strongly condemns the Poles and Soviets, who failed to help Jews in their time of need.

Baker, Leonard. Days of Sorrow and Pain. New York: Macmillan, 1978. 396p.
Leo Baeck headed the Reichsvertretung, an organization of German Jews who together faced the Nazis when Hitler came to power. Baeck was a uniting factor among Jewish groups. He worked secretly with emissaries from abroad to assist in the emigration of a large number of Jews. Rather than flee, however, Baeck, a rabbi, remained with his people. The sixth time the Nazis arrested him, Baeck was sixty-nine. He was sent to Theresienstadt. Forced to haul trash carts during a punishing work day, this heroic man organized educational programs for other prisoners at night. After the war, he worked with equal energy for the reconciliation of Germans and Jews.

Barkai, Meyer, ed. The Fighting Ghettos. Philadelphia: Lippincott, 1962. 407p.
There are more than 2,000 memoirs and other primary records gathered near Haifa, Israel, at the Ghetto Fighters House. Barkai has selected from that material documents by fighters who survived the ghettos and concentration camps. Also included are the notes and memoirs of many who perished but who left behind evidence of their humanity and what they were forced to undergo.

Bauer, Yehuda. Flight and Rescue. New York: Random, 1970. 371p.
This is a well documented account of the organized escape of Eastern European Jewish survivors, 1944-48. Almost 300,000 Jews who survived the Holocaust began to move out of Eastern Europe at the end of World War II in what has been called the largest spontaneous and illegal migration in recent history. The movement was known as Brichah ("flight" in Hebrew), the name of the underground organization that aided in coordinating this enormous effort. Bauer's typically solid scholarship, combined with readability, is evident throughout.

Cholawski, Shalom. Soldiers from the Ghetto. New York: Barnes, 1980. 182p.
Details of the resistance against the Nazis made by the Jews of Nesvizh, before the Warsaw Ghetto uprising, are hardly known. Because the Nesvizh Jews realized what the enemy (with the aid of Polish sympathizers) would do to them, they burned

their ghetto, fought with homemade weapons, and formed a partisan army in the forest. From there they harassed the German troops advancing toward Russia in very effective ways. The author, a platoon leader who commanded Jews, Poles and Russians, recalls the inside story of their individual and collective heroism.

Druks, Herbert. <u>Jewish Resistance during the Holocaust.</u> New York: Irvington, 1983. 132p.
  Druks makes two points in this work. First, the Warsaw Ghetto uprising was not the sole instance of resistance by Jews during the Holocaust; second, he wishes to put an end to the generalization that Jews went to their death at the hands of the Nazis like "sheep to slaughter." In a solid way, he succeeds in both areas.

Eckman, Lester, and Chaim Lazar. <u>The Jewish Resistance.</u> New York: Shengold, 1977. 282p.
  The history of the Jewish partisans in Lithuania and White Russia during the Nazi occupation, 1940-45, is the subject of this study. Several hundred partisans were interviewed for this book, including members of the Federation of Former Underground Freedom Fighters. The accounts detailed here of physical resistance against enormous odds is noteworthy, but so, alas, are the stories of atrocities committed against a nearly helpless people. The enemy turned out to be not only the Nazis but Ukranian anti-Semites as well.

Friedman, Ina R. <u>Escape or Die.</u> Reading, Mass.: Addison-Wesley, 1982. 146p.
  All survivors of the Holocaust have a story, and this book collects the terrifying adventures of twelve young men and women, all under twenty years of age, Jews and non-Jews, who outlived the Nazi's plans for them. Each is a first-person narrative and, when brought together, comprise a testimony to courage, perseverance, ingenuity, and luck. One boy was imprisoned as a spy; another saw his family and residence shattered on Crystal Night; a girl spent the first six years of her existence hiding in cellars; an eleven-year-old boy survived the misery of the Warsaw Ghetto and two death camps. These are simply written, memorable accounts.

Friedman, Philip. <u>Martyrs and Fighters.</u> New York: Lancer, 1954. 254p.
  Warsaw was the cultural and spiritual center of Polish Jewry. The Nazis first imprisoned the Jews in the Warsaw Ghetto, and systematically set about their destruction. In 1943, after suffering starvation, degradation, torture, and murder, the Jews attempted to fight back with virtually no weapons; the ensuing

hopeless battle is recounted in this book, which relies totally on eyewitness testimony. The story is a gripping one. The sources include memoirs, newspapers, diaries, archivists, and historians who were present (including some who perished), accounts by Nazis, elder citizens, teenagers, journalists--even concentration camp songs.

Garlinski, Jozef. Fighting Auschwitz. New York: Fawcett, 1975. 416p.
So secret was the underground resistance movement at Auschwitz that some former inmates claim it could not have existed. But the overwhelming evidence amassed by historian Garlinski clearly shows the heroism of those who clandestinely opposed their jailers. Not only did these individuals fight but, through their contacts with the outside, they also learned of Allied victories and thus raised the sagging spirits of the inmates--so necessary for the survival of those still alive near liberation time. The author gives details of the camp organization, the build-up of the underground, communications with the Allies, the murder of Jews, spies, various nationality groups, and escapes through the final evacuation of the camp by the Nazis.

Gross, Leonard. The Last Jews in Berlin. New York: Simon & Schuster, 1982. 349p.
A handful of Jewish men and women, calling themselves "U-boats," lived through the war in the capital of Germany. Some were concealed by Germans opposed to Hitler; several hid themselves, and others lived openly with disguised identities. All had close calls with the Gestapo, often through the machinations of traitors who turned Jews in for compensation. Satisfying accounts are given of the few who aided these people, including the work of a Swedish church in Berlin that hid Jews both on the premises and in certain houses, and helped smuggle many into Sweden.

Gruber, Samuel. I Chose Life. New York: Shengold, 1978. 158p.
Gruber was a leader of resistance fighers in Poland, and this is his memoir. For him, "to fight was to live for another day, to rest was to risk instant death." The author presents very strong scenes of the Nazi destruction of Jews, including the killing of small children. He tells of his lonely escape from the Lublin Ghetto into the forest and the hostility of some Poles, who represented as much danger to Jews as the occupying German troops.

Kluger, Ruth, and Peggy Mann. The Last Escape. New York: Doubleday, 1973. 513p.
Subtitled "The Launching of the Largest Secret Rescue Movement of All Times," this book contains the account of the so-called

illegal immigration movement and the attempts to rescue European Jews from the Nazis and their collaborators. Although the ultimate outcome is known, the story is nevertheless satisfying in certain ways.

Kohn, Nahum, and Howard Roiter. A Voice from the Forest. New York: Holocaust Library, 1980. 255p.

Nahum Kohn was a Jewish watchmaker in Sieradz, Poland, who fled the invading Nazis to the forest of Volhynia. He escaped, after a series of adventures and close calls, to join the unit of the well known Soviet resister, Medvedév, who organized an intelligence network for spying and resistance activities. During much of this period the author worked closely with Nikolay Kuznetsov, one of the legendary Soviet partisans. Kuznetsov, in fact, was actually able to infiltrate Nazi headquarters because of his facility in languages and act as a Gestapo agent under the name of Captain Paul Siebert.

Kulski, Julian Eugeniusz. Dying, We Live. New York: Holt, 1979. 304p.

A personal chronicle of a young freedom fighter in Warsaw from 1939 to 1945, this book tells the story of Julian Kulski, the Protestant son of the mayor of Poland's largest city. He was only ten years old when the Nazis invaded Poland. In spite of his age, Kulski joined the Polish resistance movement. He was jailed by the Gestapo, released, and joined the Polish Home Army. With this unit he fought in its valiant, two-month battle with the Nazis in August and September of 1944. Captured, Kulski was incarcerated in a prisoner-of-war camp inside Germany at the age of fifteen. The journal form of the memoir provides a certain engaging immediacy.

Kurzman, Dan. The Bravest Battle. New York: Pinnacle, 1978. 458p.

The twenty-eignt days of the Warsaw Ghetto uprising are covered by this comprehensive account. When, in April, 1943, Nazi troops under General Jurgen Stroop entered the Warsaw Ghetto to complete the annihilation of the Jews there, they met an unexpected and fierce resistance. Under the leadership of Mordechai Anielewicz, the poorly armed Jews held out for four weeks, inflicting heavy losses on the Germans. Using their meager weapons judiciously (some of them handmade grenades), the resisters fought soldiers who had planes, tanks, artillery, machine guns, flame throwers, and a supply line, advantages not available to the defenders.

Lambert, Gilles. Operation Hazalah. Indianapolis: Bobbs-Merrill, 1974. 235p.

Thousands of Jews in Hungary were rescued near the end of World War II by an imaginative, daring group of young Zionists known as Hazalah ("rescue" in Hebrew), first organized in Budapest in 1944. They had no weapons, no contacts with the Allies, no support from any national resistance group. In fact, some Jews actually tried to discourage their efforts in the hopes of not irritating the Nazis, as they couldn't believe that the Nazis would try to eliminate 900,000 of them--but the Hazalah members knew better. False identification papers were produced; Jews were assisted to pass as Christians, agents from neutral embassies, police, even as Nazi SS troops. Although 700,000 Hungarian Jews were murdered, the Hazalah youth were credited with saving about 100,000 more.

Latour, Anny. The Jewish Resistance in France (1940-1944). New York: Holocaust Library, 1981. 287p.

Increasing documentation has recently surfaced to indicate that there was a great deal of Jewish resistance to Nazi aggression. Anny Latour, who participated in some of the events she chronicles here, interviewed hundreds of persons from various "rescue networks" in France who aided Jews in various ways. Some of these groups included Christians who risked their safety to help Jews. The story is a noble one and is well written.

Mark, Ber. Uprising in the Warsaw Ghetto. New York: Schocken, 1975. 209p.

Twice revised as new materials became available, this is a Polish historian's study of Jewish resistance in Poland's capital city. On April 19, 1943, over 2,000 Nazi troops entered the Warsaw Ghetto to destroy the last of the Jews; the event was to serve as a birthday present for Hitler on the next day. The house-to-house Jewish resistance, by both women and men, is an amazing story. How, with a few hand weapons and immense courage, Jews resisted armored troops is told from eyewitness accounts, hastily scribbled notes made by those about to die, and documents found in various archives after the war.

Meed, Vladka. On Both Sides of the Wall. New York: Holocaust Library, 1979. 276p.

At age seventeen, when the Nazis occupied her native Poland, Meed joined the underground. This Jewish girl with an Aryan appearance became an important carrier, literally, serving on both sides of internment barriers. Much is treated here: identity cards, the Polish police, forced labor, the Warsaw Ghetto, Polish friends, resistance, blackmailers, hiding, particular individuals, forged documents, labor camps, and the eventual return after the war, with family remnants reuniting briefly and uneasily. There is much information and adventure to be found in this valuable document.

Perl, William. <u>The Four-Front War.</u> New York: Crown, 1979. 376p.

A group known as "The Action" helped save 40,000 Jews in the Second World War. But their foes were not only the Nazis and their collaborators; the British, too, seen by some as enemies of Jewish refugees, receive significant attention here. The author is one who helped, before the war, to organize and direct The Action. This first-hand narrative tells an appalling story of bureaucratic ill-will, extraordinary efforts, and dignity in the face of personal destruction.

Rashke, Richard. <u>Escape from Sobibor.</u> New York: Houghton, 1982. 432p.

Little attention has been paid to what has been called the largest escape of Allied prisoners during World War II. In October of 1943, about 600 Jews crashed through the confines of the Sobibor death camp in Poland. Approximately half escaped, but only 50 survived the war. This volume is based on the accounts of 18 participants. Since only three German documents about the Sobibor camp exist, this is a particularly valuable contribution.

Shepherd, Naomi. <u>A Refuge from Darkness.</u> New York: Pantheon, 1984. 291p.

Wilfred Israel, British-born heir to a German-Jewish business fortune, used his wealth and social standing to ransom, protect, and otherwise rescue Jews during the Holocaust. A gentle man, an intellectual, shunning celebrity, Israel was a dissident Zionist and pacifist. Early in the Nazi era, he realized the implication of Hitler's Jewish policies. He worked against Nazism, on refugee policies, and eventually helped provide asylum for 10,000 children. When the war broke out, Israel left Germany but continued his saving work. Naomi Shepherd had access to hundreds of pertinent documents and interviewed many of the people who benefited from his efforts.

Sim, Kevin. <u>Women at War.</u> New York: Morrow, 1982. 286p.

Five heroines who resisted the Nazis and survived are the focus of this book. The stories are based in Paris, Warsaw, Hamburg, Birmingham (England), and Baltimore. They each portray personal triumphs: of a British agent in France; a housewife who helped Norwegian Jews to safety; a Polish Communist; a German who had breathtakingly close calls in helping prisoners; a Jewish teen-ager who survived Auschwitz. Based on interviews with hundreds of men and women, these true tales offer high adventure.

Stroop, Jurgen. <u>The Stroop Report.</u> New York: Pantheon, 1979. unp.

Some 60,000 Jews fought the Nazis in the Warsaw Ghetto in April of 1943. The group had only homemade hand grenades, nine rifles, fifty-nine pistols, and about fifteen bullets for each weapon. They faced crack German troops armed with flame throwers, armored vehicles, and limitless ammunition. The outcome of the confrontation was never in doubt, but the civilians held off the Nazis for a longer period than the entire Polish army was able to defend its nation against the invaders. Some Jewish chroniclers have provided eyewitness accounts of the heroics and horrors; now the official, documented Nazi version, by the commanding officer of Hitler's troops, has become available. In daily reports to his superior, General Stroop details the slaughter in self-congratulatory terms. On May 3 he wrote of apprehending 1,392 Jews, shooting 95 of them, and "transferring" 177 more; this made the "total number of Jews apprehended to date" 41,806. By the end of three weeks the figure reached 56,065. Stroop lies when he indicates the number of his own casualties, deliberately downplaying his losses. When on trial for his life, Stroop never denied the numbers of Jews destroyed under his command. He was condemned by his own writings; they are necessary reading.

Suhl, Uri, ed. The Fought Back. New York: Schocken, 1975. 327p.

Somehow the phrase "like sheep to the slaughter" has been linked to Jews murdered in the ghettos and death camps. Much is implied in such a statement: first, the notion that armed resistance is the only form of defiance--negating any concept of a higher, spiritual resistance. Second, also implied is the idea that no Jews ever fought back physically. This volume refutes these implications. Jewish resistance groups were formed in nearly every ghetto, every concentration camp, every death factory. Sabotage and armed revolt continued throughout the war. In thirty-four essays by a series of authors, these events are clearly and powerfully depicted.

Syrkim, Marie. Blessed Is the Match. New York: Knopf, 1947. 361p.

One of the earliest accounts of Jewish resistance to the Nazis, this book follows Jews through the Second World War and the resistance movement in Europe to their conflicts with the British in Palestine. While terror and killing by the Nazis are part of this story, so is survival. So, too, is the meaning of Palestine as a place of security, as a territory where the concept of responsibility by Jews for other Jews might solidify.

Temchin, Michael. The Witch Doctor. New York: Holocaust Library, 1983. 184p.

From eastern Poland, Temchin led a band of partisans who fought the Nazis from hiding--keeping a certain distance from his anti-Semitic countrymen and women, as well as the invaders. A man filled with hope and possessing important leadership skills, the author also had a fine facility in languages, which aided him in his survival. Self-confidence and a sense of responsibility for others were also a part of this man's makeup. He kept on going despite the loss of his wife, father, and two brothers.

Trunk, Isaiah. Jewish Responses to Nazi Persecution. Briarcliff Manor, N.Y.: Stein & Day, 1979. 371p.

As the title indicates, this volume contains accounts--sixty-two of them--of survivors of Nazi persecution. Trunk not only provides eyewitness accounts of tortures, murders, and insurrections, but also indicates where the narrator has had a memory lapse and made an error of chronology, name, number, or other fact. Trunk further shows how the accounts overlap and substantiate each other. The volume begins with a long introduction by the author outlining the historical antecedents to the Holocaust (the Crusades--and Jewish resistance to them; the catastrophe of the Marranos in Spain; etc.). He discusses Jewish attitudes during the Emancipation period, one of gratitude for a certain new freedom; hence their loyalty and patriotism towards their national governments. He maintains that German Jews believed that once Hitler assumed power, he would become a responsible leader and abandon the extravagances of his anti-Semitic programs. Trunk also outlines the responses to the Nazis made by Jews. Passive resistance was a manifestation of Jewish courage; there was also a great deal of Jewish armed resistance. And again, as Trunk illustrates, there is not one recorded instance of armed insurrection by Gentile inmates of a concentration camp during World War II. The basic themes of the eyewitness accounts are: resistance, the attitudes of non-Jews (even when they aided Jews, it was often for personal gain); the suffering of children; and conditions of imprisonment.

ASSISTANCE
AND BETRAYAL
IN NAZI-OCCUPIED
TERRITORIES

This chapter contains the stories of Samaritans, non-Jews who helped Jews escape the Nazis. If any part of this book should be more substantive, it ought to be this one. An overwhelming response would, in fact, have meant that no such massive persecution of the Jews could have taken place. But only a few accounts are found here. Some are famous; others are obscure.

Also included in this chapter are the stories of how the official churches, both Roman Catholic and Protestant, failed to denounce the Nazi persecution, even though, it has become increasingly clear, religious leaders were well informed about the situation of the Jews. Readers may also wish to refer to several histories of Christian anti-Semitism that were described in chapter 1 and to Conway's book on the churches under the Third Reich, described in chapter 2.

Anger, Per. With Raoul Wallenberg in Budapest. New York: Holocaust Library, 1981. 192p.

Wallenberg is said to have participated, directly and indirectly, in the rescue of nearly 100,000 Jews from the Nazis. A fellow Swedish diplomat, Per Anger, assisted Wallenberg and tells his story. Their work took tireless effort; there was tremendous personal risk involved; worldly rewards were not offered. But the saving mission was hugely successful. When the Russians came to liberate Budapest, Wallenberg vanished and only rumors of his appearance in various Soviet prison camps fuel the hopes that he survived.

d'Aubigne, Jeanne Merle, and Violette Mouchon. God's Underground. St. Louis: Bethany, 1970. 238p.

CIMADE is the acronym for a Christian organization that in France, during World War II, transformed itself into a Christian witness movement attempting to assist those suffering at the hands of the Nazis--Jews in particular. While Roman Catholic participation in CIMADE now exists, this was not the case during the period in question. The authors tell of the group's activities and the support it received from the World Council of Churches. The pain and death, the deportations, border crossings, escapes, and much more are chronicled here. But so are stories of humanity, of kindness through risk, of people saving people just because the victims are people--not for money, not for gain of any kind.

Bartoszewski, Wladyslaw, and Zofia Lewin, eds. The Samaritans. New York: Twayne, 1970. 442p.

More Polish Jews were massacred in the Holocaust than Jews from any other nation. Of some 3,100,000 Polish Jews in 1939, about 2,700,000 died under Nazi occupation. Many Poles cooperated with the invaders in this mass destruction and the general history of this collaborative effort is quite well documented and known. But there were heroic people who risked their lives to save Jews. This anthology of personal narratives provides a major portion of that aspect of history. The bravery of certain individuals in the Polish underground, in particular, is revealed.

Bertelsen, Aage. October '43. New York: Putnam, 1954. 246p.

The title refers to the date on which the Nazis were thwarted in their plans to deport Danish Jews to concentration and death camps. This was a time when non-Jewish Danish citizens showed their humanity, decency, and courage. The author was one of the leaders who worked to smuggle Danish Jews across the channel to Sweden; his reticent style adds to the authenticity of the story.

Bierman, John. Righteous Gentile. New York: Viking, 1981. 256p.

Winston Churchill is one of only two honorary citizens of the United States. This book is a biography of the other, Raoul Wallenberg. He was a Swedish diplomat who helped rescue up to 100,000 Hungarian Jews; when he came into contact with the Russians, however, he disappeared. The second half of this book deals with what is believed to have happened to him in Soviet concentration camps. The author makes a strong case for Wallenberg being alive even into the 1980s; other researchers have drawn far less optimistic conclusions.

Falconi, Carlo.   The Silence of Pius XII.   Boston: Little,
    1970. 430p.
    Although some historians hold that Pope Pius XII failed to
speak out against Nazi atrocities because he feared reprisals
against Catholics, and others claim that the pontiff was a coward,
the Italian Falconi (a papal historian) impressively registers
a different thesis. He blames Pius's reliance on and confidence
in Vatican diplomatic channels, and what must be labeled "German-
ophilia." In this balanced volume, the author makes a forceful
case for the pope's strong religious commitment and indicates
incidents when he acted courageously, but concludes that Pius
was destructively wrong in his silence. Falconi is also convincing in his argument that no one knew more about what was happening to Jews in Poland than Pius XII.

Fein, Helen.   Accounting for Genocide.   New York: Free Press,
    1979. 468p.
    Accounting for Genocide concerns the victims and survivors
of the Holocaust; it is an investigation of the structure of
the forces and events that helped either to stem the tide or
facilitate the Jewish tragedy throughout Europe. The causes
of the Holocaust are probed, and there is a lucid examination
of the history of Christian anti-Semitism. This volume contains
analyses of personal accounts of Jews from Poland and Hungary,
and the reader is given a picture of the behavior, psychology,
and social history of the Jewish communities of various nations.

Flender, Harold.   Rescue in Denmark.   New York: Holocaust
    Library, 1980. 281p.
    In occupied Denmark in 1943, the Germans began to implement
a policy of deporting Jews to both concentration and death camps.
But while the Nazis successfully carried out their plans in other
countries, the Danes as a whole intervened to save their Jewish
cocitizens. At great physical risk to themselves, the Danish
people initially hid the Jews, helped them flee to Sweden in a
variety of ways, and performed important acts of sabotage. No
one answer explains why the Danes acted in unison, while total
populations elsewhere did not. Flender suggests that the traditions of Danish democracy can be partially credited.

Friedlander, Saul.   Pius XII and the Third Reich.   New York:
    Knopf, 1966. 238p.
    Written for the general reader rather than the scholar, and
admittedly relying on incomplete documentation (since Vatican
files were not open to historians at the time), this volume makes
a strong case for Pope Pius's attitude favoring Germany (particularly since he spent many years in that nation as the Holy See's
papal nuncio). What Pius feared most of all was a Communist

takeover of Europe; hence he shied away from criticizing German policies. Friedlander's objectivity may be criticized, but this is nevertheless a helpful work. His documents from the files of the Nazi ministry of Foreign Affairs and British, American, and Zionist archives in Jerusalem are published for the first time.

Friedman, Philip. Their Brothers' Keepers. New York: Holocaust Library, 1978. 232p.

Christians who helped Jews escape the Nazis are the subject of this book. One was Lithuanian Anna Simaite, a leading literary critic, who was so obsessed with the pain she witnessed that she said, "I was ashamed that I was not Jewish myself"; she organized a rescue group. Jania Bucholc-Bukolska falsified identification papers to help rescue Jews. In Croatia, Archbishop Stepanic said, "I have ordered priests and nuns to continue wearing this sign [the yellow star] belonging to the people from whom the Savior came." (This happened after the Germans rescinded the order to wear the star.) Jesuit Father Pierre Chaillet was a hero of the French Resistance. A chapter is devoted to concerted governmental noncooperation in Finland on the "Jewish Question," and another chapter to Raoul Wallenberg in this testimony to human solidarity.

Hallie, Philip. Lest Innocent Blood Be Shed. New York: Harper, 1980. 303p.

Le Chambon is a French Huguenot village where, during World War II, many Jews were saved in a prolonged (some four years), community-wide program of risk and courage. The Protestant minister who helped organize the resistance was André Trocmé. With his comparably heroic wife Magda (she carried on the rescue of Jewish refugees after her husband had to flee the Nazis) Trocmé, a committed pacifist, became especially involved. Hallie's book is actually on ethics, built around a story of "how goodness happened." The events are unusual, engaging, and always bordering on the tragic. Quite moving is the fact that the rescue efforts were continued even after the Trocmé's eldest son hanged himself at age fourteen.

Hanley, Boniface. Maximilian Kolbe. Notre Dame, Ind.: Ave Maria, 1982. 80p.

Canonized a Roman Catholic saint in 1982, Maximilian Kolbe is considered one of the Christian heroes of the death camps. He perished at Auschwitz in 1941, exchanging his life for that of a family man condemned to death (who lived long enough to testify at Vatican canonization proceedings on behalf of the Franciscan priest). Subtitled "No Greater Love," this book tells the story of Kolbe the minister, the Catholic publisher, his mission to Japan, the tortures he endured at the hands of his captors and, finally, what is called his "final victory." Charges of anti-Semitism laid at Kolbe's feet are overlooked in this volume.

Hellman, Peter. Avenue of the Righteous. New York: Bantam, 1981. 165p.

At Yad Vashem, the Holocaust Memorial Center in Jerusalem, a special area is set aside to honor non-Jews who, at great risk to themselves, helped Jews during the Holocaust. While the total of such heroes is small, they deserve to be honored; this volume depicts a number of their stories. For example, there is the story of one woman who sacrificed her honor to pretend that she had a "love child," and in this way keep a Jewish youngster safe. Another woman, with her family, protected a newfound "cousin," exposing all to prolonged danger. Some rescued individuals; others helped hundreds to escape.

Helmreich, Ernst Christian. The German Churches under Hitler. Detroit: Wayne State Univ. Pr., 1979. 616p.

A major study of the churches under the Nazis, within the context of the historic relations between Christian churches and the state, this work concludes that "the Catholic as well as the Protestant churches had in the eighteenth century been turned largely into servants of the state (Staatskirchentum)." This position contributed to much of the evil that befell German Christianity. The work opens with a summary perspective on Catholic and Protestant churches in Germany from the Reformation to the end of World War I. Helmreich then discusses the situation of many groups under Hitler: Catholic, the large Protestant Land churches, the smaller Free churches, and a number of sectarian groups. The volume is authoritative, quite complete.

Iranek-Osmecki, Kazimierz. He Who Saves One Life. New York: Crown, 1971. 336p.

Produced as "a testament to the behavior of the Polish nation," this book is a necessary contribution to the story of righteous behavior during the Holocaust. While the author may not stress strongly enough the fact that a higher percentage of Polish Jews was murdered than Jews from any other country, and that some Poles killed surviving Jews after the war when they returned to their homes, this volume is a necessary corrective to the generalization that all Polish people are anti-Semitic. Documented evidence of Polish men and women who risked their lives to hide Jews, feed them, help them financially, rescue them, falsify documents to aid in their escape from the Nazis, etc., is provided. The sources vary from eyewitness testimony to findings from postwar investigation, newspaper accounts, wartime bulletins to the exiled Polish government, and other official documents.

Joffroy, Pierre. A Spy for God. New York: Harcourt, 1971. 319p.

Kurt Gerstein is a most ambiguous Nazi figure. An SS man, he is said to have become desperate on learning of the plan for the "Final Solution" to the "Jewish problem." His personal pain was compounded, according to Joffroy, by his conviction that Hitler would win the war and therefore be able to implement his murderous policies unchecked. A profoundly religious Christian, Gerstein did much to disrupt the massacre of Jews. The conquering Allies saw it differently. They arrested Gerstein and charged him with complicity with war crimes. In solitary confinement, he hanged himself. When his widow applied for a postwar pension, a local Denazification Court denied it on the basis of her husband's Nazi activities. Gerstein made reports on Nazi atrocities, reprinted here. This is a stunning biography, haunting in the questions it raises about the life of one who may have been supremely misunderstood.

Leboucher, Fernande. Incredible Mission. New York: Doubleday, 1969. 165p.

A French Capuchin priest, Father Marie-Benoit, was a true hero of the Holocaust. The author collaborated with him in his mission of humanity. Less than a documentary, this book stems rather from Leboucher's recollections, those of the priest, and some of his notes. Marie-Benoit initially operated out of Marseilles and later became the head of what was to be Roman Jewry's most successful relief agency. He helped thousands of French and Italian Jews escape the Nazis by making available to them, through various resources, false identification papers. He also helped many hide in Church institutions. This rewarding book is written in a popular, rather than scholarly, style.

Lester, Elenore. Wallenberg. Englewood Cliffs, N.J.: Prentice-Hall, 1982. 183p.

Written by the author of the New York Times Magazine cover story on Raoul Wallenberg (which is credited with bringing international attention to his case), this is the story of the Swedish diplomat who risked his life to save thousands of Jews, only to lose his freedom to Russian authorities. Wallenberg's early biography, his heroics, and what is known about his disappearance are all registered here.

Lewy, Guenter. The Catholic Church and Nazi Germany. New York: McGraw-Hill, 1964. 416p.

A great deal of controversy continues to surface over the

silence of the official Roman Catholic Church concerning the Nazi slaughter of over five million Jews. That Pope Pius XII did not speak out against it is seen as consistent with the Church's relations with Jews throughout many centuries, according to the author. Lewy's criticism also focuses on the German bishops who, he insists, understood with the Vatican what was happening to Jews under Nazi domination. Lewy is careful to cite Catholics who behaved heroically during the Holocaust, and he makes no sweeping indictments.

Lipschitz, C. U. Franco, Spain, the Jews and the Holocaust. New York: Ktav, 1984. 237p.

The despotic Generalissimo Francisco Franco did a remarkable job in helping protect Jews during the Holocaust. As leader of neutral Spain during the war, his stance helped save approximately 45,000 Jews from death. From the study of a great deal of documentation and after an interview with Franco himself, Lipschitz presents an informative and convincing account of the Spanish government's protection of Jews. Particularly fascinating is the author's conversation with Franco. While Lipschitz expresses skepticism at certain of Franco's remarks (for instance, when the Generalissimo said he helped Jews "because of an elementary feeling of justice and charity") and is puzzled at others (the dictator's anger at having the name of the nation Israel mentioned), there is much to ponder here. At one point the rabbi asks the role the Vatican played in assisting Spanish rescue of Jews. "I do not recall" is the abrupt reply. There is also the interesting matter of Franco's continued intervention on behalf of Jews in Arab countries after the war ended.

Matheson, Peter. The Third Reich and the Christian Churches. Grand Rapids, Mich.: Eerdmans, 1981. 103p.

An eleven-year period (1933-43) is represented in this anthology of sixty-eight documents that provide grist for the discussion of the role of Christian churches during World War II. Some churches tried to remain both faithful to God and loyal to Hitler; others caved in completely. Still others tried heroic resistance. While this book would benefit from an index, a better table of contents, and better editing (with notes, first names of those referred to, etc.), the documents--by Pope Pius XI, Karl Barth, and other luminaries--are valuable.

Morley, John. Vatican Diplomacy and the Jews during the Holocaust 1939-1943. New York: Ktav, 1980. 327p.

In his introduction to this book evaluating the Vatican's responses to Nazi atrocities, Morley, a priest, notes that "the Holy See has loudly and repeatedly proclaimed its uniqueness as a religious and moral power. If the records demonstrated that its diplomatic activity during the Holocaust was parochial and self-serving, it would of necessity, stand condemned by its own criterion." From Pope Pius XII, who held the Chair of Peter during the entire period, to Secretary of State Luigi Cardinal Maglioni, papal nuncios, and other Vatican representatives in various nations, the history is a tragic one. While the official Church occasionally reacted sympathetically to stories of the suffering of some individual Jews, in the main it was apparently indifferent to their plight and, on several occasions, even in favor of it. Basically, the Church interceded only for baptized Jews. Wider humanitarian views were not served. Certain documents quoted here prove to be very harsh: a lack of concern for Jews, a fear of Zionist successes, and downright anti-Semitism are all in evidence, as are expressions of self-flattery for the few actions taken. Not all nations are surveyed, but the story is much the same everywhere in Europe: Romania, France, Slovakia, Germany, and Poland.

Ramati, Alexander. The Assisi Underground. Briarcliff Manor, N.Y.: Stein & Day, 1978. 181p.
 Relatively few non-Jews came to the aid of Holocaust victims. One was an Italian peasant who became a priest, Rufino Niccacci; he saved about 300 Jews in Assisi. The historical narrative in this book is told in the first person. The priest relates how, a few hours after he learned of the Nazi takeover of Rome, the "entire course of my life changed suddenly. I was to become a cheat and a liar--for a good cause, mind you, but nevertheless a sinner, although I am sure that I have long since made my peace with God and that he has forgiven me my trespasses." These trespasses included dressing Jewish refugees as monks and nuns, finding jobs for others, using false identity cards, and forming a whole network of collaborators--some who served for money, others from a sense of moral outrage. Not one person who was part of this underground ever betrayed it.

Rosenfeld, Harvey. Raoul Wallenberg, Angel of Rescue. New York: Prometheus Pr., 1982. 261p.
 A Swedish diplomat who helped prevent the murder of some 100,000 Jews, Wallenberg was arrested by the Russians after World War II (possibly by the young Leonid Brezhnev) and has apparently disappeared from the earth. Hundreds of eyewitnesses have testified to Wallenberg's bravery. Moscow has insisted continually that the Swede died in 1947, but a number of former Soviet prisoners claim to have seen him alive at least up to 1980. Wallenberg's career and intervention on behalf of Jews, plus a balanced view of his mysterious postwar disappearance make this a fascinating book. The tale of intrigue surrounding Wallenberg includes the names of Stalin, Eleanor Roosevelt, Dag Hammerskjold, Averell Harriman,

Pope Pius XII, Einstein, and others. Not all come in for praise; neither do many members of the Swedish government, and surprisingly some Israeli officials are also cited for errors of judgment.

Thomas, John Oram. The Giant Killers. New York: Taplinger, 1976. 320p.

Most of Denmark's 7,000 Jews escaped to Sweden. The story of how the Danes collaborated to get them away from the Nazis is one of the few bright spots of the Holocaust era. Amply illustrated, here are the stories of a choir club that specialized in sabotage; of an underground press; of students who resisted; of farmers and fishing people who hid Jews at great personal peril; of a militant priest; and of common people in general who behaved in very uncommon ways.

Werbell, Frederick E., and Thurston Clarke. Lost Hero. New York: McGraw-Hill, 1982. 284p.

The mystery of Raoul Wallenberg is the focus of this volume. This Swedish diplomat helped rescue nearly 100,000 Jews in 1944 through espionage, threats, bribes, and by taking great personal risks. How he decided to do this forms one part of the biography; his mysterious disappearance after a secret meeting with Russian officers forms the remainder. The authors claim that there is evidence to suggest that Wallenberg might have been alive in the Soviet Gulag even into the 1980s.

Winowska, Maria. The Death Camp Proved Him Real. Kenosha, Wisc.: Prow Books, 1971. 192p.

Originally published in 1952 as Our Lady's Fool, this is a biography of Franciscan priest Maximilian Kolbe, who volunteered to be starved to death at Auschwitz in place of another hostage. While filled with useful information about Kolbe's life, this is basically a "puff" book, a promotion to enhance Kolbe's chances for canonization (which indeed happened on October 10, 1982, thirty years after this book was first published). As this, therefore, is not a "warts and all" portrayal, the level of objectivity is not high.

Yahil, Leni. The Rescue of Danish Jewry. Philadelphia: Jewish Publication Society, 1969. 536p.

Anti-Semitic Nazism clashed dramatically with Danish democracy--and lost. Recounted here are the initial persecution of Jewish Danes by the conquerors; the failure of this persecution; the position of the Jewish community during the crisis; the actual, thrilling rescue operations; and the important role played by many Swedish people. Particularly valuable in this work is Yahil's clarification of certain legends that grew up around Denmark's King Christian X and his deeds on behalf of his Jewish subjects.

The king was indeed supportive of Jews, but some stories about him are false and are corrected here.

Zahn, Gordon C. <u>German Catholics and Hitler's Wars.</u> New York: Sheed & Ward, 1962. 232p.

Roman Catholic Church officials not only did not refuse to cooperate with many of Hitler's war aims, but they also endorsed some of them with vigor. How they encouraged the laity to participate in the German effort shows "the social control [employed by the Church] inducing Catholic conformity to the requirements of the Nazi military effort." Zahn, an angry Catholic, provides authenticity by including German originals (in footnotes) of the important documents translated in the body of the text. He tells how, among other condemnable actions, German bishops denied the sacraments to Catholics who refused to bear Nazi arms until just before their execution.

------. <u>In Solitary Witness.</u> New York: Holt, 1965. 277p.

Franz Jagerstatter was an Austrian peasant who refused to fight for Hitler. Rather than betray his conscience, Jagerstatter, a devout Catholic, remained firm in his belief that the Nazi position was immoral in spite of enormous pressure from others, including his priest and bishop. In 1943, he was beheaded after a military trial. The implications of his refusal are developed by the author through the use of Robert K. Merton's analysis of social deviance. Jagerstatter's insights on contemporary problems are included here, as is his prison statement and his letter of advice to a godson. Zahn narrates his life with clarity and intensity.

INTERNATIONAL INDIFFERENCE

The Allies' response to the Holocaust is a story of consistent indifference and failure. From the beginning of Hitler's rise, which was partially aided by certain powerful American and British industrialists (see chapters 1 and 2), through liberation, during which insensitivity and incompetence often endangered those released from the camps, the Allies did not come to grips with the plight of the Jews. Notable is not only the failure to divert military strength against the camps, but also the failure to receive Jewish refugees and, primarily, the failure to even protest as Nazi aims and actions became clear. The confused reactions of American Jewish leaders are another part of this story. The books discussed here describe the information that did reach both the governments and populations of the Allies during the Holocaust, and clearly condemn their inaction.

A few books discuss the ironic activities of the Japanese during the Holocaust. Believing in the fraudulent Protocols of the Elders of Zion, the Japanese sheltered some 18,000 German and Polish Jews in the hopes of profiting from the refugees' supposed political and economic influence.

Abella, Irving, and Harold Troper. None Is Too Many. New York: Random, 1983. 336p.

This book, winner of the National Jewish Book Award, tells the sad story of Canada's refusal to do much to assist Jewish refugees for a fifteen-year period, beginning in 1933. An account of pettiness, misunderstandings, and deliberate ill will is shocking in some aspects. Only 4,000 Jews were admitted into Canada during this entire period.

Bauer, Yehuda. American Jewry and the Holocaust. Detroit: Wayne State Univ. Pr., 1981. 523p.

How successful was American Jewish assistance to Europe's threatened Jews during the Holocaust? Bauer traces the activities of what became the representative Jewish agency, the American Jewish Joint Distribution Committee (JDC). Aid and rescue depended on available funds as well as political pressure. All of this was based on American Jewish awareness of the realities of the Holocaust. While a great deal of data was available on the subject, the seeping of this knowledge was a slow process not completed even by the war's end. JDC acted as best it could, Bauer concludes, though sometimes its work was considerably misunderstood.

Dinnerstein, Leonard. America and the Survivors of the Holocaust. New York: Columbia Univ. Pr., 1982. 222p.

While some evidence is produced in this book documenting the staunch efforts of some U.S. citizens to aid Jewish survivors, what stands out are indifference to such suffering and blatant anti-Semitism. The American and British governments not only did very little to help these refugees, but they also actually hindered the process of their rehabilitation. The U.S. State Department also made it very difficult for Jews to obtain visas. General George Patton shipped displaced persons back home (and in many cases back into danger) against the orders of General Eisenhower. Allies, incredibly, put former Nazis in charge of centers for displaced persons. One of the major ironies in this story is that while American Jews were successful in getting displaced persons into this country, it thus became possible for former Nazis to sneak in as well.

Dobkowski, Michael N., ed. Politics of Indifference. Washington, D.C.: Univ. Pr. of America, 1982. 474p.

As the title suggests, this is a volume about people who didn't want to get involved. The author writes: "In the beginning the Nazis watched closely whether there would be reactions, whether there would be reprisals, and it was only when it appeared that the world did not give a damn, that the Nazis began implementing their plan. Thus, we are survivors not only of one unthinkable doctrinal bestiality, but also of a widespread indifference." This work is in two parts--diplomatic efforts on behalf of refugees, and how America received them. The authentic story is not a happy one.

Druks, Herbert. The Failure to Rescue. New York: Robert Speller, 1977. 108p.

Referring to President Roosevelt's policy regarding the rescue of Jews as "two-faced, tricky and disastrous for Jews" and accusing Britain's Anthony Eden of acting as one of the refugees' greatest stumbling blocks, Herbert Druks has written a damning book. He also records several unsuccessful rescue attempts, such as the Europe Plan, the Brand scheme to trade Jews for trucks, and the sailing of the St. Louis. The failure of the Allies to bomb railroad tracks leading to the death camps is also censured. Jewish leaders come in for their share of criticism, too, for failing to present a strong united case for assistance.

Feingold, Henry L. The Politics of Rescue. New York: Holocaust Library, 1970. 416p.

One of the major questions arising from the Holocaust is why the United States government did so little to aid European Jewish victims. This presentation is balanced, providing a persuasive critique of the Roosevelt Administration, given what did and did not happen. It is the author's purpose "to move beyond the moral aspect to examine the political context in which America's response was conceived." The conclusion is a painful indictment of "callous Allied indifference." The people so indicted include a host of well known names; perhaps none is more culpable than Assistant Secretary of State for Special Problems Breckenridge Long, who in his anti-Semitism linked communism and Jewish internationalism. This is a depressing, but necessary, book.

Friedman, Saul S. No Haven for the Oppressed. Detroit: Wayne State Univ. Pr., 1973. 315p.

United States policy towards Jewish refugees during the period 1938-45 was hardly admirable. This was true on all levels, including government officials, American citizens in general, and even certain American Jews (as well as people of other Western nations). Friedman draws on archival government materials as well as private sources; he examines Jewish communal records and publications of various labor groups. The question that continues to nag: What if the United States, Great Britain, and other nations had accepted the Jews when Hitler tried to exile them? Friedman discusses more than this topic alone in his wide-ranging, well documented volume.

Gilbert, Martin. Auschwitz and the Allies. New York: Holt, 1981. 368p.

The dreadful story of Allied unwillingness to recognize or acknowledge what was going on in the most infamous of the Nazi death camps is revealed here. Aerial photographs, eyewitness accounts, even Hitler's public threats were all ignored. Some blame can be placed on typical bureaucratic incompetence, but most such lack of recognition was deliberate, done by real people in both high and low offices; if some of these individuals had

been tried at Nuremberg, they might well have been found guilty.
Britain's Anthony Eden, of course, is one such person; Breckenridge Long, Assistant Secretary of State, who failed to pass on
vital communications to the proper channels, is another. Names
such as John J. McCloy (Assistant Secretary of War), Sir A. W. G.
Randall of England's Refugee Section (who worried about "a quite
unmanageable flood of possible escaping Jews"), and even Allen
Dulles (whose technical approach to the horrors was so "typical")
are recorded here. Illustrative maps and photos add to the value
of this work.

Gottleib, Moshe R. American Anti-Nazi Resistance, 1933-1941.
    New York: Ktav, 1982. 426p.
    Jewish agencies in the United States attempted to organize
serious boycotts against German goods during the period just
before America's involvement in World War II in response to Nazi
treatment of Jews. Many problems arose, including internal differences among American Jews; some believed that such actions
might make the situation even worse for Jews living under Hitler.
Several labor groups encouraged the boycott and, in 1938-39,
some sympathetic Christian organizations were formed. The author
gives the history of this era a dispassionate presentation and
concludes that such boycotts were probably, in actuality, not
very effective, although he does cite German documents that indicate that this manner of resistance had a considerable impact.

Gruber, Ruth. Haven. New York: Coward, 1983. 335p.
    One thousand refugees, mostly Jews, were brought to the United
States during World War II as "guests" of the government by order
of President Roosevelt. The author of this book headed that
mission. On ship she assisted the victims, heard their stories,
and became involved with Jews, Protestant, Catholic, and Greek
Orthodox Christians, and some of the soldiers. She wrote down
their stories, hoping to bring them to the attention of the president and the rest of America. When the refugees landed, instead
of gaining immediate liberty, they were forced to live in an
internment camp; this, too, is a major part of the volume.

Kranzler, David. Japanese, Nazis and Jews. New York: Yeshiva
    Univ. Pr., 1976. 644p.
    About 18,000 German and Polish Jews found haven from the
Nazis in Japanese-occupied Shanghai. This book chronicles a
little-known aspect of World War II and is based on over 20,000
primary sources including diaries, archives of captured German
and Japanese documents, confidential files of Jewish relief organizations, and a large number of interviews. The Japanese
thought that the Jews possessed enormous world political and economic power, and therefore were anxious to have Jews immigrate.

It is interesting to learn that the Japanese sent out peace feelers to the United States through Jewish intermediaries, and fascinating to learn of a rich Jewish cultural life established in Shanghai.

Laqueur, Walter. The Terrible Secret. New York: Little, 1981. 262p.

It is no secret that the Holocaust was no secret. Laqueur, in a volume subtitled "Suppression of the Truth about Hitler's 'Final Solution,'" unites the ideas found in previous works--and much more--regarding the topic. He believes that most Germans knew the facts, as there were so many involved in the operation. For example, a whole bureaucracy was employed in the selling off of expropriated Jewish property. Victims had to be declared dead by certain officials, neighbors had to know this, reports had to be filed, typed, approved, etc. The author also proves that the neutral nations such as Switzerland, Sweden, and Turkey were almost fully aware of the plight of the Jews. So were the Vatican and the International Red Cross. Why, then, such little response? How could the New York Times publish articles on the slaughter of at least a million Jews and not put such pieces on the front page? Much of what Laqueur documents is not new information, but his attempt at objectivity is commendable. He does not attempt to blame, but raises the question of what information was available to the world, in order to try to understand why the Holocaust was, in effect, kept a secret.

Morse, Arthur. While Six Million Died. New York: Random, 1967. 420p.

Subtitled "A Chronicle of American Apathy," this volume "concentrates on the bystanders rather than the killers or the killed." The author observes that "a combination of political expediency, diplomatic evasion, isolationism, indifference and raw bigotry" in America played right into Hitler's hands. Among those receiving a serious share of criticism are President Roosevelt himself, Undersecretary of State Sumner Welles and his chief, Secretary of State Cordell Hull. Assistant Secretary of State Breckenridge Long may prove to be the most infamous American citizen in this story with his deliberate obstructionism. Opportunities for rescue were ignored while more than a million places in the U.S. immigration quota system went unfilled from 1933 to 1943.

Penkower, Monty Noam. The Jews Were Expendable. Champaign: Univ. of Illinois Pr., 1983. 302p.

This careful study is solidly documented, revealing that saving Jews during the Second World War was not a very important item on the Allied agenda, since it did not directly contribute to victory. Initially, England, the Soviet Union, and the United

States were primarily concerned with their own survival. From 1943 to 1945, as the conduct of the war shifted, Allied interest in the safety of the Jews did not improve. The author is excellent on the inexcusable silence of the International Red Cross, and his chapter on the failure to rescue the Jews of Hungary is superb.

Ross, Robert. So It Was True. Minneapolis: Univ. of Minnesota Pr., 1980. 374p.

In a thoroughly documented study of fifty-two Protestant periodicals from 1933 to 1945, the author shows that hundreds of articles, editorials, letters to the editor, and paid advertisements directly dealt with the misfortunes of Jews under Hitler-- from their initial humiliations to their eventual murder. Thus it is inaccurate to state that Americans could not have known that the Holocaust was happening. While it is true that a few writers saw these events as God's judgment on the Jews, by far the great majority decried what was happening. This work basically asks two questions: Did American Protestants know? Ross's reply is an emphatic "Yes." The second question he does not answer directly: "Why was there not more intervention on behalf of Jews?" In an indirect reply, Ross effectively points to the moral outrage exhibited in the American Protestant press over the atomic bombing of Hiroshima and Nagasaki, when there were pleas for the Christian church to become stronger, truer to its calling. The whole tone of the discussion of the bombings was on a far more "effective" level than that of the Holocaust.

Thomas, Gordon, and Max Morgan Witts. Voyage of the Damned. Briarcliff Manor, N.Y.: Stein & Day, 1974. 317p.

The authors have written an absorbing novel of the tragic voyage of the ship St. Louis, with its 937 Jewish refugees fleeing from Nazi persecution. The book is in a day-by-day diary format, and is divided into three parts. The first, entitled "Chance to Live," begins with the passengers' elation on learning that they will be allowed to leave Europe. It is followed, however, by "Chance to Die," when joy turns to grief. The final section is properly named "The Final Solution." More than the story of the agony of the victims, one of the better known episodes of the Holocaust, it is also an account of the machinations of the German Secret Service and how it worked to smuggle classified material out of the United States.

Tokayer, Marvin, and Mary Sagmaster Swartz. The Fugu Plan. New York: Paddington, 1979. 287p.

The Protocols of the Elders of Zion was a proven forgery, but the Japanese thought that this plan documenting a Jewish attempt to control the world's economics and politics was authentic, and thus overestimated the influence of Jews throughout the

Western world. So, between 1934 and 1940, the Japanese government developed a secret plan to save many Jews; they believed
that they could benefit greatly by having Jewish technical experts
and industrialists settle in Manchuria to develop that area into a
buffer zone against the Soviets. This amazing story is re-created
here with the aid of Jewish refugees who moved to Japan before
that nation declared war on the United States. The Dell paper-
back edition is titled Desperate Voyages (1980).

Wasserstein, Bernard. Britain and the Jews of Europe 1939-
    1945. New York: Oxford Univ. Pr., 1979. 389p.
    In 1939, a British White Paper repudiated the Balfour decla-
ration of 1917 that promised a "national home for the Jewish
people." On December 17, 1942, Anthony Eden, the secretary for
foreign affairs, told the House of Commons (speaking in the name
of the Allied governments) that the Nazis were "now carrying
into effect Hitler's oft-repeated intention to exterminate the
Jewish people in Europe. . . ." Within a year the British knew
that ninety percent of all Polish Jews had died. Yet almost
nothing was done to help European Jewry, and this lack of action
forms the theme of this work. While failure was often due to
stupid judgments rather than ill will, nevertheless anti-Semitism
was a considerable factor, as reflected in this account.

Wyman, David S. The Abandonment of the Jews. New York:
    Pantheon, 1984. 445p.
    Franklin Roosevelt's most spectacular failure as president,
according to Wyman, was involved in the American failure to aid
Jews during the Holocaust. The State Department refused to act
when instances of genocide were authenticated. The same is true
of the Office of War Information. Members of Congress (including
seven Jews only one of which, Emanuel Celler, acted honorably
on this subject) were negligent, as were Christian churches, the
media--including the Jewish-owned New York Times and Washington
Post--and prominent Jews unable "to break out of a business-as-
usual pattern. Too few schedules were rearranged. Vacations
were seldom sacrificed." The military refused to bomb the death
camps, although targets within five miles of Auschwitz were attacked.
All of this and so very much more appears in this authoritative
volume, a major work. Wyman credits those who deserve it, but unfortunately there is vastly more blame he finds he must distribute.
His concluding suggestions regarding what might have been done to
help save Jews are valuable as a pattern for thinking about future
disasters.

------. Paper Walls. Amherst: Univ. of Massachusetts Pr.,
    1968. 306p.
    Wyman notes three principal reasons why the United States

granted only 150,000 visas to Jews fleeing Europe from 1938 to 1941: unemployment, nativism, and anti-Semitism. Add to these a certain amount of indifference to the plight of these victims and a fairly clear picture emerges. When certain politicians stirred fear in their constituencies by warning that foreigners were taking their jobs, evidence that proved the contrary was ignored. One shortcoming in this volume is Wyman's apparent unwillingness to discuss in any depth the lack of adequately positive response by the American Jewish community to the needs of the refugees. Otherwise, this is a very strong, solid work of historical research.

JUSTICE

"Justice" is a curious word to apply to the legal responses made to the crimes against humanity committed by the Nazis and their collaborators. Retribution, penalties, punishment, even revenge are spoken of, but how can anyone hope to tally up what is due after the massacres and tortures of the Second World War? There were no precedents for the Nuremberg Trials or others. Some Allies wanted Nazi leaders executed immediately upon their capture. (Joseph Pulitzer, the St. Louis publisher, demanded the execution of one-and-one-half million Germans after he visited death camps at the end of the war.) Legal questions were raised, procedures were argued over, and remarkably puzzling sentences were handed out. If a man was sentenced to death for being responsible for the death of 100,000 persons, another, guilty of "only" 7,000 murders, might receive a fifteen-year term. The bargaining between judges, the various nationalistic approaches, the legal ramifications, the manner of investigations, the attitudes of the accused, the world's reactions--all are included within the titles in this chapter.

The works described here cover not only the Nuremberg Trials but also the kidnapping-arrest of Adolf Eichmann and his trial in Israel along with the other activities of the Nazi hunters. Many also describe how U.S. authorities helped secure safety for some war criminals, often to gain information from the Nazis about Soviet activities.

Blum, Howard. Wanted. New York: Quadrangle, 1977. 256p.
One of the first to focus public attention on the fact that some U.S. government officials assisted Nazis to enter this coun-

try in anonymity, the author tells of four Nazis who came to America, how they lived their lives, and how they were tracked down. Tales of stolen government files, inexplicable Immigration Service delays, State Department footdragging, and interference by certain congressmen are presented. The chief figure in this puzzling account is Immigration Service investigator Anthony DiVito who, after bringing one Nazi criminal to justice, established a list of fifty-nine others living in this country. He tried to search them out, but found a major obstacle in the U.S. government.

Bosch, William J. Judgment on Nuremberg. Chapel Hill: Univ. of North Carolina Pr., 1970. 272p.
    Bosch focuses on four main questions in this book dealing with the trial of Nazi war criminals: How was the law interpreted by the responsible personnel? Were some who participated in the proceedings representatives of governments that were also guilty of crimes comparable to those for which the Nazis were tried? Were the sentences too lenient? What value did this trial have for the future? The answers provided by the author, while not fully satisfying, are illuminating. American views of the trial are also investigated to show how they reveal the national character of this country. (Nearly all major groups studied support what was done at Nuremberg, with the notable exceptions of historians and experts in international affairs.)

Bower, Tom. The Pledge Betrayed. New York: Doubleday, 1982. 462p.
    The failure of the United States and Great Britain to deal properly with Nazi war criminals is the focus of this book. In spite of the Nuremberg Trials, which showcased the prosecution of certain notorious Nazis, far too many went unprosecuted. A significant number of these was even appointed by the Allies to supervise the reconstruction of war-demolished Germany. Bower cites many reasons: self-interest, corruption, incompetence, petty antagonisms, and much else. Thus, for example, Gustav Wagner, deputy commandant of the Sobibor death camp, was on the United Nations list of most wanted men but was released from internment by the U.S. Army and escaped to South America. Many other instances recorded in this book are equally disquieting.

Conot, Robert. Justice at Nuremberg. New York: Carroll & Graf, 1984. 593p.
    Conot not only gives a thorough account of the Nazi war crimes trial, but also reconstructs the various offenses with which each of the twenty-one defendants was charged. He thus provides the historical setting, a characterization of the main figures, and examines with due caution the manner in which the

prosecution, defense, and sentencing were handled. Readers also meet the judges, learn of their deliberations and how they arrived at their verdicts. The importance of what happened at Nuremberg cannot be overestimated. As one of the U.S. prosecutors, Supreme Court Justice Robert Jackson, noted: "Never before in legal history has an effort been made to bring within the scope of a single litigation the developments of a decade, covering a whole continent, and involving a score of nations, countless individuals and numerous events. . . . This trial has a scope that is utterly beyond anything that has ever been attempted that I know of in judicial history."

Davidson, Eugene. The Trial of the Germans. New York: Macmillan, 1966. 636p.
A long recap of the Nuremberg Trials is the subject of this book. The writer attempts to understand what led up to the criminal acts perpetrated by the defendants by examining their careers. He interviewed three defendants (Doenitz, Schacht, von Papen), the widow of one of the executed Nazi generals (Jodl), concentration camp survivors, and the prisoners of war. Perhaps most interesting is the author's reflections on the proceedings. Some have held that they were absolutely necessary, others that they violated legality. Davidson believes that the unusual nature of the crimes required an extraordinary response for both political and psychological reasons. Some errors were made, he grants, but what came out of the trials was an account so overwhelming that it stunned the world.

Friedman, Tuviah. The Hunter. New York: Doubleday, 1961. 286p.
While some may believe that the author exaggerates his role as a hunter of Nazi war criminals, there is no question that he did have an important part in this activity. He helped prove the circumstances of many Nazi crimes, find the perpetrators of a number of them, and aided greatly in bringing them to trial. Whether or not he takes too much credit for the apprehension of Adolf Eichmann has been raised by a number of informed persons. Nevertheless, this is a fascinating and illuminating memoir.

Gilbert, G. M. Nuremberg Diary. New York: Farrar, 1947. 471p.
Captain Gilbert was the prison psychiatrist at Nuremberg. His chief duty was to remain in close contact with Nazi war criminals being tried by the Allies, and to report to the prison commander on the inmates' morale. He was to help, if he could, to ensure order in the trial and to collaborate with psychiatric commissions when their work with the Nazis was deemed necessary. Gilbert, fluent in German, talked freely with these men and was able to understand their informal conversations at lunch and

when court sessions ended each day. One special value of this extraordinary book is found in Gilbert's technique: he appears very little in the book, allowing the quotations of the Nazis to have their own frightening impact.

Glock, Charles; Gertrude Selznick; and Joe Spaeth. The Apathetic Majority. New York: Harper, 1966. 222p.
The trial of Adolf Eichmann was widely covered in the United States, with evening reports by television journalist Jim Bishop. Yet, as this study indicates, few Americans were very moved by the trial, which took place in Jerusalem, or by all of the horrors disclosed. In fact, few in this nation were greatly interested in the proceedings, and those who knew the most about the trial proved to be the most critical of the way Israel handled the case. (The opinions of blacks in this country, however, were generally directly opposite that of the majority populace.) The investigative conclusions of this book are based on 463 interviews done in Oakland, California; while the methodology does not appear to be beyond question, the work has value on several levels.

Harel, Isser. The House on Garibaldi Street. New York: Viking, 1975. 265p.
As chief executive of the Secret Services of Israel, Isser Harel directed the manhunt, capture, and abduction from Argentina of Adolf Eichmann. It took fifteen years to bring to justice the man who, in 1945, is said to have bragged: "I will leap into my grave laughing because the feeling that I have 5,000,000 human beings on my conscience is for me a source of extraordinary satisfaction." This detailed account goes from the first tentative identification of Eichmann, by a blind man, to the suspense-filled kidnapping and flight from Buenos Aires.

Harris, Whitney. Tyranny on Trial. Dallas: Southern Methodist Univ. Pr., 1954. 608p.
Here is one of the best books on the Nuremberg Trials, written by a man on the prosecutor's staff for the United States. Harris says that "this is a book of tragedy. It is a story of what dictatorship really is, and what tyranny and terror really mean. It tells of incredible crimes and unbelievable events." It also tells of the judicial process, from the inside. The author's obvious pride in the legal precedents set at Nuremberg, and his analysis of their significance, make this a readable and important book.

Hausner, Gideon. Justice in Jerusalem. New York: Harper, 1966. 528p.
This book suffers from being written in a language not the author's native tongue. Furthermore, Hausner has been criticized

for being less than convincing concerning the jurisdiction of the Eichmann trial, the theme of the volume. Nevertheless, because he was the attorney general of Israel and the prosecuting attorney at the Eichmann trial, he lends an unprecedented authority to the subject. Hausner had access, of course, to all available evidence on Eichmann, and has combined accounts of both victims and victimizers in this book in what can only be described as terrifying glimpses of human bestiality. This work not only reaffirms Eichmann's guilt, but also accuses Pope Pius XII, most of Europe's clergy, and much of the world for its interaction with Nazi Germany in the prewar period.

Hill, Mavis M., and L. Norman Williams. Auschwitz in England. Briarcliff Manor, N.Y.: Stein & Day, 1965. 293p.

In 1964, a doctor who had been a Polish prisoner of the Nazis sued Leon Uris for libeling him in the novel Exodus, in which the physician was accused of performing 17,000 medical experiments without anesthetics. The trial, which took place in England, brought victims to testify of sexual mutilations and other tortures they underwent. Because of the law, the jury had to find for the plaintiff. However, they also set the amount to be paid the doctor by Uris and his publishers: "One Ha'penny."

Jackson, Robert. The Nuremberg Case. New York: Cooper Square, 1972. 268p.

Documented here is the case against the major Nazi war criminals as presented by the chief counsel of the United States, Robert Jackson. This is a summary of the United States' argument and includes the fascinating cross examination of several of Hitler's notorious accomplices. Jackson's deep sense of idealism is apparent in most of this work. The Nuremberg Trials were, of course, precedent-setting, so this account is of great importance.

Jewish Black Book Committee. The Black Book. New York: Duell, 1946. 560p.

One of the earliest indictments against the Nazis for their innumerable atrocities committed against European Jews, this volume was prepared under the direction of a number of organizations including the World Jewish Congress; the American Committee of Jewish Writers, Artists, and Scientists; plus others. Carefully compiled, this work presents documentation given to the United Nations War Crimes Commission as evidence. Based mainly on eyewitness testimony and contemporary press accounts, the book makes constant reference to other documents, many of which are reproduced.

Klarsfeld, Beate. Wherever They May Be. New York: Vanguard, 1975. 344p.

"Three weeks after I was born, Hitler entered Prague." So begins this work, written by a Nazi hunter who is both a German and a Christian. She married a French Jew who witnessed Nazi terrorism firsthand and when she learned, through him, the horrors of the Holocaust, she began a personal crusade against freed war criminals. (Klarsfeld spat in the face of West German Chancellor Kurt Kiesinger--a former Nazi--to protest the political power he had gained, and she did it at a public party session at the Congress Palace, getting worldwide publicity.) Klarsfeld is a person of conviction, willing to risk arrest (another incident was a sit-in at Dachau to convince her government of certain legalities concerning Nazi criminals) as well as physical danger in her activism. This autobiography gives a picture of this much honored woman.

Knoop, Hans. The Menten Affair. New York: Macmillan, 1978. 164p.

Pieter Menten, a Dutch multimillionaire and art collector, took part in the killing of Polish Jews by the Nazis during the Second World War. He was brought to trial and found guilty. The author of this volume, a Dutch journalist, tracked Menten down and helped bring him to justice; this is a record of the detective work.

Lang, Jochen von, and Claus Sibyll, eds. Eichmann Interrogated. New York: Farrar, 1983. 293p.

These transcripts from the archives of the Israeli police are taken from the pretrial testimony of the mass murderer whose defense was "I obeyed. Regardless of what I was ordered to do." It is clear that Eichmann wanted to exonerate himself before history, to leave a record of a man not responsible for crimes but almost virtuous in his loyalty. As his major interrogator, Avner Less, notes, Eichmann would lie until defeated by documentary proof; he would present himself merely as a cog in a machine; he would finally fall back on "orders from above." Eichmann tried to present himself as sympathetic to Jews, as one who even attempted to combat the extreme anti-Semitism of certain Nazis. He insisted he was only a transportation officer, in charge of moving victims, not of killing them. The picture that emerges is that of a man who would condemn himself morally while trying to escape legal blame. As we read his words here, we learn of a man who said, "If they had told me that my own father was a traitor and I had to kill him, I'd have done it."

Loftus, John. The Belarus Secret. New York: Knopf, 1982. 196p.

While the author does not prove his thesis in a totally convincing fashion, there is enough evidence to make his case--that

Nazi war criminals were deliberately smuggled into this country by the State Department's chief of intelligence--very believable. Loftus says that Frank Wisner, who committed suicide in 1965, sneaked important Nazis into the United States to use them in helping in the fight against communism. Loftus writes of Radislaw Ostrawsky, the president of a Nazi-appointed Byelorussian puppet government who lived for many years in Benton Harbor, Michigan, until his natural death. Emanuel Jasiuk, who presided at a camp where 5,000 Jews were massacred, is also named. So is Stanislaw Stankievich, the mayor of a town where 7,000 Jews were shot to death after having been forced into predug mass graves. Adding irony to what may already be an ironic story is Loftus's conclusion that many of the Nazis were, in fact, working for the Soviets to begin with, so that the project was to have a reverse effect in many ways.

Miale, Florence, and Michael Selzer. The Nuremberg Mind. New
    York: Quadrangle, 1976. 302p.
    Sixteen major Nazi war criminals tried after the war are analyzed through interpretations of the Rorschach tests given them. This attempt at psychohistory will both please and alienate. The methodology of the Rorschach is rather thoroughly explained, although some have seriously questioned its applicability. Given this, the volume is fascinating, though perhaps more confirming of prejudgments made by the test administrators than valuable for independent conclusions. Short, helpful biographical sketches of each of the Nazis are presented, but were they adequate background for the testers?

Mitscherlich, Alexander, and Fred Mielke. Doctors of Infamy.
    New York: Schuman, 1949. 172p.
    Nazi doctors performed horrifying, totally useless medical experiments on prisoners. The subject of this volume is the Nuremberg medical trial and the historical events preceding it. It is grim reading, not only in spite of but also perhaps due to the understatements of the atrocities contained in the quoted records. The medical and legal documents form a moving structure for this painful book. Three additional authorities have added useful comments to this work: Telford Taylor, chief counsel for the war crimes, gives a historical overview; psychiatrist Leo Alexander offers an analytic preface; and remarks on medical ethics are given by Albert Deutsch.

Neave, Airey. On Trial at Nuremberg. Boston: Little, 1978.
    348p.
    The enigma posed by the Nuremberg Trials of Nazi war criminals is addressed by the author in this interesting analysis. Should the trials have been held at all? Winston Churchill

thought not; he wanted the Nazi leaders summarily executed. Details of some of the crimes with which these men were charged are given. But, of more importance, Neave raises philosophical questions that go to the heart of the value of the Nuremberg Trials. Were they simply the justice of the victors? Should they have been held at all? How are the lessons from the trials to be applied in the future?

Neumann, Bernd. Auschwitz. New York: Praeger, 1966. 433p.

A reporter who was present at each day of the longest trial in German history (twenty months), Neumann gives us the account of day-to-day occurrences at the Frankfurt trial of twenty-two SS officers who eventually were given sentences ranging from thirty-nine months to life in prison for their roles at Auschwitz. The defendants mocked the proceedings, refused to take responsibility for their acts, and claimed to be as innocent as their victims: "I knew only one mode of conduct: to carry out the orders of superiors without reservation" was a typical response. Another was "I naturally sought to save the lives of as many Jewish prisoners as possible." What is told about actual camp life is very sad; the author's objective rendering is noteworthy.

Pearlman, Moshe. The Capture and Trial of Adolf Eichmann. New York: Simon & Schuster, 1963. 666p.

An exciting account of the hunt and kidnapping of one of the Nazis' most notorious leaders, finally found in Argentina and spirited away by Israeli agents, is recounted here. It is followed by a more stolid account of the Eichmann trial in Jerusalem. There is much detail here in a volume that, contrary to the conclusions of Hannah Arendt's Eichmann in Jerusalem, gives unqualified praise for the conduct of the trial. The author writes at length to convince readers of the precedents, moral and legal, justifying the right to try Eichmann.

Saidel, Rochelle G. The Outraged Conscience. Albany: State Univ. of New York Pr., 1984. 208p.

A small number of men and women in the United States are vigorously pressing the government to seek justice for Nazi war criminals living freely here. Morally angry, these people basically work as individuals; there is no nationwide, organized effort. These action-oriented persons are diverse in nature but have in common what this book calls "the outraged conscience." This volume also examines general moral questions: Is there any justification for the U.S. government's allowing known Nazi criminals into this country after the war? Why hasn't there been more moral outrage on the part of American Jewish organizations, veteran groups, and the news media?

Smith, Bradley F.   Reaching Judgment at Nuremberg.   New York:
Basic Books, 1977.   349p.

Many of the details of what happened before the war crimes
trials of Nazis are described in this interesting book.   Where
would the trials be held?   Who would make up the prosecution
team?   Which defendants would be selected?   The volume is divided
into three sections.   Initially, the background is covered; next
the specific crimes are documented; finally, the individual verdicts are presented.   Much is contained here not only about law
and the defendants, but about the judges, too, and how they bar-
gained for sentences and acquittals.

------.   The Road to Nuremberg.   New York: Basic Books, 1982.
303p.

Smith's solid, readable scholarship provides a detailed account of how the U.S. government concluded that summary executions of Nazi war criminals, favored by some Allies, would be
wrong and that trials ought to take place.   The original concept
for the court proceedings was developed by Murray Bernays of the
War Department but it was not easily accepted.   The Treasury
Department, as well as the Navy and State departments, had serious
objections.   Questions arose: Who should be tried?   Who should
judge?   Were new codes to be drawn up covering new crimes?   Should
prosecution be limited to war crimes or should the atrocities
committed against civilians also be included?   The format here is
a daily account of the planning, strategy, and objections as they
occurred.

Wiesenthal, Simon.   The Murderers among Us.   New York: Bantam,
1968.   346p.

The best known of the Nazi hunters and a Holocaust survivor
is the author of this unusually arranged memoir.   Joseph Wechsberg,
who edited the volume, includes profiles of the autobiographer
as chapters 1, 2, 11, and 18.   The remaining 22 chapters are
Wiesenthal's as told to Wechsberg.   The work contains information
on ODESSA, the secret escape organization of the SS underground.   It gives accounts of Wiesenthal's activities throughout
the world in trying to track down war criminals.   And it closes
with a warning from one of his Nazi captors, "a good SS man,"
who told him that if Wiesenthal ever got to America and told
people what was happening within death camps, "they wouldn't believe you.   They'd say you were crazy."

REFLECTIONS ON THE HOLOCAUST

In the philosophical sense, the Holocaust was an absurd experience. How could it have a meaning? And yet, we are almost condemned to try to plumb its depths, all the while knowing that this is impossible. Many writers, therefore, have attempted interpretations of the Holocaust either through theological inquiry, psychological analysis, historical perspective, dialectic (my book with Elie Wiesel), confession (Littell's The Crucifixion of the Jews), hope (Peck's anthology), despair (After Auschwitz, by Richard Rubenstein), and other approaches. Works attempting various kinds of analyses are described in this section, as are works on Jewish-Christian relations that bear more or less directly on the Holocaust.

This chapter has been divided into three parts. In the first, Historical and Philosophical Reflections, the broadest questions are raised: How did it happen? What is the uniqueness of the Holocaust? How responsible were the collaborators? Are the victims themselves to blame? In the second part, Psychological and Sociological Reflections, the tools of two disciplines are brought to bear on the psychological structures and habits of both perpetrators and victims, giving rise to many fruitful perceptions about human behavior in the presence of evil. The third part, Religious Reflections, ranges in scope from the meaning of Jewish faith after the Holocaust, to Christian-Jewish relations, to the meaning of Christian faith after the Holocaust. Questions of Jewish law in dehumanizing situations are raised in two titles, as well.

HISTORICAL AND PHILOSOPHICAL REFLECTIONS

Arendt, Hannah. Eichmann in Jerusalem. New York: Viking, 1963. 275p.

Certainly one of the most controversial of the books dealing with an aspect of the Holocaust, this opus is subtitled "A Report on the Banality of Evil." Arendt deals only briefly with the trial of Nazi criminal Adolf Eichmann. She concentrates more on his participation in the process of murdering European Jews in Hitler's "Final Solution." The author is extremely critical of the trial, claiming that it was a political show of revenge rather than an instrument of justice. Eichmann is portrayed as an ignorant braggart, emotionally immature and, in short, a banal person. Arendt shows not a monstrous criminal but a pathetic product of a totalitarian system, a truly mediocre man--himself victim as well as murderer. Another startling element of the work is Arendt's insistence on Jewish complicity in Hitler's plans, which she claims could not have been so effective without the cooperation of the intended victims. Arendt has been both pilloried and praised for her insights in this provocative essay.

Aycoberry, Pierre. The Nazi Question. New York: Pantheon, 1981. 257p.

Three questions give this volume its focus. The first asks to what extent Hitler was really in charge. (Some have theorized that the Nazi party was far less centralized than is generally believed.) The second examines the question of who actually placed the Nazis into power. (In doing so Aycoberry blasts the simplistic Marxist analysis that Hitler was a product of big business.) Finally, the author looks at the controversy over whether Adolf Hitler was himself basically the result of centuries of German history or more accurately representative as a phenomenon of this century. The author does not give facile answers for the direction he believes future scholarship should take. This is not, as Aycoberry tells us, a history of Nazism, but a history of the images of Nazism.

Bauer, Yehuda. The Holocaust in Perspective. Seattle: Univ. of Washington Pr., 1978. 181p.

Four essays compose this volume by one of the great Holocaust scholars. The first discusses how humans learn and warns about the difficulties in assessing the point at which information becomes knowledge. He applies his subject to the problem of the Holocaust and American Jewry. The next section discusses the uniqueness of the Holocaust which, nevertheless, has potential genocidal parallels. Bauer here studies those who try to deny the tragedy, as well as those who try to turn it into mystical experience. Chapter 3 looks at the problem of the bystanders.

There were a number of different responses by non-Jews in the Axis nations themselves, in Nazi-occupied territories, in Allied countries, and in the neutral ones. Intelligent thoughts are presented, although the enigma is not solved. Bauer's last chapter is centered on the sensational mission of Joel Brand and his attempt to trade trucks (needed by the Germans) for Jews--the history and morality of the barter try.

------, and Nathan Rotenstreich, eds. The Holocaust as Historical Experience. New York: Holmes & Meier, 1981. 288p.
A very strong anthology is the result of a 1975 New York conference titled "The Holocaust--a Generation After." Among the important contributors are the editors themselves, Raul Hilberg, Henry Feingold, Alice Eckardt, Isaiah Trunk, Abba Kovner, Uriel Tal, and others. A number of viewpoints on a series of crucial questions are offered on such problems as: Could the Holocaust have been prevented? Why did Jews die in massive numbers in some countries occupied by the Nazis while in other nations so many were able to survive German occupation? Could the Holocaust have been predicted? What was the function of the Judenrat? How is Jewish resistance to be regarded? The participants in this forum are often in disagreement and are always stimulating.

Cargas, Harry James. Harry James Cargas in Conversation with Elie Wiesel. New York: Paulist Pr., 1976. 126p.
Less of a dialogue than a question-and-answer book between a Christian author and a leading Jewish authority on the Holocaust, this work ranges in topics from the massacre of 6,000,000 Jews to the life and works of Wiesel himself. Each chapter of conversation is preceded by an excerpt from a Wiesel publication and is followed by Cargas's commentary. Wiesel's comment on mystical madness, the need for understatement in literature, the "Jewish condition," Soviet Jewry, Christianity and, of course, the Holocaust, is important reading.

Dawidowicz, Lucy S. The Holocaust and the Historians. Cambridge, Mass.: Harvard Univ. Pr., 1983. 187p.
Many historians have neglected the Holocaust, Dawidowicz states, and some who do not ignore it use an approach of which she is very critical, including Raul Hilberg, Hannah Arendt, and Bruno Bettleheim (though the last two are not historians, and Hilberg calls himself a political scientist). Soviet and Polish anti-Semitism and anti-Zionism, as found in their histories, are discussed. German historical writing since the war has been perverted, according to the author, in order to link nazism-fascism with an international movement rather than showing it to be the particularly German phenomenon that it was. American

and British historians give little attention to the Holocaust, she writes, because of the pervading German influence on their thought, an influence that sees Jews as outside the mainstream of history.

Fackenheim, Emil L. The Jewish Return into History. New York: Schocken, 1978. 196p.

Perhaps Fackenheim's best known sentence reappears in this volume: "The authentic Jew of today is forbidden to hand Hitler yet another, posthumous victory." The Jews, this Canadian philosopher insists, are first of all commanded to survive. He says this particularly in the light of the Holocaust: "Transcendance is found at Auschwitz in the form of absolute Command." The impact of the attempted annihilation of Jews is at the center of this thinker's deliberations. He then adds another element, the centrality of the State of Israel. He sees the nation as a moral necessity after the Holocaust.

Fleischner, Eva, ed. Auschwitz: Beginning of a New Era? New York: Ktav, 1977. 469p.

An international symposium on the Holocaust was held in New York's Cathedral of St. John the Divine in 1974, and this is a compilation of the talks given at that time. The editor's introduction to each section is very helpful and the chapters themselves have a general excellence. Irving Greenberg's initial essay on the world after the Holocaust sets the tone for what comes after. "Let us offer, then, as working principle the following: No statement, theological or otherwise, should be made that would not be credible in the presence of burning children." Catholic theologian Rosemary Radford Ruether develops her thesis that anti-Semitism in the West is a direct outgrowth of Christian theological anti-Judaism. Father John Pawlikowski explores the "teaching of contempt" of Jews. Several speakers explore the relationship between the Holocaust and the State of Israel, and there are pieces on the pathology of "Jew-hatred," blacks and Jews, and "Art and Culture after the Holocaust" (Elie Wiesel) in this immensely important volume.

Friedman, Philip. Roads to Extinction. Philadelphia: Jewish Publication Society of America, 1980. 616p.

There were 150,000 Jews living in Lvov, Poland, when the Second World War erupted. About 1,000 survived. One of them was established historian Philip Friedman who, at age forty-three (in 1944), dedicated himself to writing about the Holocaust. He has been called the first historian to apply the methods of objective and critical study to this highly emotional subject. He is also credited with inspiring survivors to write their stories, to collect letters, photographs, anything else which might be of value in recapturing the lost period of Jewish culture. This collection of essays is one of the major fruits of his efforts. He looks at the Holocaust from two viewpoints here, from that of German policy and from that of Jewish reaction. One long essay is on the annihilation of Lvov's Jews (which Friedman witnessed); another deals with Ukrainian-Jewish relations under the Nazis, and a series of chapters deal with historical approaches to the Holocaust.

Jaspers, Karl. The Question of German Guilt. New York: Capricorn Books, 1961. 123p.
One of modern Germany's most distinguished philosophers tackles the major question of the book's title. Here are some sentences from various parts of the book: "But each one of us is guilty insofar as he remained inactive." "It is nonsensical, too, to lay moral guilt to a people as a whole." "This way of purification by reparation is one we cannot dodge." Jaspers has produced a profound book that gives no easy answers, but explores deeply the relationship all of us have regarding the Holocaust and its aftermath.

Kruger, Horst. A Crack in the Wall. New York: Fromm International, 1982. 292p.
With a subtitle "Growing Up under Hitler," this is a despairing book about the German national character. The author was raised in a suburb of Berlin and wrote this book in the 1960s. However, in an afterword for the edition that appeared nearly two decades later, Kruger maintains that nothing much has changed, in his opinion. Hitler came to a people who had an iron sense of place and of rank; people who kept tight rein on their emotions, and who lived out a daily military regimen. Kruger's sense of guilt is strong as he wonders what he would have done if assigned to a position of responsibility in a death camp, since nearly all Germans were indoctrinated to obey.

Mayer, Milton. They Thought They Were Free. Chicago: Univ. of Chicago Pr., 1971. 346p.
The question the author set himself was: How did the "average German" react to Nazi rule? An American Jew and a journalist, Mayer moved to Germany for a year in the early 1950s and lived in a small town to find out. The stories of ten Germans Mayer came to know--and like, surprising even himself--are here retold. These are followed by reflective comments by the writer. One important finding is that these people all saw themselves as good, decent individuals although they had collaborated with the Nazis.

Mosse, George L. Toward the Final Solution. New York: Harper, 1980. 272p.
Presented here is a solid chronicle of racism and nationalism

and how both of these aspects of twentieth-century history combined to form a climate in Germany capable of permitting a Holocaust. Topics covered include how racism and nationalism interact in a society, racism as science (so incredibly foisted on society by Hitler and his propagandists), racism as ideology, and how both racism and nationalism contributed to genocide.

Rings, Werner.   Life with the Enemy.   New York: Doubleday, 1982.
   408p.
   Swiss historian Rings has marshaled evidence to prove that most Europeans who had a choice opted to collaborate with Nazi occupation forces, rather than to resist them. In the sixteen countries under German domination, including a population of some 180 million adults, there was not only a large amount of actual betrayal and even persecution of co-citizens, particularly Jews, but, all the more subtle forms of collaboration as well. He cites the businessmen who easily allowed their industries to support Nazi war efforts, as well as blue collar workers who, among other things, kept the Nazi trains running--many filled with human cargo sent for destruction. The two million Europeans who voluntarily left their countries to work in Germany are also criticized. Rings does not fail to mention the group of men and women who seemed to serve Germany during the day while resisting in the underground at night.

Robinson, Jacob.   And the Crooked Shall Be Made Straight.
   New York: Macmillan, 1965.   406p.
   Hannah Arendt's very controversial analysis, Eichmann in Jerusalem, is rebutted here by an authority on international law and modern Jewish history. Robinson participated as a consultant to the chief prosecutor at the Nuremberg tribunal and served similarly during Eichmann's trial. The author criticizes Arendt for being contradictory, wrong, confused, ambiguous, and unreliable on many points. Major reviewers found the scholarship behind this work awesome but the conclusions inadequate. The argument about Arendt's contribution is far from settled.

Rubenstein, Richard.   The Cunning of History.   New York: Harper, 1975.   113p.
   It is written here that "we are more likely to understand the Holocaust if we regard it as the expression of some of the most profound tendencies of Western Civilization in the twentieth century." The author insists that the exterminaton of Jews in World War II was a "Final Solution" for the British as well as the Germans. This is because, writes Rubenstein, the culture that made death camps a possibility was indigenous to the West and a result, however unintended, of the West's fundamental religious traditions. There is additional controversial material

here, including the charge that the overwhelming number of Jewish victims did not resist. Rubenstein fears that the Nazi genocide program will influence future population planners as a way to reach desired goals. And he makes a strong plea for the way to prevent future holocausts: "The power to injure remains the most credible deterrent to a would-be aggressor's violence." This volume is nothing if not provocative.

Swarsensky, Manfred E. Intimates and Ultimates. Madison, Wisc.: Edgewood College Pr., 1981. 196p.
Swarsensky, a rabbi, was a Holocaust survivor who saw the great synagogues of Berlin destroyed by the Nazis. In this selection of his addresses, his conciliatory approach may be found summarized in an introductory paragraph: "It is my hope that the spirit of the Judaeo-Christian tradition upon which our American heritage rests will remain the spiritual and moral foundation of our country's faith and strength." Whether he spoke about the need to build bridges beyond Auschwitz, in praise of that great German teacher Leo Baeck, on Holocaust victims, or on a wide variety of other important issues, Swarsensky was always insightful, relevant, and pro-humanity on a grand scale.

Wiesel, Elie. One Generation After. New York: Random, 1970. 198p.
The title refers to the period following the Holocaust. Wiesel is haunted by a realization that the awesome events of the World War II period and certain reflections on them have failed to have a significant impact on the present. "Nothing has been learned; Auschwitz has not even served as warning. For more detailed information, consult your daily newspaper." The writer is also obsessed with needing "to face the dead, again and again, in order to appease them, perhaps even to seek among them, beyond all contradiction and absurdity, a symbol, a beginning of promise." Wiesel's thoughts on the state of Israel are of great relevance here.

------; Lucy S. Dawidowicz; Dorothy Rabinowitz; and Robert McAfee Brown. Dimensions of the Holocaust. Evanston, Ill.: Northwestern Univ. Pr., 1977. 63p.
A professor at Northwestern University wrote a book claiming that the Holocaust never took place, that it was a hoax perpetrated on the world by Zionists. In response to the furor that resulted, the university sponsored a series of lectures that are gathered in this volume. Elie Wiesel speaks as an eyewitness of the events and about the literature. Historian Lucy Dawidowicz tells of documents, not just those produced by survivors but captured German papers as well. Dorothy Rabinowitz's "The Holocaust as Living Memory" contains a complaint against many who would

revise the true history of the Holocaust, including authors Bruno Bettelheim, Hannah Arendt, and filmmakers Marcel Ophuls and Lena Wertmuller. Robert McAfee Brown discusses "The Holocaust as a Problem of Moral Choice."

PSYCHOLOGICAL AND SOCIOLOGICAL REFLECTIONS

Beradt, Charlotte. The Third Reich of Dreams. Chicago: Quadrangle, 1968. 177p.
From 1933 to 1939, the author interviewed Jews and non-Jews of various age groups who lived under Hitler to see if their dreams were in some way significant. Reviews have been mixed about Beradt's findings, although in a concluding essay psychiatrist Bruno Bettelheim writes that "it is a shocking experience, reading this volume of dreams, to see how effectively the Third Reich murdered sleep by destroying the ability to restore our emotional strength through dreams." More than 300 dreams were "collected" from people of varying backgrounds, and the dreams are certainly fascinating. People dreamed of being Hitler's associates; of denouncing people; of identity papers proving the dreamer to be Aryan and not Jewish; of street signs printed with unutterable words.

Bettelheim, Bruno. The Informed Heart. New York: Free Pr., 1960. 209p.
Bettelheim was imprisoned in Dachau and Buchenwald before they became death camps. He was ransomed to the United States and became a leading psychiatrist here. He developed a thesis which, boldly stated, claims that those who survived best in the concentration camps were those who became as arrogant as their captors, self-centered and possessing a willingness to adopt a "me-first" attitude.

------. Surviving and Other Essays. New York: Knopf, 1979. 433p.
The survivor/psychiatrist here has a series of essays on Nazi concentration camps, extreme situations, the victims, surviving, a generation after the Holocaust, the lessons that Anne Frank and Eichmann have left, etc. On the psychological appeal of totalitarianism Bettelheim will spark much thought on the part of his readers.

Cohen, Elie Aron. Human Behavior in the Concentration Camp. New York: Norton, 1954. 295p.
The psychiatrist who has perhaps done the most important study of concentration camp survivors is a man whose work is not listed in this bibliography--Norwegian Leo Eitinger. Although many

of his articles are available in English (some appear in anthologies listed in this book), no book of his valued contributions has been published in the United States. Elie Cohen, like Eitinger, is a Jewish psychiatrist who survived Auschwitz. This Dutch citizen, in a remarkably dispassionate volume, analyzes the mentality of the prisoners and their SS persecutors. While not a particularly well written presentation, this is nevertheless an important book.

Frankl, Viktor E. Man's Search for Meaning. New York: Washington Square, 1963. 226p.
Along with Freud and Adler, Frankl is one of the three founders of major schools of psychology in Vienna. His concept of Logotherapy was developed out of his experiences as a prisoner in Nazi camps. The author squarely faces such topics as the meaning of suffering, life's transitoriness, collective neuroses, and the meaning of life. In Frankl's view, what most aided death camp inmates to survive was an ability "to retreat from their terrible surroundings to a life of inner riches and spiritual freedom." This book, originally entitled From Death-Camp to Existentialism, is far removed from Bruno Bettelheim's thesis that those who could become more like their tormentors had the best chance of living.

Kren, George N., and Leon Rappaport. The Holocaust and the Crisis of Human Behavior. New York: Holmes & Meier, 1980. 176p.
The authors here indicate historical and psychological developments that led up to the Holocaust. They analyze these elements from various perspectives as they try to render original insights into Nazi policies and personnel. Victims, resisters, and neutral bystanders also receive attention.

Krystal, Henry, ed. Massive Psychic Trauma. New York: International Universities Pr., 1969. 369p.
A collection of essays on the psychological after-effects of major disasters, these papers cover a wider range of topics than the Holocaust alone--including the atomic attack on Hiroshima--and are valuable on several levels. The similarities and differences of cases are instructive.

Luel, Steven A., and Paul Marcus, eds. Psychoanalytic Reflections on the Holocaust. New York: Ktav, 1984. 239p.
The ongoing impact of the Holocaust on survivors and especially on society in general is the subject of this collection of essays by scholars and psychoanalysts. Some writers discuss the broader psychological, moral, cultural, and societal implications of the legacy of the Holocaust. As the editors indicate

in their introduction, an extensive literature of a clinical nature dealing with the treatment of Holocaust survivors and their children is available, but relatively little exists in the way of psychoanalytic reflections on the Holocaust as such, and on its broader ramifications. This volume tries to remedy that lack.

Mitscherlich, Alexander, and Margarete Mitscherlich. The Inability to Mourn. New York: Grove, 1975. 322p.
Subtitled "Principles of Collective Behavior," the book deals, from a psychoanalytic viewpoint, with the unresolved conflicts of certain German patients deriving from a commitment to Hitler and a reaction to the downfall of their society. Included here is an analysis of the unwillingness (or inability) of many of these persons to accept any responsibility for the atrocities of World War II. Alexander Misterlich was a figure in the Nuremberg Trials, serving as a member of the German Medical Commission to the American Military Tribunal at that court. Many case histories and observations make up the foundation for this book's eight chapters. There is valuable material here, as Robert Jay Lifton's preface attests.

Pawelczynska, Anna. Values and Violence in Auschwitz. Berkeley: Univ. of California Pr., 1979. 170p.
"The few who were able to 'love their neighbors as themselves' attained the value of highest heroism. By their conduct they proved that existence did not determine consciousness: by their attitude they defied camp conditions, simultaneously reducing their material needs below the minimum." So writes Polish sociologist Pawelczynska who thus, with this book, effectively rebuts Bruno Bettelheim's teachings that those who identified with their aggressors were best able to survive in the concentration camps. Her conclusions are based on much study and analysis of prisoners. This is a methodical, readable, important book with an excellent introduction by translator Catherine S. Leach.

Ryan, Michael D., ed. Human Responses to the Holocaust. New York: Mellen Pr., 1981. 278p.
Ryan's compilation here covers perpetrators, victims, bystanders, and resisters. In the first category there is an article on Hitler and another by Leon Wells, a survivor, who has continually involved himself as a witness at Nazi war criminal trials. Among the other chapters are pieces on the Danish rescue of Jews, the response of the Dutch churches to Jewish persecution, an article on Helmuth James van Moltke, who gave Christian witness, and one on the less spectacular approach of Adam von Trott. In "The Witness Role of American Jewry: A Second Look," Henry

Feingold indicates some important points of failure by American Jews to come to the effective aid of those suffering in Europe. The final three essays in this volume contain post-Holocaust theological and ethical reflections by Robert McAfee Brown, Jacob Agus, and Alice Eckardt.

Steinert, Marlis G. Hitler's War and the Germans. Athens: Ohio Univ. Pr., 1977. 387p.

Steinert analyzes the moods and attitudes of the German populace during the Hitler era. She examines the interplay between public opinion and the attempted manipulation of the people through various intense propaganda techniques employed by the totalitarian states. As elsewhere, opinion is not exclusively conditioned by official propaganda. There are other sources, including historical myths and images that have proven to be extremely enduring. There are also leading figures in primary and secondary groups, as well as (and this above all) the evidence of personal observation. There are limitations, then, to manipulating public attitudes. Where Germans did express criticism (most often within boundaries tolerated by the Nazis) Hitler and his men were quite responsive to it and either halted, moderated, or concealed their intentions.

Weinstein, Fred. The Dynamics of Nazism, Leadership, Ideology and the Holocaust. New York: Academic, 1980. 168p.

The author's goal here is to try to comprehend "how it was that Hitler and the Nazi movement, inspired by and promoting a particular kind of ideological commitment, could have intervened in what was, from the standpoint of large numbers of people, an unexpected, unanticipated, potentially chaotic social situation and have unified and mobilized a heterogeneous population from the early 1930's through the war and the Holocaust. . . ." With fresh insights and approach, Weinstein achieves that aim. Nazism succeeded in great part because it was able to sell the masses on the idea that it was the only available political force that might both unite the nation and fight communism. He is convincing in showing, contrary to some earlier works, that Nazism's appeal was not limited to the lower strata of society, but had wide acceptance in all classes. Some readers may be put off by the writer's psychoanalytic approach.

RELIGIOUS REFLECTIONS

Berkovits, Eliezer. Faith after the Holocaust. New York: Ktav, 1973. 180p.

Berkovits is an understandably angry Jewish writer who addresses himself to major theological questions after the Holocaust.

Where was God at Auschwitz? Where was God at the times of other bloody acts in history? Where does humanity's responsibility end in history and God's begin? His analysis of the contribution of Christianity to the misery of Jews is powerful. So are his statements on the necessity of the existence of the State of Israel. Berkovits is one of the most provocative of modern Jewish writers.

------. With God in Hell. New York: Sanhedrin, 1979. 166p.
     The burden of this volume is a plea for Jews to develop a greater sense of resistance--both military (as a final resort) and on other levels as well. Berkovits insists that "the moral obligation of withstanding evil, even when directed against oneself, must be incorporated with the value system of Judaism." The Holocaust, he writes, proves the need for resistance. "It is our duty in the presence of God." Berkovits's pride in the faith of Jews during the crisis of the Holocaust permeates this little volume. Examples of heroic religious practice were remarkable. Prayer and faithfulness to God outlasted Nazi Germany and he further observes that "the authentic Jew did not escape into spirituality but simply lived the life of the Jew in the circumstances in which he found himself." In another beautiful commentary he says that the true Jew believed that "what I am doing here does count; indeed, it is of supreme importance.. That I have to burn the contents of garbage cans, that does not matter. That is not my doing; that is done to me. My doing is being a Jew under all conditions and circumstances. That alone is what I am doing." Berkovits's anger and rhetorical style, while perhaps understandable in a Holocaust survivor, may detract from his insights.

Cargas, Harry James, ed. When God and Man Failed: Non-Jewish Views of the Holocaust. New York: Macmillan, 1981. 238p.
     The twenty sections of this book include chapters by many of this nation's finest Christian commentators on the Holocaust. The editor has two articles dealing with literature; Robert McAfee Brown discusses the Holocaust as a problem in moral choice; Franklin H. Littell looks at ethics after the death camps; Eva Fleischner explores the importance of the Holocaust for Christianity. Alice and Roy Eckardt examine how contemporary German thinkers view the Holocaust; and the Holocaust as a technological triumph is W. Robert McClelland's topic. Included are two moving poems by William Heyen and a lengthy bibliography.

Cohen, Arthur. The Tremendum. New York: Crossroads Bks., 1981. 110p.
     Can the Holocaust be understood? Does it have meaning? Most serious commentators answer with a definitive "No." Arthur Cohen

takes a tremendous risk in this small volume, subtitled "A Theological Interpretation of the Holocaust." One of the risks is that he will be misunderstood. He says early in the book that the Holocaust as an event has no meaning. But the death camps have ended one argument forever: unmistakably, utterly, the Jews are a chosen people. Auschwitz was a celebration of death and the Jew may have been the ideal victim because of "his refusal to die throughout four millenia. . . ." The event must be seen from the perspective of all of human history, not simply of Jewish existence. The second of four chapters here is crucial. It is a most definitive treatment of theological evil resulting from the Holocaust. In the third section, the author treats specific writers (Halevi, Buber) and also speaks to Christian theologians as well. It is worthwhile noting that in the Introduction to this book, David Tracy, a priest, observes that contemporary Jewish theologians are thinking in their own tradition but also on behalf of all theologians in all traditions. The final chapter attempts "a redefinition of the reality of God and his relations to the world and man, but as well a reinvestment of the passive receptiveness of the world and the active freedom of man with significant meaning."

------, ed. Arguments and Doctrines. New York: Harper, 1970. 541p.
   The controversial Jewish theologian Arthur Cohen has here collected essays, most of which appeared in Judaism and Commentary magazines, on Jewish thinking following the Holocaust. The subjects are wide-ranging, including Will Herberg's conversion from Marxism to Judaism and one on the enigmatic Simone Weil's anti-Semitism (which is an arguable piece). In general the topics are important, the writers provocative, and Cohen's own commentaries, including disagreement with one writer, are illuminating. While the Holocaust is central for some of the thinkers here, the overall impact probably fails to give a clear view of just how important it was in Jewish thought of the sixties.

Davis, Alan T. Anti-Semitism and the Christian Mind. New York: Herder & Herder, 1969. 192p.
   "The Crisis of Conscience after Auschwitz" is the telling subtitle of this significant work. Davies, a Christian theologian, takes a penetrating look into the many challenges that traditional Christian thought must face in its perception of the Jew in the aftermath of the Holocaust, and the responsibility of Christians and Christianity for that tragedy.

Eckardt, A. Roy. Elder and Younger Brothers. New York: Scribner, 1967. 188p.
   Eckardt is one of the most important Christian figures in

postwar ecumenism, and this volume on the encounter of Jews and Christians is probably his most significant work. It is not specifically about the Holocaust, but helps put that tragedy into a certain perspective by investigating Jewish-Christian relations before the Holocaust. Eckardt also examines new ways to close old wounds stemming from Christian anti-Semitism.

------, with Alice L. Eckardt. A Long Night's Journey into Day. Detroit: Wayne State Univ. Pr., 1982. 207p.
The Eckardts, students of Jewish-Christian relations and of the responsibility of Christians as Christians in the Holocaust, have subtitled their book "Life and Faith after the Holocaust." The authors insist that the deliberate massacre of Jews during World War II is as much a Christian event as a Jewish one. They write of the need to remember, the singularity of the event (not just unique but "uniquely unique"), the dangers and opportunities inherent in exploring the tragedy, and of certain responses to the Holocaust. That this is extremely important for the Eckardts is seen in their quotation, with approval, of a Dutch pastor who wrote that "only by understanding Auschwitz can we be Christian again." This volume is extremely outspoken and will irritate many Christian readers.

Hay, Malcolm. Thy Brother's Blood. New York: Hart, 1975. 356p.
This volume was previously published under two other titles. Originally it was called The Foot of Pride (1950) and later renamed Europe and the Jews (1960). The three titles clearly indicate what the contents cover. This is a history of Christian anti-Semitism written by an Episcopalian minister who, like Edward Flannery and Rosemary Reuther after him, takes a penetrating look at the Christian roots of anti-Semitism and the final destructive consequences.

Littell, Franklin H. The Crucifixion of the Jews. New York: Harper, 1975. 153p.
Franklin Littell is the dean of American Christian Holocaust scholars. This Methodist minister has certainly been the most influential and probably the most productive of such scholars, given his years of teaching, preaching, writing, scholarly work, and organizational planning. This volume is among his most important contributions in the field. He briefly traces the history of Christian anti-Semitism, discusses the German church struggle and the Jews (1933-45), has a chapter on "The Meaning of the Holocaust," and then looks at the State of Israel and the crisis its existence causes Christianity. The book ends with a moving Christian liturgy for Holocaust commemoration.

------, and Hubert G. Locke, eds. The German Church Struggle and the Holocaust. Detroit: Wayne State Univ. Pr., 1974. 329p.

An anthology of papers given at a 1970 conference by leading Christian and Jewish authorities, this book covers a wide range of thought on how the churches behaved under the Nazis. Roman Catholic author Gordon Zahn, for example, classifies the Catholic Church's response to Hitler as a failure, despite the highly moral conduct of certain Catholics who performed well as individuals. Richard Rubenstein and Elie Wiesel have contributed to this important volume, as have many others.

McGarry, Michael. Christology after Auschwitz. New York: Paulist Pr., 1977. 119p.

Author McGarry, a Catholic theologian, begins by emphasizing that supercessionism (the idea of the Church as a new and therefore better Israel) has no place in the Jewish-Christian dialogue. He surveys post-Holocaust formal Christian documents on Jews and Judaism and concludes that at the very least, "None of the statements claimed a complete break from the Jewish religion, but saw rather in Jesus a new beginning or a new covenant." A survey of scholarly theological opinion follows and is perhaps best summed up in the words of one document: "It is a tragedy of history that Jesus, our bond of unity with the Jews, has all too often become a symbol and source of division and bitterness because of human weakness and pride."

Neusner, Jacob. Stranger at Home. Chicago: Univ. of Chicago Pr., 1981. 213p.

Jacob Neusner throws out a challenge: Does the Holocaust pose a major theological question for Jews? His unusual answer, in a book with the subtitle "Holocaust, Zionism and American Judaism," is in the negative. He observes that problems raised by the Holocaust, including that of radical evil, have existed since biblical times. Neusner criticizes what he labels as the overemphasis, in the United States, on commemorating and studying the Holocaust.

Peck, Abraham J., ed. Jews and Christians after the Holocaust. Philadelphia: Fortress, 1982. 111p.

Seven very intelligent essays on how Christian-Jewish relations have been affected in the light (or darkness) of the Holocaust are collected here. Rosemary Radford Ruether claims that it was Christian theology that developed the reprobate status of the Jew in history; the German church struggle is the topic for John Conway; a Protestant view is tendered by Allan Brockway, who insists that religious values were at the heart of Hitler's final solution; Irving Greenberg, a rabbi, is powerful as he writes from both theological and secular perspectives, while David Tracy, a priest, is eloquent on the need for certain re-evaluations in Christian theology. Here is one of the finest collections of its kind.

Pilch, Judah, ed. The Jewish Catastrophe in Europe. New York: American Assn. for Jewish Education, 1968. 230p.

The Holocaust raised major questions: Where was God? Where was humanity? Where were the churches? How should what happened be conveyed to future generations? Five authors here try to face these issues squarely by tracing Jewish life between the two world wars; analyzing the "Jewish Question" in the Third Reich; by a presentation of the bare facts of the years of the Holocaust; discussing Jewish resistance; briefly examining some Holocaust literature; looking at the world, which was silent as the destruction of Jewry took place; and looking at the years that followed.

Rosenbaum, Irving J. Holocaust and Halakah. New York: Ktav, 1976. 177p.

How did Jews conform to the pattern and norms of Halakhic Judaism during the Nazi era? This book is centered, mainly, on rabbinic response written in Germany, Poland, Hungary, and Lithuania, covering 1933 to 1945, and including rulings from ghettos, concentration camps, and death camps. Many topics are covered, including the justifiability of murder, suicide, and abortion under the dehumanizing conditions. The factual data surrounding each case is presented, as is a summary of the legal arguments leading to the rendered judgment.

Rubenstein, Richard L. After Auschwitz. Indianapolis: Bobbs-Merrill, 1966. 287p.

The author of this highly controversial analysis of the meaning of theology after the Holocaust insists that the murder of millions of Jews has overwhelmingly negative implications for both Judaism and Christianity. He concludes that, contrary to Jewish teaching, the ideas that God in some way rules over history and that the Jews are somehow in a special relationship with the Lord are false. How can the murder of all of these victims be a part of God's plan? Rubenstein writes: "I would rather live in an absurd, indifferent cosmos in which men suffer and die meaninglessly but still retain a measure of their integrity, than view their tragedies as imposed by a punitive God on a guilty humanity." The author opts for a pagan kind of Judaism in this startling and provocative book.

Ruether, Rosemary Radford. Faith and Fratricide. New York: Seabury, 1974. 294p.

The roots of Christian anti-Semitism are found in the Christian Testament, according to this Roman Catholic theologian. Christian faith has somehow resulted in a long tradition of almost unrelenting hatred of the Jews. This was in great measure pro- legomena to the culminating event in this century, the Holocaust. She follows a psychopathological approach here: Christian detes- tation of Jews is symbolic self-loathing. Ruether urges a kind of relativization of the meaning of Christian scripture and says that the Church must see Jesus more as a paradigm of the eschata- logical experience. Drawing primarily on the Gospels, St. Paul, and the Fathers of the Church, Ruether's discussion here has pro- voked much in the way of dialogue between Christians and Jews and among Christians themselves.

Zimmels, H.J. The Echo of the Nazi Holocaust in Rabbinic Literature. New York: Ktav, 1977. 372p.
Many troubling questions on Jewish law were raised during the Holocaust. This volume, after outlining the history of the Third Reich, then investigates such topics as the Nazi desecra- tion of cemeteries and synagogues, mixed marriages, reburial, unclaimed property, and adoption. The authorities here emphasize the importance of saving of life, which will allow for paradoxical rabbinical decisions in emergencies.

SURVIVORS
AND THE
SECOND
GENERATION

Although the shortest section of the bibliography, it is by no means unimportant. What has happened to Holocaust survivors and their children, and to the persecutors and their children, is one of the most neglected areas of Holocaust study. From the few books (and more significantly, the many articles, particularly in journals dealing with psychology and psychiatry) we learn how deeply the Holocaust affected the torturers as well as their victims, and some titles deal with problems faced by the descendants of the Nazis.

Amery, Jean. At the Mind's Limit. Bloomington, Ind.: Indiana
    Univ. Pr., 1980. 111p.
    "No one can become what he cannot find in his memories." So writes Auschwitz survivor Jean Amery. He was raised a Catholic, but the fact of a (long dead) Jewish father caused the young man to be designated a Jew by the Nazis. His personal dilemma is implicit in the title of one chapter: On the Necessity and Impossibility of Being a Jew. An agnostic all of his adult life, Amery nevertheless accepted his Semitic identification, but with it the concentration camp and torture. It is the experience of torture that caused him to write this book. As an intellectual, he found his idealistic system and principles meaningless under the beatings and bone dislocations he suffered. He stated that the very first blow caused one to lose trust in the world and become transformed completely into flesh. And once one had succumbed to torture, he or she was never again "at home" in the world. Amery insisted that torture was the very essence of the Third Reich, not merely an accidental quality. Communism, he

observed, could de-Stalinize itself, but the Nazis "tortured because they were torturers." As for the victim, that person is indelibly marked: "Whoever was tortured, stays tortured. Torture is ineradicably burned into him. . . ." (This statement was given personal authenticity by Amery on October 17, 1978, when he took his own life.)

Ben-Ami, Yitzhaq. Years of Wrath: Days of Glory. New York: Speller, 1982. 599p.

Ben-Ami has written about the evolution of Jews from survivors of the Holocaust to founders of the State of Israel. He was an important leader in the resistance against Nazis, and developed plans for saving Jews and finding safety for them in Palestine. This book covers three phases of Jewish life that occurred in one generation: the massacre of European Jews in the Holocaust; the rebellion against British authority in Palestine; and the establishment of the State of Israel.

Bergmann, Martin S., and Milton E. Jucovy, eds. Generation of the Holocaust. New York: Basic Books, 1982. 338p.

The first in-depth study of the psychological effects of the Holocaust on the children of the survivors, this book utilizes the data from thirty such families from around the world. Analyzed by authorities, a keen picture emerges of the agonies suffered by the second generation of boys and girls, men and women. The editors first present a background for this study followed by the problems and difficulties faced by the families. Some of the editors' conclusions may prove "too Freudian" for a number of readers, but they certainly provide a new focus. The final section, Theoretical and Clinical Aspects, discusses such areas as recurrent problems in the treatment both of survivors and their children, hysterical features among the second generation, and some thoughts on superego pathology.

Brenner, Robert Reeve. The Faith and Doubt of Holocaust Survivors. New York: Free Pr., 1980. 266p.

Dull as portions of this book are to read (it seems to be an unmodified Ph.D. dissertation), the facts are certainly arresting and worth the effort. Brenner traces the impact of the Holocaust on the Jewish faith of the survivors. He surveyed 708 men and women (100 in person, the rest by mail), and fifty-two percent responded that the catastrophe had little or no effect on their religious behavior. Of those who said they did change, there is no way of knowing if such shifts would have occurred anyway, under more normal circumstances. Yet when those who were surveyed tell their stories, they speak profoundly. Some believed they found faith under duress; others cannot deny God but continue to express their rebelliousness by way of protest.

Not one of these Jews saw the camp as a personal spiritual birth-place (as did a number in Solzhenitsyn's Gulag Archipelago, for example).

Day, Ingeborg. Ghost Waltz. New York: Viking, 1980. 244p.
The author was born in Austria, where her father was a Nazi police officer; she is haunted by the question of his role in the persecution of Jews. Day also feels that she is somehow afflicted by anti-Semitism and does not know how she acquired it. This is not a solid book. The writer, in the end, seems to let her father off too easily and overcomes her own prejudices in rather too pat a manner. Nevertheless, it is a book that shows that the Holocaust affected not only children of the victims but also children of the persecutors, as well.

Des Pres, Terrence. The Survivor. New York: Oxford Univ. Pr., 1976. 218p.
Subtitled "An Anatomy of Life in the Death Camps," the book begins with these words: "My subject is survival, the capacity of men and women to live beneath the pressure of protracted crisis, to sustain terrible damage in mind and body and yet be there, sane, alive, still human." Des Pres looks at survivors in fiction, with an emphasis on the work of Camus, Malamud, and Solzhenitsyn. Then he moves to documents of the Holocaust, discussing such authors as Chaim Kaplan, Alexander Donat, Primo Levi, and others. Following is one of the most remarkable chapters in all of Holocaust literature, titled "Excremental Assault." Des Pres tells of the living conditions for those who were covered with their own filth, even the excretion of others from the bunk bed situations--and fed "soup" meals that readily ran through the bodily system. In the book's final chapter, Des Pres writes of the survivors as "the first of civilized men to live beyond the compulsions of culture, beyond a fear of death which can only be assuaged by insisting that life itself is worthless. The survivor is evidence that men and women are now strong enough, mature enough, awake enough, to face death without mediation, and therefore to embrace life without reserve."

Dimsdale, Joel, ed. Survivors, Victims, and Perpetrators. New York: Hemisphere, 1980. 474p.
A medical doctor, Dimsdale has collected essays that deal primarily with the emotional effects of the Holocaust on survivors, their children and, perhaps most significantly, a socio-psychological view of World War II Nazis as they are today. In a survey of 300 former SS members, investigation showed that they were generally well integrated into society, rarely regretted their Nazi activities, enjoyed each others' company, and were no longer looked down on in German society. These men were often

divorced, very aggressive, and tended not to be church affiliated, but rather associated with a revival of paganism.

Epstein, Helen. Children of the Holocaust. New York: Putnam, 1979. 348p.

Children is primarily about Epstein herself, a child of two of the approximately 75,000 Jews who outlived the death camps. These survivors, with their nightmares, waking fears, obsessions with the health and happiness of their children, and the effects of all this on those children (i.e., on Helen Epstein) is the subject of this essay. Clearly, for many the Holocaust had hidden effects: imagine the feelings of a child whose mother, in anger, rages: "Did I leave Auschwitz for you?" Epstein is properly concerned with her relation to history, Israel, her parents, and the children of other survivors. What happens when one of these youngsters is hospitalized for a minor ailment and shares a room with a "normal" child who is visited by grandparents, aunts, uncles, and cousins, and who is struck by the realization that there are no relatives around to visit her? What does it mean when a child of survivors has children? (It can mean a victory against Hitler.) The patterns that she and others, including psychiatrists in many countries, have found cannot be denied. They are a part of the ongoing tragedy of the Holocaust.

Heymont, Irving. Among the Survivors of the Holocaust--1945. Cincinnati: American Jewish Archives, 1982. 111p.

After liberation, many Jewish survivors were assigned to displaced person's camps until they could be sent to permanent homes. Large numbers did not wish to return to their native lands; most sought to go to Palestine or the United States. While in these camps, they were often badly treated by their liberators. These Jews no longer considered themselves to be Russians or Poles or Germans, but Jews. American army personnel had a difficult time with this idea and with certain demands made by these Jews, and much else. In fact, things got so bad that when they were brought to President Truman's attention, he took immediate action, noting that "as matters now stand, we appear to be treating Jews as the Nazis treated them except that we do not exterminate them." The author of this book was in charge of a camp outside of Munich, and what he saw is recorded here in the letters, preserved by his wife, that he sent her. The problems of governance, sanitation, allowing for rituals, conflicts among Jews themselves, camp strikes, attempts at retribution against Nazi prisoners, etc., are chronicled. The volume is particularly helpful to one interested in the psychology of the survivors.

Moskovitz, Sarah. Love despite Hate. New York: Schocken, 1983. 320p.

When the Second World War ended, the British government permitted a thousand child survivors, ranging in age from three to eleven, to enter England. Sarah Moskovitz interviewed twenty-four of these individuals, most now living in Israel or the United States. The suffering they continue to experience, as well as the guarded optimism they have for life, becomes evident. Nearly all are involved in ethical and spiritual activities in their communities. One conclusion of this child therapist is that serious emotional disability does not necessarily follow childhood trauma. It may have implications for wider applications (for example, in considering the effect of unfortunate early environment on criminals), with far-reaching ramifications.

Rabinowitz, Dorothy. New Lives. New York: Knopf, 1976. 242p.
Biographical information about survivors of the Nazi death camps now living in the United States makes up the bulk of this book. The perspective, by men and women who have lived here for twenty-five to thirty years, is unique. The details are seen in reflection, rather than in the heat of living. Rabinowitz interviewed 108 refugees, but concentrates on the stories of a handful. Nevertheless, she could not have selected segments as artistically or historically significant if the basic groundwork had not also been done. There are various people here, some uneducated, one who married an older woman who could not conceive children (he lost three children and his wife in the Holocaust), still another who visited her former concentration camp and crawled into an oven to gather ashes as a reminder.

Sachar, Abram L. The Redemption of the Unwanted. New York: St. Martin's 1983. 320p.
What happened to the relatively few Jews (400,000) who survived World War II? Most were hungry, diseased, and mentally troubled. They were free from the death camps but not free from the memories and pain. This is a book about Jewish redemption and the establishment of the State of Israel. Sachar covers American and British attitudes toward aiding Jewish victims; he also examines such topics as Polish death camps, resistance movements, the Nuremberg Trials, displaced person's camps, and more.

Steinitz, Lucy, and David Szonyi, eds. Living after the Holocaust. New York: Bloch, 1976. 149p.
The editors of this collection, themselves children of Holocaust survivors, have gathered a series of essays, discussions, poems, and reflections on what it means to be a member of the "Second Generation." How the younger people reacted to the tales their parents told them is revealing, and the lessons they learned even more. "In some way, everything they told me annihilated the

validity of my own experiences and feeling," said one. "Except for a tragic accident of history I would be living in Germany now," observed another. A third noted that she "really didn't realize that people had grandparents until I came to Israel and America--that really is a possibility for Jews."

Wiesenthal, Simon. The Sunflower. New York: Schocken, 1976. 216p.

A dying German officer requests that any Jewish prisoner be brought to him, because he feels that he wants to ask for forgiveness. While the SS man does not actually ask forgiveness, it is implied. The prisoner (Wiesenthal himself?) remains silent. The Catholic officer dies, unabsolved by the Jew. After the war, the Jew visits the mother of the dead soldier and closes the first part of the volume questioning whether he should have forgiven the dying man. The second portion of the book contains commentaries on the event by prominent Christians and Jews, survivors, Germans, and others including Jacques Maritain, Cynthia Ozick, Abraham Heschel, Edward Flannery, and Herbert Marcuse.

THE
ARTS

It should not be surprising that this is the largest section of the bibliography; humanity's responses to major events in both the history of individuals and the history of international affairs have frequently been expressed in artistic form. A statistically documented presentation on the Holocaust may be very informative, but hardly as moving as a poem by Nelly Sachs or a novel by Andre Schwarz-Bart. A short drama by Shimon Wincelberg (see Skloot) or Elie Wiesel's cantata (Ani Maamin) can prove as gripping as any factual work. Monuments to the dead (Rieth) can have greater impact than anthologies of archive documents, and the literary criticism of Holocaust fiction and poetry can lead to a deeper comprehension of its tragic aspects. Here, then, are titles from those groupings. An overview of Nazi Cinema is included as well. Some of the listings are first rate; others, like Gerald Green's Holocaust and William Styron's Sophie's Choice, are only entered for the reasons indicated in the discussion. There is much that is truly excellent in this section; Holocaust literature may prove to be one of the great subgenres of world writing.

This chapter is divided into sections on fiction, drama, poetry, art, and criticism.

FICTION

Aichinger, Ilse. Herod's Children. New York: Atheneum, 1963. 238p.
The nightmare story of the Holocaust is told in nightmare fashion through the eyes of innocent children who confuse reality

and fantasy in this highly imaginative novel. This tale of a group of Jewish children in Vienna during the war depicts a terrifying world so lacking in rationality, so frightening, that the children have to create a world within a world in order to survive. The reader sometimes has difficulty distinguishing between the reality and the make-believe, which is appropriate to the message of the novel. While the young people seem a bit too precocious for their ages, and too many are too full of insight, their encounter with chaos is met with very satisfyingly.

Appelfeld, Aharon. The Age of Wonders. Boston: Godine, 1981. 224p.

The time is 1937; the location a small town in Austria. The narrative is related through the perspective of a ten-year-old boy named Bruno whose parents are assimilated Jewish intellectuals, the father a highly regarded writer. Both of Bruno's parents despise the Jewish middle class, even going so far as to denounce its members, particularly those engaged in business. They also refuse to consider the possibility that the growing anti-Semitism in Austria could somehow affect them. They prove to be wrong and their lives are destroyed. The marriage is wrecked and Bruno is deported, as are his mother and adopted sister. The novel ends some years later when Bruno returns to the town, now totally without Jews, to recall the past and somehow to atone for his father's sins.

------. Badenheim 1939. Boston: Godine, 1980. 148p.

During a comfortably warm summer just before the onset of World War II, Jews are being brought into a small, pleasant Austrian community, but nobody seems to know why. Intellectuals, aristocrats, musicians, and others of the middle class interact, but not in the carefree way they had previously; something is wrong. The visiting Jews begin to be frightened by nightmares; they become fearful of the future and develop a nostalgia for the past. Finally, they all board the boxcars that will take them to their fate. The final sentence of this Holocaust novel is powerfully ironic: "If the coaches are so dirty it must mean that we have not far to go."

Arnold, Elliott. A Night of Watching. New York: Scribner, 1967. 441p.

Filled with brief, anecdotal chapters that shift focus from this character to that, this novel is about the Danish underground that worked so hard and risked so much to save Jews from the occupying Nazis. The characters are rather well drawn, some even memorable. They include the leader of the resistance forces, Hansen; a Prussian general enthusiastic about the war but embarrassed by underhanded Gestapo methods; a chief rabbi who did not believe in running away; and Buhle, a German officer moved by the sacrifice and heroism of his adversaries. There is also some humor, and the author successfully portrays Danes with their failings as well as their strengths.

Becker, Jurek. Jacob the Liar. New York: Harcourt, 1976. 266p.

Born in Poland in 1937, the author was a victim of the Lodz Ghetto and several concentration camps. From those experiences he has written a novel about one man's personal victory in the midst of the Holocaust. Jacob Heym, a simple person, by example communicated the will to live to an entire community. The ghetto is a lifeless place but Jacob, a "nobody" before the war, spreads invented rumors about Allied advances, providing the ghetto dwellers with hope to replace their despair. Some people think that he gets his information from a contraband radio; since this endangers them, they ask him to give it up. His response is simple and convincing: "Since the news reports have circulated in the ghetto, I know of no incident where anyone has taken his life." This is a very engaging tale.

Bercovitch, Reuben. Hasen. New York: Knopf. 1978. 142p.

The 1978 Ernest Hemingway Foundation Award for best first novel was given to this fictional work about two boys who live in a forest that abuts a Nazi concentration camp. Thirteen-year-old Ritter and Perchik, a year younger, stay alive primarily through their ability to successfully hunt hares (Hasen) with which they bribe Hoegel, the camp commandant. Then they learn that Perchik's ten-year-old brother Dudie has just been taken prisoner. A very complex plan is devised to free the child and the tension in this well written tale reaches near break-point. The two major characters must come to grips with the problem of exposing their own vulnerability to save another.

Berger, Zdena. Tell Me Another Morning. New York: Harper, 1961. 243p.

"Fictional autobiography" is the proper category for this memorable book. Ostensibly the tale of Tania, a fourteen-year-old Czech child, much of the story is told through vignettes that create an authentic atmosphere. The girl lost her family in a concentration camp. How is she to survive physically, emotionally, spiritually? Here is the answer--one of pain and of hope. This book works both as a novel and a memoir.

Borowski, Tadeusz. This Way for the Gas, Ladies and Gentlemen. New York: Penguin, 1967. 180p.

The author, a non-Jewish survivor of the Holocaust, committed suicide in 1951. In this collection of short stories he portrays the horrible conditions in the death camp with remarkable under-statement. In one story, a prisoner who feels no pity for other, even less fortunate victims is comforted by another: ". . . it is natural, predictable. . . . Why, I'd even call it healthy." Another story finds burial detail prisoners involved in a soccer game while new prisoners are being brought in; the match goes on while the bestiality continues. "A Day at Harmenz" is the descrip-tion of an average twenty-four-hour period rendered in matter-of-fact terms. Death is present, of course; so is theft--as prisoners steal rations from their comrades in desperate efforts to survive. The corrupt power of the Kapo (prisoners with certain authority) is portrayed, as well as the general inhumanity of Auschwitz. There is a story of heroic resistance; another on revenge after libera-tion. Most of all this is a rare, tension-filled collection of perhaps the best short fiction on the Holocaust.

Braunburg, Rudolf. Betrayed Skies. New York: Doubleday, 1980. 366p.
Written by a former Luftwaffe pilot, this is a beautiful novel: lyric, celebrating flight in the manner of St. Exupery. Taking place in World War II, it concerns a German pilot who wants to become a commercial flier in Berlin after Germany wins the war. But in the air, he learns that he cannot kill--killing is incompatible with the true romance of flying. On reflection, he concludes that Germany must lose the war if civilization is to continue.

Chaneles, Sol. Three Children of the Holocaust. New York: Avon, 1974. 192p.
Naomi and Deborah, aged twelve, and Michael, six, spent years in the horrid environment of a concentration camp. When the war ends, Auschwitz is liberated and these three orphans begin to face a totally different kind of life. A wealthy American couple adopts them, brings them to New York, and raises them under privi-leged circumstances. What eventually happens to them is a major part of this intelligent novel.

Eliach, Yaffa. Hasidic Tales of the Holocaust. New York: Oxford Univ. Pr., 1982. 266p.
A compilation of stories written after the Holocaust as well as during that experience itself, this wide-ranging anthology is both a testament to the human spirit, as well as a record of it. All the stories are by Hasidim and the editor's eclectic efforts are far-reaching.

Elon, Amos. Timetable. New York: Doubleday, 1980. 349p.
A frightening novel, enhanced in its terror because it is based on fact, this is the story of a reported deal offered by

Adolf Eichmann: Jews for trucks and supplies. Eichmann sent Joel Brand to deliver the proposal. Brand was a Jew active in the resistance. When he told the Allies that a million Jewish lives might thus be saved, the reactions here recorded are monumentally disappointing. Could Brand be believed? Was the offer authentic? How much would this damage the war effort? Where could such an influx of refugees be kept? This fiction is about one of the must puzzling events of World War II.

Epstein, Leslie. King of the Jews. New York: Avon, 1980. 309p.
One of the most remarkable novels written about the Holocaust, this work of fiction is courageous in both its concept and execution. The conquerors of a small Jewish town decide to commit a horrendous crime on such a scale that they resolve to make the Jews perform it for them. They particularly single out I. C. Trumpelman; he is designated "King of the Jews." Trumpelman is a liar, a rogue, a lecher, a doctor without credentials, and conversely a savior. He is willing to assign hundreds to their deaths--in order to save thousands more--in this gripping, exuberant, fascinating, amazing story.

Frank, Anne. Anne Frank's Tales from the Secret Annex. New York: Doubleday, 1984. 136p.
In a journal, separate from her now well known diary, teenaged Anne Frank wrote short fiction, essays, fables, and vignettes of her life. This collection contains all of these in one volume, some of it not available elsewhere. The stories are very brief, quite imaginative, and hold the interest of those who know Anne's Diary and her fate. There is special poignancy in her references. For example, a kindly grandfather is presented in one three-page tale that ends with the narrator/author observing the old man making a canoe for his grandchild: "I wish I had that kind of grandpa." There is some good humor in the essays here, whether on finding a flea in her clothing or in a piece titled "The Sink of Iniquity" that begins: "Don't worry, I'm not going to give you a list of examples to illustrate my title."

------. The Works of Anne Frank. New York: Doubleday, 1959. 332p.
This compilation contains both The Diary of a Young Girl and most (though not all) of the fables, short stories, reminiscences, and essays found in Anne Frank's Tales from the Secret Annex. Of special value to this edition is the strong introduction to the book by Ann Birstein and Alfred Kazin.

Fuks, Ladislav. Mr. Theodore Mundstock. New York: Ballantine, 1969. 223p.
This novel is about the effects and implications of the Holo-

caust on an old man's sensibilities. Part of the process of discovery here centers around what happens when a person finds out that the real is fantastic, incredible--in fact absurd. The author creates a tension in Mundstock based on the opposition of reality and illusion, and hope and death. The main character is not one who even asks for an affirmation of life but merely looks for a way out of the overwhelming horror of it all.

Gladstone, Frances. Anne's Youth. New York: Schocken, 1984. 113p.

Hitler does continue to have posthumous victories, the kind that philosopher Emil Fackenheim warned us against permitting. Here is a fictionalized account of how the Holocaust troubles second and third generation survivors. Anne is a young daughter of concentration camp survivors. Her parents seem to desire only to live normal lives as Jewish Americans. But the father routinely beats Anne; her mother has a contempt for her daughter as well as for herself; and all of this appears to result from Holocaust-shaped experiences. It is as if Anne represents to her parents what they might each have become if they had had the opportunities they were denied.

Green, Gerald. Holocaust. New York: Bantam, 1978. 408p.

This rather sentimentally told novel of a Jewish family's odyssey and partial destruction at the hands of the Nazis was the basis for a nine-and-one-half hour NBC television program of the same title. Not a critical triumph, this volume was commercially successful; many have read of the Weiss family's plight, as well as the rise of Nazi Erik Dorf at the expense of Jews during the Holocaust.

Habe, Hans. The Mission. New York: Coward, 1966. 319p.

As fiction, this effort is not highly recommended; as the story of an actual event in Holocaust history, however, it is riveting. Author Hans Habe covered a 1938 conference at Evian-les-Bains, where representatives from thirty-two nations discussed the saddening situation of some 500,000 German and Austrian Jews, who were urgently in need of refuge. This documentary novel is based on the reporter's eyewitness experiences at the meeting. The fictional protagonist, an elderly Jewish professor from Vienna, carries a secret proposal to the meeting. The Nazis will sell individual Jews for $250 and a family for $1,000. Disgusting as such bartering might be, the professor concludes that this is the only way these unfortunate people can be saved. But the man soon discovers that the very nations that will make up the Allies during World War II are not seriously interested in rescuing Jews. The hero of the book is well drawn, unlike the other characters, but the writing is often sentimental; even so, the facts on which the novel are based compel the reader's attention.

Hersey, John. The Wall. New York: Knopf, 1967. 706p.

A long, wrenching novel about the Warsaw Ghetto, Hersey's book covers the period from its creation through its further isolation, caused by the wall, to the Jewish uprising and subsequent destruction of the Ghetto by the Nazis. Based on factual evidence, the work is often devastating, as when a Jew has to smother a baby to keep its cries from betraying a hiding place to German soldiers.

Hochhuth, Rolf. A German Love Story. Boston: Little, 1980. 269p.

The title of this novel has a double meaning. On the surface it concerns a love affair between a Polish prisoner of war and a German village woman. Because it violates Nazi racial laws, the man is executed. On another level the novel is an exploration of Germany's national love affair with death. Hochhuth accepts Nietzsche's insight that "insanity is a rare thing in individuals but habitual to groups, parties, nations, and ages." Called "a true life novel," this powerful work has intercalated chapters of effective philosophical musings.

Jacot, Michael. The Last Butterfly. Indianapolis: Bobbs-Merrill, 1974. 231p.

Because he made a joke about Hitler, a half-Jewish clown with failing talents is sentenced to perform for the Jewish children of the concentration camp in Terezin. Antonin Karas's sensitivities in this novel are juxtaposed to the deliberate Nazi cruelties towards inmates of this model camp (used to deceive International Red Cross workers about the true purpose of Nazi concentration camps). The spiritual resistance and hopefulness give this fictitious work a certain charm that is at once satisfying and yet incredible (since only some 1,300 out of 140,000 who went through Terezin survived). Very short chapters (often only a page or two) are appropriate for such an absorbing story.

de Jong, Dola. The Field. Sagaponack, N.Y.: Second Hand Pr., 1980. 215p.

Dola de Jong, a Dutch writer who escaped from Europe during World War II, gives a penetrating presentation of what can happen to a makeshift family of refugees forced into a precarious existence by the common atrocities of war. (This novel was originally published in 1945 as And the Field Is the World.) Lies and her husband, Aart, fled Holland with their own family, picking up needy children along the way. Aart attempts to farm on barren land just outside Tangiers, and the frustrations of the impromptu

group multiply. There is the usual collection of domestic squab-
bles, some jealousies, and sexual attraction between a pair of
the nonrelated youngsters. Lies, growing weary of her maternal
responsibilities, snaps at the children. Eight-year-old Luba
runs away to become the mistress of a curious European. Aart is
mistaken for a lawbreaker and, when he resists arrest, is imprisoned. Seventeen-year-old Hans then takes over the family (which
includes, among others, pre-schooler Pierre, whose leg amputation
is yet another grief). Hans improves the group's lot; when Aart
returns from jail, an archetypal conflict takes place between the
two. The death of Lies, following a miscarriage, is another woe,
but the family's hopes are raised with the prospect of emigration
to the United States. A final, overwhelming tragedy remains, however, and the novel ends with a sense of impending doom.

Kanfer, Stefan. The Eighth Sin. New York: Random, 1978.
299p.

The Eighth Sin is the story of a Gypsy, Benoit, who survived
the Nazi massacres of Gypsies in World War II. Benoit comes to
the United States as a teen-ager, is adopted by a college professor
and his wife, gets into trouble for shoplifting, and is institu-
tionalized. All the while, his own important skill, an ability to
paint portraits, is being developed. As a painter, he will make a
very good living, but this is not important to him; his death camp
experiences haunt everything that he does and infect everything
that he is. This theme is played out as Benoit seeks another
Gypsy, Eleazar Jassy, who survived by brutalizing other Gypsies
at the will of the Nazis. As a child, Benoit was horrified by
Jassy's ability to maim and kill; as an adult, Benoit remains
horrified as he recalls what he saw Jassy do. There appears only
one purgation for Benoit--to track down and kill Jassy. Much of
the novel is an adventure story--picking up clues, finding Jassy,
then confronting him. But there is more to the book than merely
the chase. Character delineation is excellent. Stefan Kanfer's
sense of detail is highly sensitized, and he writes in a gripping
style that will not let the reader go.

Karmel, Ilona. An Estate of Memory. New York: Houghton,
1969. 444p.

While not one of the better known Holocaust novels, this
touching story tells of four women who are prisoners in a Nazi
concentration camp in Poland. Covering the period 1943-44, the
novel ultimately becomes a tale of hope, which is symbolized as
the women work together to ensure the secret birth of a baby.
Children were, of course, not allowed to exist in the camps because they would have been unproductive, wasteful consumers rather
than helpful workers. Nevertheless, how the child was safely de-
livered and smuggled to freedom makes for a satisfying adventure.

Karmel-Wolfe, Hema. The Baders of Jacob Street. Philadelphia:
Lippincott, 1980. 321p.

Halma Bader, this novel's main character, belongs to a Jewish
family that has lived on Jacob Street in Krakow, Poland, for generations. How the young woman reacts to the Nazi occupation of
her neighborhood is the theme of this sometimes moving, sometimes
rather flat story. Perhaps the main failure is in the portrayal
of the central figure, who does not seem capable of holding the
reader's interest for the entire novel. Still, the book gives valuable insights into this human spirit, into the daily history of
this sad episode in Europe, and remains an honest, if not artistic,
achievement. For example, the author does not spare the Nazi
appointed Jewish ghetto government (the Judenrat) from criticism.

Kosinski, Jerzy. The Painted Bird. New York: Pocket Bks.,
1966. 214p.

A young boy is this novel's main character. He is abandoned
by his parents and forced to see the miseries of war from an
innocent perspective. Violence abounds, most of it graphically
related. Kosinski sees no other way to tell such tales of sadism.
The child has so many close calls, sees so many truly horrifying
experiences, that for a long period of time he becomes literally
speechless. Vivid images abound in Kosinski's fiction.

Kuznetsov, Anatoly. Babi Yar. New York: Dell, 1967. 399p.

Called a "documentary novel," this story of the massacre of
thousands of Jews by the Nazis near Kiev, Russia, is told from the
perspective of a Russian boy. The author was twelve when the Germans conquered Kiev in 1941. In the nearby ravine of Babi Yar,
not far from Anatoly's home, the Nazis slaughtered almost 200,000
persons; about 50,000 were Jews. Kuznetsov vowed that if he lived
he would tell the full story and this book, which caused a sensa-
tion when it was published in the U.S.S.R., fulfills that promise.

Langfus, Anna. The Whole Land Brimstone. New York: Pantheon,
1962. 218p.

A wrenching autobiographical novel, this book is almost unbearable in its presentation of torture and winter death, of escape,
recapture, and imprisonment. Maria is a lovely, pampered young
woman who escapes the Warsaw Ghetto into which her family is forced.
In the outside world she finds tremendous anti-Semitic persecution
from non-Jewish Poles. After a series of endured hardships, she
and her husband are captured and accused of being spies for the
Russians. He is shot, Maria is tortured and sentenced to death.

Laqueur, Walter. Farewell to Europe. Boston: Little, 1981.
336p.

Farewell to Europe is a sequel to The Missing Years (see

following entry). Laqueur's low-keyed approach to the events described is similar to that of his earlier fictional volume. This work opens in Berlin with the war over, but not its effects. The portrait of Berlin in The Missing Years was memorable; so is this description of the postwar era. The main figure of the two books, Lasson, now widowed, a Jew who stayed in Germany throughout the war, becomes a mini-celebrity when he is identified as a victim of Nazism. He leaves for America in 1946. The novel is then mainly concerned with his two sons, whose complicated lives take one to Israel and the other to America. Best known for his nonfiction writing, Laqueur proves himself a fine novelist as well.

------. The Missing Years. Boston: Little, 1980. 281p.
This is a curious and surprisingly riveting novel. Surprising because this work of fiction contains very little dialogue, little in the way of graphic description, and almost no dramatic incidents. Furthermore, much of the book reads like a series of tracts. However, the novel has a representative (rather than individualistic) narrator who is Jewish, a survivor of the Holocaust in Berlin. What holds the reader, as critic Terrence des Pres has noted, is the probable connection between the author (who did not undergo the experiences here, though he did lose his family in the Holocaust) and his material, a "fictional autobiography."

Levin, Meyer. Eva. New York: Simon & Schuster, 1959. 311p.
Eva Korngold, a Jewish girl who escapes from the Nazis in Poland disguised as a Ukrainian, narrates this novel. In disguise she finds employment in a German household, working as a servant. Later she finds a place in a government office, but eventually is caught and sent to Auschwitz. On a death march, she again escapes and ultimately finds a haven in Israel. Some may find the ending of this fictional work rather gratuitous, with Jews gaining revenge that seems inappropriate to the theme of an innocent's survival.

Lind, Jakov. Landscape in Concrete. New York: Grove, 1966. 190p.
Writing in a subgenre that has been called the "literature of extremity," Jakov Lind portrays the insanity of violence, random murder, and wild sexuality. Set near the end of the war, this allegorical novel is about Gauthier Bachmann, a soldier who went mad on the Russian front and was discharged from the German army. Various Nazis encounter Bachmann as he wanders through Europe and manipulate him for monstrous purposes. He has been conditioned to follow orders, so he willingly kills without conscience while seeing himself as longing for the finer

things of life. The result is a powerful indictment of Nazism by an author that some critics place in the top rank of Holocaust novelists and short story writers.

Linn, Meritt. A Book of Songs. New York: St. Martin's, 1983. 309p.

The story of this novel is of concentration camp inmates struggling not to become as psychologically brutalized as their captors. They find in a violin-playing child inmate the possibilities of the world beyond the barbed wire. The tension the author creates, as inmates sacrifice to help the boy escape into childhood, is skillfully handled, as are the episodes of failure-- the sections in which Jewish prisoners succumb to the pressure of hunger, psychological and physical terror, loneliness and alienation. The chapter in which the prisoner/narrator, fulfilling a promise to another Jew, approaches a man to mercifully put him out of his misery is almost unbearable.

Lustig, Arnost. Darkness Casts No Shadows. Washington, D.C.: Inscape, 1976. 144p.

While the author seems more adept in the short story form than longer fiction, this novel is, nonetheless, a solid achievement. It is actually based on Lustig's escape, as a teenager, with a friend from a Nazi transport. Their adventures, especially in the dark forests of Germany, are gripping. Their hunger and fears are delicately transmitted. There is also a rather jarring change in the point-of-view, and the ending is a little too pat, but like most Holocaust literature, the book really helps stretch our understanding of what fiction can do.

------. Diamonds of the Night. Washington, D.C.: Inscape, 1978. 234p.

Volume 3 in Lustig's Children of the Holocaust series, this book contains nine compelling stories that have come out of the author's own concentration camp experience. The horror of existence under the Nazis is powerfully rendered in stories such as "The Lemon." In it, a boy has to obtain a lemon for his dying sister, who has a vitamin deficiency. To get enough money, the boy knocks the gold teeth out of his recently dead father's corpse. The impact on the child is profoundly measured here. An old man watches helplessly as his elderly wife dies in "The Old Ones and Death"; medical help is not available to these victims. Lustig communicates the pain of the Holocaust with enormous skill.

------. Night and Hope. Washington, D.C.: Inscape, 1976. 206p.

Seven short stories written in a documentary style make up this work. They are based on actual records of ghetto and camp experiences. "The Return" is about a man who escapes from a transport for Jews, but rejoins his people after a time on the outside. "Rose Street" is about the death of a woman beaten by a Nazi, and the compassion for her humanity felt by another Nazi. "Stephen and Anne" concerns two children who shared their first kiss; before their love can blossom, she is removed from his life by a Nazi transport. Lustig writes primarily about children, and is a master storyteller.

------. A Prayer for Katerina Horovitzova. New York: Harper, 1973. 165p.

Like a modern Judith and Holofernes tale, the theme of this novel is of innocence defeating evil. The shattering climax, in which a lovely young Jewish woman, going to her concentration camp death, destroys her Nazi tormentor before she is killed, is at once surprising and satisfying. This story begins in Italy, where twenty American Jews are about to be killed by Nazis. They try to negotiate for their freedom but lose their money in a cruel hoax. Among them is the young Katerina, frightened of death when she has so much of her life before her. How she faces her end with courage and quiet determination is beautifully rendered by one of the best writers of Holocaust fiction.

Neshamit, Sarah. The Children of Mapu Street. Philadelphia: Jewish Publication Society of America, 1970. 324p.

A strong novel about children caught up in the devastation of the Holocaust, this is set in Kovno, Lithuania's capital, on a street where a number of Jewish families live. The happy courtyard where the children once played became something else when the German army appeared. The author writes of the children's feelings as they heard their parents trying to decide whether to flee or remain; the fury unleashed by their neighbors, reacting against them because they are Jews; of life in the ghetto; and of a few non-Jews who were heroic in saving Nazi victims-- even to the point of losing their own lives.

Oliner, S. P. Restless Memoirs. Judah L. Magnes Memorial Museum (2911 Russell St., Berkeley, Calif. 94705), 1979. 104p.

Sam Oliner, a young Polish Jew, survived from age nine to fifteen through courage, quick thinking, and good fortune. His family was destroyed by the Nazis. This "nonfiction novel" begins when the twelve-year-old child is urged by his stepmother to flee a ghetto just before its destruction. Then the work turns back to prewar days and proceeds more chronologically--a very effective style. The second half of the book finds the young hero "passing" as a non-Jew, working for an anti-Semitic family. It is, in fact, a Polish Gentile woman who enables the boy to save himself in a very moving story.

Orler, Uri. The Lead Soldiers. New York: Taplinger, 1980. 234p.

How did children survive the Holocaust with their minds intact? Uri Orler partly answers this question in this autobiographical novel of a young boy's journey from a Warsaw suburb to its ghetto, and then to the Bergen-Belsen camp. The way he coped, with his younger brother, was to metamorphose the horrors they were experiencing into children's games. This is a very original triumph.

Rawicz, Piotre. Blood from the Sky. New York: Harcourt, 1963. 316p.

In this powerful novel the narrator, surviving the destruction of a Jewish community in the Ukraine, now lives in a group of refugees and assorted "down-and-outers" in Paris, people who are simply letting life take its course. Boris's life is recounted from scraps of his journal and some of his poetry. Rawicz uses an audacious symbol, Boris's penis, as the sign of his destiny. His circumcision is not only that which ties him to his people; it is also the mark by which he is betrayed to the Nazis. And it is, in addition, a signifier of Boris's connection to life.

Schaeffer, Susan Fromberg. Anya. New York: Macmillan, 1974. 489p.

This is a moving and important novel of one woman's survival of the Holocaust. Anya, a Jew, abandons her baby daughter on convent steps in order to save the child's life. At the book's close Anya indicates that her life is perhaps meaningless because she gave it no direction herself--"Hitler chose for us." Schaeffer is a novelist with a beautiful style; her word descriptions are absolutely satisfying. She provides readers with everything they want or need to know. However, her plot construction is weak.

Schwarz-Bart, Andre. The Last of the Just. New York: Bantam, 1961. 411p.

There is a Jewish tradition holding that the world is being preserved because of the existence on earth of one Just Man. What Schwarz-Bart does in this highly regarded novel is to trace the legend, as he has adapted it, from the twelfth century to the Holocaust era, making it appear as if each incarnation of the Just Man were the continuation of a single biography. A long, depressing history of the abuse of Jews is portrayed in this novel. A number of memorable characters appears until we meet Ernie Levy, who chooses to perish in the Holocaust rather than live in such a world. He even deliberately refuses to act like a human being, opting to behave like a dog rather than like them, and the story ends with prayer: "And praised. Auschwitz. Be. Maidanek. The Lord. Treblinka. And praised. Buchenwald.

Be. <u>Mauthausen</u>. The Lord. <u>Belzec</u>. And praised. <u>Sobibor</u>. Be. <u>Chelmno</u>. . . ." The currency of history is a magnificent element of this novel.

Semprun, Jorge. <u>The Long Voyage</u>. New York: Grove, 1964. 236p.

While not an artistic triumph, this novel is a readable story about the events of a five-day journey in a cattle car. It takes place in 1943 and the narrator, a Spaniard in the French Resistance, is among the 120 prisoners transported from France to a Nazi concentration camp near Weimar. Apparently autobiographical, the tale is one of suffering: padlocked in a boxcar without sufficient food or water, no facilities, and facing terrible fear. The author tries to transmit all this experience of isolation and terror to the reader. While not a totally successful novel, many of the details of what such a trip was like appear to be valid.

Siegal, Aranka. <u>Upon the Head of a Goat</u>. New York: Farrar, 1981. 214p.

Aranka Siegal's childhood recollections in Hungary during the World War II period are presented here from the viewpoint of Piri Dawidowitz, the nine-year-old narrator of this book. Piri recalls ordinary scenes from her childhood, which take on tragic aspects under Nazi occupation. Her youthful innocence erodes as adult responsibilities are thrust upon her. This Jewish girl is expelled from school and her non-Jewish friends become former friends. There is gentleness and love, too, in this essentially tragic tale of suffering and death.

Singer, Isaac Bashevis. <u>Enemies, a Love Story</u>. New York: Farrar, 1972. 280p.

Nobel Prize-winner Singer portrays a very complicated hero who has three wives in this compelling story. He tells us much about Jewish life in Poland and New York as the major characters are haunted by the lingering effects of their Holocaust experiences.

Steiner, Jean Francois. <u>Treblinka</u>. New York: Simon & Schuster, 1967. 415p.

A documentary novel, this is the story of Nazi brutality and Jewish resistance at Treblinka, the death camp in Poland that was noted for its efficient massacre of nearly a million Jews. Steiner vividly relates the ambiguity of situations where the line between heroism and villainy is obscured, or where the line between excruciating pain and dulled senses cannot be drawn. Perhaps most memorable is the prisoner uprising, where 600 escaped but were hunted down, with the aid of Polish peasants, so effectively that at liberation time only 40 escapees survived.

Stern, Daniel. Who Shall Live, Who Shall Die? New York:
Lancer Bks., 1963. 319p.
In the Nazi death camps some died and some did not. Was
there any logic to this situation? This is the kind of question
that plagues all those who came out alive. Set against the background of a concentration camp, this novel deals with two men as
they compete to establish their own version of personal morality.
The inexorable climax, which involves the suicide of one of the
major figures, is compelling.

Styron, William. Sophie's Choice. New York: Random, 1979.
515p.
A controversial novel with its roots in the Holocaust, this
book focuses on three characters: a narrator, who falls in love
with Sophie as he learns about life; an insane Jewish scientist,
who is Sophie's lover; and Sophie herself, a Polish Catholic
survivor of the Nazi death camps who is forever haunted by the
choice she had to make--a choice forced on her by one of her
captors--as to which of her two children would be allowed to
live. The outline of the story indicates its powerful emotional
pull. However, Styron's development of the characters, while
complex, includes sensational sexual passages that cheapen the
work considerably in the eyes of many critics.

Suhl, Yuri. On the Other Side of the Gate. New York: Avon,
1975. 127p.
Lena and Hershel are about to have a baby. But the circumstances are terrible: they live in the Warsaw Ghetto; they are
confined by Nazi troops; and the order is out that pregnancies
for Jews are henceforth forbidden. Their doctor counsels abortion; and although their fears are great, their belief in the
future causes them to bravely, clandestinely bear the baby and
smuggle it to new life outside the Ghetto, as the title of this
strong novel indicates.

Uris, Leon M. Exodus. New York: Doubleday, 1958. 626p.
A monumental novel tracing the history of European Jewry
from the end of the nineteenth century to the founding of the
State of Israel, this is a work filled with adventure. The characterization is not strong, however, and the near stereotyping
of the Arabs and the British weakens it as a work of art. Some
have been irritated by the pro-Zionist tone.

------. QB VII. New York: Bantam, 1972. 564p.
In this novel, a libel suit is brought against a New York
writer by a doctor who worked for the Nazis. Uris basically
describes what happened when the Polish physician, portrayed as
having experimented on thousands of concentration camp victims,

tried to deny the writer's claims. As part of the trial, the testimony of eyewitnesses and victims gives readers a chance to learn much about Nazi terror.

Weil, Grete. My Sister, My Antigone. New York: Avon, 1984. 203p.

The writer apparently uses this novel in an attempt to work out of her system some of the spiritual pain she experienced during the Nazi years. Born in Germany, she was a student of German literature. She and her husband moved to Holland in 1935, but he was killed in the Mauthausen concentration camp. Weil worked with the Jewish Council in the Netherlands and later with the underground. With the collapse of her world and a feeling of guilt for surviving (a not uncommon phenomenon), she found a parallel between her own life and that of the tragic figure from classical Greek drama, Antigone.

Wiesel, Elie. The Gates of the Forest. New York: Holt, 1966. 226p.

Young Gregor flees the Nazis in Hungary, and is saved through the sacrifice of another. Part of the escape process entails his passing as a mute child to whom townspeople willingly entrust their greatest secrets. When they discover the truth about him, he must run again. He survives the war but must face the awesome question of how to live in a world that God has abandoned. Here is vintage Wiesel in a spellbinding, philosophical work of fiction.

------. Legends of Our Time. New York: Avon, 1970. 237p.

Fifteen tales are included in this deeply moving collection. The first deals with the death of Wiesel's father at the hands of the Nazis. In another, the author reflects on his dead teacher, who had no burial: "Perhaps I, his disciple, am nothing more than his tombstone." Family life and religious practice is the subject of another piece. The story of Pinhas, who fasted on Yom Kippur in the death camp out of defiance to God rather than love, is followed by another revealing what the narrator did after the war when he had an accidental opportunity for revenge. The figure of Moshe the Madman that so haunts Wiesel is the focus of another tale. "The Last Return" is about a visit to his home city of Sighet in Transylvania. Another entry is about a visit to Germany, where the author was surprised to learn that he could not hate. The volume ends with "A Plea for the Dead," Wiesel's most direct and angry statement about those who complain that the Jews should have put up stronger resistance during the Holocaust.

Wiesenthal, Simon. Max and Helen. New York: Morrow, 1982. 163p.

A "nonfiction novel" based on the effects of concentration

camp experience, this gripping work is a love story with an unhappy ending. Simon Wiesenthal, known as the "Nazi hunter," tracks down a war criminal noted for the pleasure he took clubbing victims to death. A survivor of that commander's camp, Max (a physician) has the opportunity to testify against the former Nazi but he and his beloved Helen refuse to do so. She has a terrible secret that will be revealed if the case comes to trial and, for humane reasons, Wiesenthal refuses to press the prosecution. The secret is a son forced on Helen by the murderous commander. Max cannot abide looking at the boy, who resembles his father, and finally separates from Helen.

DRAMA

Eliach, Jaffa, and Uri Assaf. The Last Jew. New York: Smader, 1977. 138p.

Reactions to the Holocaust by survivors and by their children are transcribed in this moving drama. It takes place in Israel a generation after the Nazi atrocities. Flashbacks from the European past of several characters make a strong impact. Central to the play is the problem facing the younger generation: how to live without constantly being subjected to the effects of the Holocaust.

Frisch, Max. Andorra. New York: Hill & Wang, 1964. 88p.

Written as a fable, this drama is about a boy who thinks, incorrectly, that he is Jewish. The anti-Semitic citizens of Andorra, to which he was brought as a baby, also think he is a Jew and they mistreat him accordingly. Ultimately they kill him because he is Jewish and only then discover the truth. This is extremely powerful drama.

Goodrich, Frances, and Albert Hackett. The Diary of Anne Frank. New York: Random, 1956. 174p.

One of the best known Holocaust works is Anne Frank's Diary. The dramatized version of that book has been widely produced around the nation. Audiences seem to appreciate not only the suspense inherent in the situation of a family in hiding, living in fear of the Nazis, but also the characterization developed by the playwrights. Anne is not alone in her concealment in a warehouse; there are her parents, a sister, and others including three members of the Van Daan family, the son of which provides the young girl's romantic interest.

Hochhuth, Rolf. The Deputy. New York: Grove, 1964. 352p.

A thesis drama on the explosive topic of the failure of Pope Pius XII to come to the aid of the Jews during the Holocaust, this long, highly controversial five-act play was initially produced in 1963. There is a serious question about whether the author has been amply refuted by responses. This edition of the drama contains an informative historical appendix in which the playwright attempts to support his case. While not great drama, it may prove, in the long run, effective on another level. The hero, a Roman Catholic priest who tries to fight the Vatican's lack of involvement in the "Jewish question," may seem quite unbelievable in the scope of his relationships, but some of his arguments are damning to the character of the pope.

Miller, Arthur. <u>Playing for Time</u>. New York: Bantam, 1981. 151p.

This screenplay is based on Fania Fenelon's memoir of the same title (see page 54).

Ruffini, Gene. <u>The Choice</u>. New York: Anti-Defamation League, 1980. 83p.

Are atonement and redemption possible for Holocaust crimes? That is the painful question posed by the author of this two-act drama. It is set in New York City, in a Catholic mission for teen-agers. The play opens with a novelist, who has dedicated her life to exposing Nazi war criminals in hiding, revealing that one of the priests who heads the mission is a former SS officer responsible for the slaughter of more than 2,000 Jews in a small Polish community. The problem that the dramatist sets out to explore is treated better in philosophical than aesthetic terms.

Skloot, Robert, ed. <u>The Theatre of the Holocaust</u>. Madison: Univ. of Wisconsin Pr., 1982. 333p.

Four very powerful dramas that make a valuable contribution to the worlds of art and psychology are collected here. <u>Resort 76</u>, by Shimon Wincelberg, is hard hitting, inspiring, depressing, filled with black humor--all in superb balance; it is basically the story of how ghetto Jews suffer, survive, and perish under the Nazis. Mordechai Rumkowski, head of the Lodz Ghetto Jewish Council, is the focus of <u>Throne of Straw</u>, by Harold and Edith Lieberman. Betrayal of Jew by Jew is the unsettling theme of this play. Surreal technique describes George Tabori's <u>The Cannibals</u>, where characters are faced with starvation or eating human flesh. Some persons die, then live again as sons symbolically assume their dead fathers' identities. Charlotte Delbo contributes <u>Who Will Carry the Word?</u> to this anthology. The author is obsessed with the role of witness and survivor, but also with the increasing number of people who wish to be ignorant of horrifying truths. The editor's introduction is a helpful essay on these plays and on Holocaust theater in general.

POETRY

Borenstein, Emily. Night of the Broken Glass. Mason, Tex.: Timberline Pr., 1981. Unp.

Prose-poetry is the form in which this book, which deserves a much wider reputation, is written. The hybrid style seems exactly right for what the author attempts in this chilling volume. The Prologue sets the tone: "I fashion my poems out of the ashes of dead Jews." Agonies are portrayed; a baby is strangled so the hiding place of Jews will not be betrayed. Starvation and torture are such that an almost despairing persona asks: "In what language shall we cry out?" There is another question posed: "It is Hanukkah in the Lodz Ghetto./Where are the Maccabees?" It is clear that the author has absorbed Elie Wiesel's memoir Night. Several lines of his are practically appropriated for Borenstein's purpose and she is absolutely correct in her usage of them.

Gillon, Adam, ed. Poems of the Ghetto. New York: Twayne, 1969. 96p.

Some of the poetry found in this volume was written by major poets living in relative comfort in the United States or Great Britain. More was written in a basement, a concentration camp, or even a death van. The poets included are Czeslaw Milosz, Tadeusz Rozewicz, Jerzy Pietrkiewicz, and a dozen more. As the editor says in his introduction to these poems, "They are . . . a testament written by lost men, an awful indictment of humanity; but in at least some of its [the book's] pages one finds a glimmer of hope which, like a lonely star, shines over the sombre wilderness of the Nazi jungle."

Haushofer, Albrecht. Moabit Sonnets. New York: Norton, 1978. 204p.

While in solitary confinement awaiting death, chained hand and foot, the author wrote a series of eighty sonnets. Many of these poems are of praise and love, but some are angry and others express sorrow over the ravages of World War II. Sonnet IX even expresses compassion for the enemy: "Prisoners--they too. Will they understand that? Tomorrow? Later? Even?" Haushofer was executed just before the war's end. When his body was found three weeks later by his brother, his hand was clutching the manuscript hidden under his coat. This edition is in German and English.

Heyen, William. The Swastika Poems. New York: Vanguard, 1977. 82p.

Here are thirty poems by a German-American who is torn by the knowledge that two of his uncles died wearing Nazi uniforms.

There is a memorable "letter" to his father-in-law, who died for "your Fuehrer." It is followed by "My Nazi Uncle," an airman killed over Russia in 1941. The author struggles with his own father's emotions as the latter gazes at photos of his now dead brothers, who wear the uniform of the Third Reich. The narrator's response: "I often curse the two of you and spend my hours writing verses that wonder how your fiery, German romanticism started, and where, at last, if it did, it died." Another powerful poem is "Riddle," which asks, since everyone denies it, "Who killed the Jews?" Heyen is tortured by the image of "lampshade of jewskin," by the camps: "I do not think I will ever live a full day when I do not think of Belsen," and much else. Heyen's is a suffering awareness of inherited guilt.

Kolmar, Gertrud. <u>Dark Soliloquy</u>. New York: Seabury, 1975. 262p.
Translated from the German by Henry A. Smith, these lovely poems, sensitive and poignant, were written during the period of Nazi oppression. The author, also known as Gertrud Chodziesner, died at Auschwitz at forty-eight. Her work is becoming increasingly recognized--as it deserves.

Reznikoff, Charles. <u>Holocaust</u>. Los Angeles: Black Sparrow, 1975. 115p.
A founding member of the Objectivist school of poetry, Reznikoff here offers a book-length poem that is basically a collection of verse paraphrases and quotations from verbatim accounts of the trial records in this country and from Nazi confessions at the Nuremberg Trials. The volume, in twelve parts, ranges widely from "Deportation" (where 12,000 Jews are instantly shipped from their homes) through "Invasion" (in which SS men strip and beat Jews). "Research" (on ghastly medical experiments), ghetto atrocities, massacres, gas chambers and gas trucks, to work camps, the particular pathos of the situation of children, the mass graves and finally, for some, escape. There is even a segment titled "Entertainment" relating how Nazis were amused at the expense of the incarcerated. Here is powerful poetry.

Sachs, Nelly. <u>O the Chimneys</u>. New York: Farrar, 1967. 387p.
The author of this overwhelming volume of poetry was a German Jew who escaped to freedom in Sweden. She won the Nobel Prize for literature in 1966. The crematoria of the title are implicit in her every line, and the ultimate sadness is in the poems about children, in all of their innocence, being led to their deaths.

Snodgrass, W. D. <u>The Fuhrer Bunker</u>. Brockport, N.Y.: Boa, 1977. 72p.
A major American poet allows his imagination to reflect on

the last days of Hitler in all of their horror, all of their banality, all of their essence. In a series of monologues, we meet the personalities who were with Hitler to the end, when he committed suicide. Here are Albert Speer (hurt because there was no final handshake), Martin Bormann (a final letter to "Mommy-Girl"--his wife), Joseph Goebbels (concerned with appearances to the last), Eva Braun (so obsessed with marrying the Fuehrer) and, of course, Hitler himself. In an afterword Snodgrass gives a rationale for some of the details found in this work-in-progress: Eva Braun's favorite song was "Tea for Two" and Hitler did prefer "Who's Afraid of the Big, Bad Wolf" to Lohengrin, etc. Snodgrass wanted to investigate behind the public facade. "My poems, then, must include voices they would hide from others, even from themselves."

Volavkova, Hana, ed. I Never Saw Another Butterfly. New York: McGraw-Hill, 1964. 81p.

The last page of this heartbreaking book contains only the following: "A total of around 15,000 children under the age of fifteen passed through Terezin. Of these, around 100 came back." Wrenching poems by some of these children, along with their drawings, make up this moving work. They write of pain, of loss, of loneliness, of fear. Yet somehow there is also hope, love, and a sense of beauty.

Wiesel, Elie. Ani Maamin. New York: Random, 1973. 111p.

This cantata, performed at Carnegie Hall with music by Darius Milhaud, may be seen as a tremendous act of faith--given the author's experience. It is the story of Abraham, Isaac, and Jacob imploring God to have mercy, to interfere with the massacre of Jewish children during the Holocaust. But God seems unmoved through all of the pleading. The narrator's conclusion, so silently affirmative, is this: "And the silence of God is God." Eventually, a tear is seen in God's eye in this poignant work of art.

ART

Blatter, Janet, and Sybil Milton. Art of the Holocaust. New York: Rutledge Pr., 1981. 272p.

Critics have generally ignored the art produced in Nazi death camps. But rules of art need not apply to an aesthetic that came into existence after the standards were already established. This book proves the point. It is a documentary volume in the fullest sense. Not only is it a record of the art of a significant period in human history, but a collection of documents of history itself. Here are haunting portraits and self-portraits; the realistic and expressionistic presentation of torture and murder; the escapist paintings, wherein an artist might control events in a way that was not true in the subhuman concentration camps. The editors have provided two outstanding introductions. Janet Blatter gives an artistic, historical background of the era. She also tells of the difficulties the creators had with obtaining supplies. It was not even a matter of stealing ink and paper for most; that was nearly impossible. Sketching with burnt tree twigs, with the product of squeezed vegetables (which meant missing precious meals)--the ingenuity was enormous. So was the manner of hiding these paintings and works of sculpture. Sybil Milton discusses the legacy of Holocaust art, to which this volume is a testament. Over 350 works of art are pictured in this book, all from the ghettos and concentration camps. The spiritual resistance and courage, as exemplified by what can only be described as true art, found in this great book comprise a human treasure.

Constanza, Mary S. The Living Witness. New York: Free Pr., 1982. 196p.

Holocaust art--the paintings and drawings produced by inmates of the ghettos and concentration camps--is not pleasant. And yet it is uplifting. So much of it was done, consciously or not, to maintain humanity in an inhuman universe. Mary Constanza has searched out this art and some of the surviving artists to provide a moving account of the spirit of a suffering but surviving Judaism. Not only are many of the works reproduced on these pages, but interviews with seven of the artists as well. Although many of the artists did not survive the Nazis, their spirit did.

Green, Gerald. The Artists of Terezin. New York: Schocken, 1978. 193p.

Drawings add impact to Green's The Artists of Terezin. Although the author's script for the television series Holocaust and his novel of the same title are mediocre, there can be no denial of the influence Green's work has had on mass audiences. Perhaps those people who are moved by Green will begin to read Wiesel and Donat and Hilberg and Borowski and the many others who present the tragedy more vividly. In his Preface to this edition, Green writes that the seed of his Holocaust script is in this volume. Here he traces the experiences of four "main characters" in Terezin, which was showcased as a humane concentration center. Others also appear in this work; most were not artists before the war but worked at drawing and painting in Terezin. They attempted to smuggle out the art they created surreptitiously, since it told the truth about Terezin and the Nazis. Many of their efforts are reproduced in this book. Of the four protagonists, one died as a result of beatings, another was gassed, a third died soon after liberation, and one "survived." The sufferings of prisoners in Terezin, which was in actuality a collection point for Auschwitz, are clearly shown. It is significant that, as Green points out, the hearse dominated the imaginations of so many of the artists. It is also significant to note how the Red Cross, inspecting the camp, was deceived.

Heartfield, John. Photomontages of the Nazi Period. New York: Univ. Bks., 1977. 143p.

Originally named Helmut Herzfeld, the artist changed his name to John Heartfield after the Kaiser, in World War I, persuaded patriotic Germans to use the phrase "God punish England" when passing in the streets. He became one of the inventors of the photomontage technique (along with the celebrated artist George Grosz, in 1916). Bringing together apparently disparate portions of various photographs, Heartfield was able to satirize in a very effective way. Photomontage is said to show not only the facts as seen, but also to indicate the social tendency expressed by the facts. Comments on propaganda, German voters, war, Hitler, greed, and the Gestapo, have a powerful impact.

Hinz, Berthold. Art in the Third Reich. New York: Pantheon, 1980. 300p.

Not one single important work of painting or sculpture was produced by Nazi ideology; totalitarian control of art clearly militates against true creative inspiration. The Nazis used the visual arts for propaganda purposes, to further the philosophy of the Third Reich. Nationalistic and militaristic in character, this made-to-order genre was intended to glorify the ideal figure (in most cases blue-eyed, blond, always white), farmers, mothers (who raised their children in the Fascist manner), workers--whose efforts were directed toward national goals--the military, etc. Oversentimentality is, perhaps, the chief criticism of this work. The author's thesis is unusual--that the Nazi artists did such a poor job of portraying the average Germans that the results were ordinary and coarse. Nazi art, it can be concluded, actually served as anti-Nazi propaganda.

Kantor, Alfred. The Book of Alfred Kantor. New York: McGraw-Hill, 1971. 127p.

Only twenty percent of the one thousand prisoners who took part in a death march to the concentration camp at Terezin survived. The author of this book is one of those who lived. While in a displaced person's camp, Kantor produced 127 drawings that illustrated moments from his more than three years of Nazi captivity. The remarkable aspect of this art is in its innocence. As a teenager, Alfred lost his mother and his girlfriend and witnessed the terrible atrocities of the Holocaust. Some of his experience is rendered here in unique fashion. John Wykert's explanatory notes are quite helpful.

Lasansky, Maurice. The Nazi Drawings. Iowa City: Univ. of Iowa Pr., 1976.

Thirty unsettling atrocity drawings are represented in this staggering collection. Nazi murders, a woman trussed like a slab of meat, corpses, a woman impaled, and much else appears here in a volume prepared by a master print-maker.

Novitch, Miriam, ed. Spiritual Resistance. New York: Union of American Hebrew Congregations, 1981. 247p.

A collection of art from concentration camps covering the years 1940 to 1945, this book represents the work of forty-eight victim-artists. Miriam Novitch devoted thirty years of her post-war life to gathering the works. These colored reproductions cover a wide variety of art, from watercolors to gouaches. Many are in black-and-white because of the lack of materials available to the secret artists. And, of course, they had to rush their work, not having the leisure time ordinarily associated with creativity. The agony of the Jewish experience is poignantly captured here.

Rieth, Adolf. Monuments to the Victims of Tyranny. New York: Praeger, 1969. 104p.

Perhaps dated now, this volume is nevertheless a very useful collection of photographs (with a brief helpful introductory text) of sculpture and buildings that memorialize the atrocities of World War II. Israel and many European nations are represented among the 104 illustrations. There are photos of Roman Catholic, Protestant, and Jewish memorials in Dachau; of the monument to the war dead outside Leningrad; of the memorial for 360,000 murdered prisoners in the camp at Chelmno, Poland; of cemeteries; and of designs for works of art apparently still to be accepted. All are dignified and effective.

Saloman, Charlotte. Charlotte. New York: Harcourt, 1963. unp.

This picture diary is the record of a young girl's life under the Nazis. Charlotte Saloman, who perished in the Holocaust, was born of German-Jewish parents. She was in high school when Hitler came to power. She left school because she was being persecuted as a Jew and began to study art. Her parents sent her from Berlin to grandparents in France, but she found no refuge. Life with the grandparents, who could not understand her need for self-expression through art, was difficult. As the war came closer, they too became deeply affected; the grandmother, in fact, committed suicide. All of this is recorded in the eighty gouaches reprinted in this riveting volume.

Szajkowski, Zosa. An Illustrated Sourcebook on the Holocaust. New York: Ktav, 1977, 1979. 3v., 516p.

The first volume of this work is perhaps the most valuable of the three. All contain reproductions of public materials, wall posters, newspaper headlines, pamphlets, magazine covers, and cartoons from Germany, Belgium, Latvia, France, Hungary, and elsewhere. There are explanatory notes that accompany each of the figures, and while they are helpful they are less than complete. For example, documents in German, Hebrew, and other languages are not translated, merely pictured. Some 1,200 individual pieces are represented in these three volumes, mainly devoted to "popular" features that the average person could see. Included are illustrations of Jewish reaction and high spirit, as well as pro-Nazi abuse.

Toll, Nelly. Without Surrender. Philadelphia: Running Pr., 1978. 109p.

For thirteen months when a child, Nelly Toll and her mother were hidden from the Nazis by a Christian family. Young Nelly drew pictures of the atrocities she saw as she peered through boarded windows. When she matured, she became interested in Holocaust art found in the ghettos, concentration camps, and hiding places throughout Europe. She here collects eighty secretly produced works of art, made from the crudest of materials. An art historian in later years, Toll brings that expertise to the extensive narrative accompanying the black-and-white reproductions. Much of the art is extremely moving.

CRITICISM

Alexander, Edward. The Resonance of Dust. Columbus: Ohio State Univ. Pr., 1979. 256p.

Edward Alexander observes that the magnitude of the Holocaust event eliminates any possibility of its being used merely as a symbol or theme for authors. The writer understands that the psychological ambiguity of the tragedy will be reflected in the literature which cannot be sustained by a confident, controlled authorial voice. He pays special attention to the writers "who seemed to me primarily concerned with the relationship between the Holocaust and the course of Jewish history, the fate of the Jewish people" (Sachs, Wiesel, Singer, Kovner, Bellow, Kaplan). Alexander suggests that the touchstone of adequacy in Holocaust literature should be the recognition that the tragedy of the Jews is something more than material for written art. The ambiguity of the Holocaust literary response may prove a truer statement than any other kind of reply.

Bosmajian, Hamida. Metaphors of Evil. Iowa City: Univ. of Iowa Pr., 1979. 247p.

Hamida Bosmajian's exploration of modern German writers living through the shadow of Nazism is greatly influenced by Canada's enormously erudite myth-critic, Northrup Frye. Bosmajian looks at Gunter Grass, Rolf Hochhuth, Uwe Johnson, and other important figures, scrutinizing what she sees as intellectual and emotional defenses in their writings. Her discussion of metaphors and myths of evil is provocative as she analyzes the intellectual and emotional defenses of that segment of contemporary German literature influenced by the Holocaust.

Ezrahi, Sidra De Koven. By Words Alone. Chicago: Univ. of Chicago Pr., 1980. 262p.

Although this book is a valuable critique of the Holocaust in literature, it deals only with work written after the Holocaust period itself. Ezrahi's framework is original; she attempts to define a Jewish "Lamentation tradition" and examines certain authors from that perspective. She observes that the Lamentation tradition is rooted in scripture, that "the center of reference is the people and history of Israel; the ultimate assault of Nazism is on the survival and values of the community; and the Holocaust is perceived as a formative historical event." From this basis, the literature of such writers as Elie Wiesel, Tadeusz Borowski, Nelly Sachs, Arthur Miller, Saul Bellow, Andre Schwarz-Bart, and others is examined.

Friedlander, Saul. Reflections of Nazism. New York: Harper, 1984. 143p.

The preposition in the title of this analysis is important. The word is "of," not "on." Friedlander tries to show how certain artists, purposely or not, are finding a fascination with the myth of Adolf Hitler. They aesthetically rework, the author charges, a large number of Nazi rituals and symbols that tend to have great influence over audiences. The manner in which Hitler has been turned into a part of the entertainment industry troubles the author. He suggests that this is more than gratuitous reverie in many cases, more than just an expression of profound fears, but even "mute yearnings" as well. Discussed are such disparate writers and filmmakers as George Steiner, Joachim Fest, Albert Speer, Rainer Werner Fassbinder, and Hans-Jurgen Syberberg. Friedlander warns that attention has been shifted by some from the horrors of Nazism "to voluptuous anguish and ravishing images, images one would like to see going on forever."

Halperin, Irving. Messengers from the Dead. Philadelphia: Westminster, 1970. 144p.

The first book-length inquiry into Holocaust literature, this volume retains its value. Halperin is a Jew who, not having lived through the European terrors of World War II, tries to discover them and their significance through reading. He insists that the body of writings he analyzes be judged not first as literature but as moral teaching. Elie Wiesel's first five books receive their own chapter. There are inquiries into diaries and journals, and what the author calls the literature of "Spiritual Resistance" (including works by Jakov Lind, Josef Bor, Andre Schwarz-Bart, and the non-Jew Tadeusz Borowski). This is a short, valuable introduction to the genre.

Insdorf, Annette. Indelible Shadows. New York: Random, 1983. 234p.

The author has studied seventy-five films on the Holocaust, and discusses posing a question to not only the moviegoer but to the reader of books on the Holocaust as well: Where do artistic and moral integrity meet, where do they clash? Insdorf, who teaches courses on film at Columbia University and Yale, takes strong stands. She appreciates Sophie's Choice and The Pawnbroker very much. She also indicates how the Holocaust is barely touched on in such films as Julia, The Boys from Brazil, Ship of Fools, Exodus, Cabaret, and Marathon Man. The best works to come from Hollywood on the Holocaust are Judgment at Nuremberg, Voyage of the Damned, and The Diary of Anne Frank. Regarding films on television, Insdorf is less certain. She likes "Playing for Time," and cannot deny the impact of the "Holocaust" series, but questions the negative impact that commercials have on an audience that is thus interrupted in experiencing certain emotional effects. Documentary films such as The Sorrow and the Pity, Kitty: Return to Auschwitz, and particularly Night and Fog show the Holocaust with great fidelity to truth.

Langer, Lawrence. The Holocaust and the Literary Imagination. New Haven, Conn.: Yale Univ. Pr., 1975. 300p.

This work represents one of the important volumes of literary criticism about Holocaust literature. Langer writes that because of the legacy of physical horror and psychological discontinuity that writers of the Holocaust had experienced, they had to invent new ways to present their materials, be they autobiography, fiction, or poetry. This critic understands and analyzes the attempts of the various authors to confront an awesome reality that requires remembrance even while demanding a reverent silence. Wiesel, Kosinski, Celan, Aichinger, Boll, Steiner, Lind, and many others are penetratingly examined.

------. Versions of Survival. Albany: State Univ. of New York Pr., 1982. 267p.

There is no "typical" Holocaust survivor, insists Langer, nor was there such a thing as "typical" behavior of victims in the concentration camps. In this work, subtitled "The Holocaust and the Human Spirit," the author points out the inadequacies of language to cope with the problems of presenting the Holocaust to readers. Words like "suffering," "tragedy," and "dignity" cannot properly convey the full force of the awesomeness of what occurred at Auschwitz, Dora, Treblinka, etc. Focusing on the writing of Elie Wiesel, Gertrud Kolmar, and Nelly Sachs, the author indicates that not only were situations difficult in various ghettoes and camps, but also situations from time to time differed in the same ghettoes and camps. He writes that every memoir by a survivor must be read in some way as a work of imagination, at least in part, as the author selected details to relate in a process of organization.

Leiser, Erwin. Nazi Cinema. New York: Macmillan, 1975. 179p.

Hitler's ministry of Popular Enlightenment made German filmdom into an extremely efficient segment of Nazi propaganda geared toward projecting the infallibility of Adolf Hitler. Beyond that, it tried to support the concept of a master race, of the obligation to conquer the world, and the need to eliminate all Jews. Leiser analyzes widely known, as well as nearly forgotten, films, and he shows frightening examples of the use of this medium for brainwashing. Triumph of the Will shows Hitler as a New Siegfried; Jud Suss is about a Jewish criminal who rapes a German woman; a sentimental argument to justify mercy killing is the burden of Ich klage an. Part of Nazi policy was to eliminate movie criticism while insisting on the political function of each film.

Rosenfeld, Alvin. A Double Dying. Bloomington: Indiana Univ. Pr., 1980. 210p.

Alvin Rosenfeld's A Double Dying contains very important insights. He wants the literature of atrocity read on moral grounds as well as artistic. Thus, he states that "while no literature is beyond judgment, the particular body of writings under review here does not cry out in the first place, in my opinion, for aesthetic evaluation." Rosenfeld's findings are very well supported when he writes of the literature he finds to have merit (Wiesel, Wells, Levi, Borowski, for example), as well as of that which is inauthentic (Sophie's Choice in particular). Initially, the author states his theory of Holocaust literature and tells what his approach will be. He illustrates this with five chapters that apply his ideas to a large bulk of Holocaust literature. These are followed by an examination of the Nazi manipulation of the German language and a final chapter, Exploiting Atrocity, that discusses the Holocaust-for-profit motive of some authors.

COLLECTIONS

This chapter contains collections of a general nature. Placing them in a more specifically subject-oriented chapter would incorrectly limit their scope. Their importance should not be overlooked. The collections of primary documents are indispensable reading for serious scholars. The material gathered for publication in anthologies often represents the most powerful of all writings on the subject. Photograph and oral history collections contain records of unique impact.

DOCUMENTS

Arad, Yitzhak; Yisrael Gutman; and Abraham Margaliot, eds. Documents on the Holocaust. New York: Ktav, 1982. 504p.
Sources on the massacres of Jews in Germany, Austria, Poland, and the Soviet Union are contained in this excellent compendium. Extracts from Hitler's speeches and Goebbels's diary, the Nuremberg "Law for the Protection of German Blood and German Honor," the order for the liquidation of the ghettos of Ostland by Himmler, eyewitness accounts of atrocities, and much else are found here. It is depressing reading, but it is a necessary and handy compilation for those seriously interested in Holocaust studies. Entries average just over two pages each, and so there is an almost overwhelming variety of pieces from which to choose. And yet there is a sameness, too, in the uniformity of the tragic atmosphere surrounding all events referred to here.

Central Commission for Investigation of German Crimes in Poland. German Crimes in Poland. New York: Howard Fertig, 1982. 2v. in 1. 472p.

This is one of the definitive sources for study of the Holocaust. When the Second World War ended, the Polish provisional government collected an enormous amount of evidence of German war crimes, including eyewitness testimony, documents, memoirs, and photographs. Much of that is included in these two volumes. Volume 1 has chapters on the destruction of Polish Jewry, on the death camps of Auschwitz, Chelmno, and Treblinka, as well as others. The companion volume has essays on the concentration camps of Belzec, Sobibor, and Stutthof, on the liquidation of the Warsaw Ghetto, and on medical experiments in Ravensbruck. It is important to observe the book's perspective of Nazi crimes against the Jews, as nearly every part of this book emphasizes the uniqueness of the Jewish experience.

Dawidowicz, Lucy S., ed. A Holocaust Reader. New York: Behrman House, 1976. 397p.
Over five dozen documents, all primary sources, fill this book, each section helpfully introduced by the editor. These documents include anti-Semitic legislation (forbidding practice by non-Aryan lawyers, for example, and "Law for the Protection of German Blood and German Honor"), resettlement orders for the Warsaw Ghetto, eyewitness reports on Auschwitz, and the report by the commanding officer of the troops that destroyed Jewish resistance in Warsaw--and more, which highlight the first section, The Final Solution. Part 2, The Holocaust, features papers that indicate the spirit of some of the victims. Janusz Korczak's appeal for child care, songs, health care, how to wear the yellow badge (with pride), the way some confronted death, how many resisted the enemy, and other topics are also represented.

Hilberg, Raul, ed. Documents of Destruction. Chicago: Quadrangle, 1971. 292p.
Hilberg, a major Holocaust historian, brings together an authoritative and serviceable collection of previously unpublished German and Jewish documents basic to any serious study of the event. The editor's commentary is excellent.

Noakes, Jeremy, and Geoffrey Pridham, eds. Documents on Nazism, 1919-1945. New York: Viking, 1975. 704p.
The wide number of sources used makes this a valuable volume. The emphasis is on the workings of the Nazi machine and how it interacted with individuals as well as groups. It begins with an account of Hitler's recruitment into the German Worker's party in 1919 and ends with Hitler's last will and testament, written just before his suicide. All of the documents are set in context in a very useful fashion by the editors. Unfortunately, the index is quite inadequate.

ANTHOLOGIES

Chartok, Roselle, and Jack Spencer, eds. The Holocaust Years: Society on Trial. New York: Bantam, 1978. 295p.

Designed to serve as introductory material for high school students, this collection of readings works for college-level students as well. Featured are excerpts on the murder of Jews written by historians and eyewitnesses and others taken from Nazi testimony. Pieces on the Jewish situation in Europe, on prejudice and scapegoating, and on Jewish resistance follow. The Third Reich and its program for destruction of the Jews is then presented. What the Holocaust reveals about society in general is explored in some eighteen brief pieces, followed by items taken from literature and life that parallel the Holocaust; a final section "looks ahead" through ominous signs.

Friedlander, Albert. Out of the Whirlwind. New York: Schocken, 1976. 536p.

A reader of Holocaust literature, this anthology contains excerpts by some of the greatest writers of this genre: Elie Wiesel, Alexander Donat, Emil Fackenheim, Primo Levi, Chaim Kaplan, and others. There are memoirs (Donat, Anne Frank), reflections (Hans Jonas, Abraham Heschel), imaginative literature (Wiesel, Hochhuth), even a sampling of music and poetry by the victims. An interesting juxtaposition appears when Bruno Bettelheim's piece blaming Jews for participating in their own destruction is followed by Alexander Donat's authoritative rebuttal to that now-discredited thesis. This is probably the best anthology of Holocaust writings extant.

Furman, Harry, ed. Holocaust and Genocide: A Search for Conscience. New York: Anti-Defamation League, 1983. 217p.

In a diverse, one-volume approach to the Holocaust, some of the better known authors in this genre, such as Elie Wiesel, Nellie Sachs, Arthur Morse, Martin Gilbert, Terrence Des Pres, etc., are represented. Readers may be surprised to also find a satire on Eichmann by Lenny Bruce; a selection by Sammy Davis, Jr., "I Ain't Sleepin' Nexta No Nigger"; and lyrics by Bob Dylan, Paul Simon, or Mick Jagger and Keith Richards. It all succeeds very well: historical facts plus contemporary newspaper pieces; works dealing specifically with the Holocaust; others discussing racism, atrocities in Cambodia, Argentina, and elsewhere. Solid introductions and excellent questions for discussion make this a valuable text in spite of some sloppy editing.

Grobman, Alex, and Daniel Landes, eds. Genocide. Los Angeles: Simon Wiesenthal Ctr., 1983. 501p.

Subtitled "Critical Issues of the Holocaust," this is an

excellent one-volume introduction to the subject. Published as a companion to the film Genocide (an Academy Award winner), the anthology is for both the general reader and the high school or college student. Henry Feingold discusses why the Holocaust is considered a unique event by many thinkers in the opening section, followed by three short pieces on the film Genocide that place it in the context of the problem, asking whether or not there can be art after Auschwitz. Eight chapters discuss the history and culture of Jews in Europe before World War II. A powerful section entitled "Antisemitism," highlighted by a Christian view of theological anti-Semitism, is penetratingly presented by Paul Van Buren. John Pawlikowski raises the agonizing question, "The Holocaust: Failure in Christian Leadership?" Ysrael Gutman's concise history of the Holocaust is followed by a useful timeline. Other topics include contributions on German bureaucracy, SS troops, the ghettos (and their resistance movements), as well as concentration and death camp conditions. The Nuremberg Trials, Jewish religious life after the massacre, and a piece on World War II Nazis in the United States are followed by chapters on the implications of the Holocaust from Christian and Jewish perspectives.

Korman, Gerd, ed. Hunter and Hunted. New York: Delta, 1974. 320p.

This powerful anthology contains essays and excerpts of almost universal excellence, written by survivors, journalists, educators, historians, businessmen, and the Nazi hunter Simon Wiesenthal. Portions appear from Elie Wiesel's Night, Chaim Kaplan's Scroll of Agony, and Raul Hilberg's The Destruction of European Jewry; other authors include John Toland, Alexander Donat, and Kalman Friedman. The sweep of the anthology is broad and includes two views of the controversial head of the Warsaw Judenrat, Adam Czerniakow, and a poignant letter written by Max Korman to his wife about his trip on the ill-fated ship St. Louis.

Kugelmass, Jack, and Jonathan Boyarin. From a Ruined Garden. New York: Schocken, 1983. 275p.

For the purpose of commemorating the Jews murdered by Nazis and their collaborators in World War II, memorial books have been written by Eastern European survivors. This volume is a summary of over 100 such works. Arranged by topic, the organization includes communities, personalities, customs, and the Holocaust, among others. Jews in their daily activities in trades and the professions, at home, or in towns, are shown. The sadism of the Holocaust is portrayed, as are episodes of heroism. Another section describes how the few Jews who returned to their homes from the death camps were often unwelcome in certain areas-- some, as in Poland, even murdered.

Sherwin, Byron L., and Susan G. Ament, eds.   Encountering the Holocaust.   Chicago: Impact Pr., 1981.   502p.
Subtitled "An Interdisciplinary Survey," this compendium contains fourteen chapters on such topics as the antecedents of the Holocaust; international law on the subject of attempted genocide; the fiction, poetry and drama that came out of the event; and the diaries and memoirs that reveal so much of the personal anguish experienced by the victims. Also included are discussions of music, art, and film. The final section has two chapters by one of the editors, Byron Sherwin, on theological (Jewish and Christian) encounters on the subject and on philosophical reactions to--and moral implications of--the Holocaust.

Staff of the Washington Post.   The Obligation to Remember. Washington, D.C.: Washington Post, 1983. 66p.
In April, 1983, some 14,000 Holocaust survivors gathered in Washington, D.C., to commemorate those who died at the hands of the Nazis, to share memories they alone could fully comprehend, and to warn the world of future possibilities. This anthology, illustrated with photographs of the atrocities as well as those from the meeting, is a useful introduction to World War II brutalities. Included are twenty-one articles on the Warsaw Ghetto uprising, the failure of the Allies to bomb Auschwitz, theologians' views of the Holocaust, the impact of the events on children of survivors, and much more. Incorporated also is President Reagan's address at the opening ceremony, as well as a brief piece on Elie Wiesel, chairman of the United States Holocaust Memorial Council, which sponsored and organized the gathering.

Strom, Margot Stern, and William S. Parsons, eds.   Holocaust and Human Behavior.   Watertown, Mass.: International Educations, 1982. 405p.
A solid text for Holocaust studies, this is more than a collection of pieces around various themes. It is an intelligent gathering of insights on major aspects of the tragedy of World War II, with excellent introductions and transitions that are informative but not overwhelming. Such topics as society and the individual, anti-Semitism, German history before the Holocaust, who knew about the massacres--and did what--are examined. So is the problem of the Armenian genocide, a valuable inclusion. What is to be learned from all of this for now and the future is the subject of a fine final chapter.

PHOTOGRAPHS

Aptecker, George.   Beyond Despair.   Morristown, N.J.: Kahn & Kahan, 1980. unp.

A series of impressive Aptecker photographs illustrate brief quotations from Holocaust writers including Elie Wiesel, Raul Hilberg, Yehuda Bauer, and others. The black-and-white photos are at once bizarre and incisive, giving a special focus to interpreting the disaster from a unique viewpoint. Wiesel's introductory piece enhances the value of this work. Typically, he raises questions and only suggests answers: "Will there be a day when we will know what was the reality of Auschwitz? Perhaps Auschwitz never existed, except for those who left there, beneath the ashes, a part of their future in pledge." Aptecker's photographs, too, appear to record questions that only hint at responses--except, perhaps, a response of hope.

Gilbert, Martin.   The Holocaust.   New York: Hill & Wang, 1979.   59p.
Twenty-three maps and sixty photographs make up this collection by historian Martin Gilbert. Described as "a record of the destruction of Jewish life in Europe during the dark years of Nazi rule," the work is a handy visual resumé of anti-Semitism throughout the centuries. Some of the photographs, while necessarily not very sharply reproduced, are nevertheless quite moving.

Hellman, Peter.   The Auschwitz Album.   New York: Random, 1982. 167p.
Based on an album of photographs found by Lili Meier, a concentration camp survivor, this book contains 185 pictures of Jews in the Nazi death camps of Auschwitz and Birkenau. Seventeen-year-old Lili found the album in a German barracks after the war where she was recovering from typhus; it was titled "Resettlement of Jews from Hungary." Pictures of her family and friends were in it, apparently the only photos to have been taken of the millions of prisoners sent to Auschwitz. There are no scenes of overt violence in this collection, but the record of an enormous tragedy is on every page. Peter Hellman's text is an appropriate accompaniment.

Schoenberner, Gerhard.   The Yellow Star.   New York: Bantam, 1973.   288p.
With almost 200 photographs illustrating the persecution of Jews during the twelve years of the Third Reich, this is a valuable, saddening, frightening compilation. Hangings, firing squads, deportations, naked humiliations, searches, piles of bodies, the terror of children, Nazi leaders, documents, and more are contained in this nonscholarly work. The brief textual remarks are useful and add to the value of this work.

ORAL HISTORY

Rothchild, Sylvia, ed. <u>Voices from the Holocaust.</u> New York: New Amer. Lib., 1981. 456p.

There are a number of oral history projects in the United States with the goal of interviewing as many Holocaust survivors as possible. They seek to accurately record the actual events, the day-by-day living, the horrors, the heroics, and the after-effects of the Holocaust. The pages in this volume were selected from 650 hours of taped interviews taken by the William E. Wiener Oral History Library of the American Jewish Committee. The book is in three sections dealing with life before, during, and after the Holocaust. It makes for compelling reading.

INSTRUCTOR'S GUIDE

Hirt, Robert S., and Thomas Kessner, eds., <u>Issues in Teaching the Holocaust.</u> New York: Yeshiva Univ. Pr., 1981. 115p.

A result of various conferences and institutes on the teaching of the Holocaust, this guide is in two parts. The initial segment concentrates on the teaching of the Holocaust; the second section contains essays on important related topics. Some titles include: "Jewish and Psychological Factors in the Teaching of the Holocaust," "Some Counsels and Cautions in Teaching the Holocaust," "Christian Response to the Holocaust," and "Theological and Philosophical Response to the Holocaust." One important piece is "Teaching the Holocaust," in which author Norman Lamm discusses nine topics that must be a part of any Holocaust curriculum: the demonic nature of humans; racial and religious discrimination; resistance; the spectators who did not wish to get involved; the situation of Jews in the Christian world; Nazi ideology; Jewish religious resistance; the State of Israel; the obligations of the Holocaust for Jewish people.

RESEARCHING THE HOLOCAUST GUIDANCE FOR STUDENTS

Dan Sharon

A first step for the beginning Holocaust researcher would be to read the article "Holocaust" in the Encyclopaedia Judaica (Macmillan, 1972). This is a good introductory survey, with a bibliography at the end of the article listing sources for additional research. Asterisked words within the article designate topics important enough to have their own entries. One can consult the index volume for the exact volume and column number. This feature should be kept in mind, particularly if one of the starred topics is of interest for further research.

Other introductions to the subject are sections on the Holocaust in any of the following well-written one-volume histories of the Jewish people:

> Eban, Abba. Heritage: Civilization and the Jews (New
> York: Summit, 1984).
> ------. My People (New York: Behrman House, 1968).
> Roth, Cecil. A Short History of the Jewish People
> (Hartford, Conn.: Hartmore House, 1969).
> Sachar, Abram. A History of the Jews (New York: Knopf,
> 1948).

The Holocaust, by Nora Levin (New York: Crowell, 1968) is a single-volume account, written for the nonscholar, that will give a summary of the broad scope of this subject.

Dan Sharon is reference librarian, Asher Library, Spertus College of Judaica, Chicago.

A graphic introduction to the geography and chronology of the Holocaust is Martin Gilbert's The Macmillan Atlas of the Holocaust (New York: Macmillan, 1982). The well drawn maps and concise captions and notes provide basic statistics and place the subject in a geographical context.

An excellent older bibliography is Jacob Robinson's The Holocaust and After: Sources and Literature in English (Jerusalem: Israel Univ. Pr., 1973). This book-length bibliography is arranged by subject: "Roots and Essence of National Socialism with Special Reference to Anti-Semitism," "Children of the Holocaust," and "Resistance." Both books and articles are listed. A shorter, less comprehensive bibliography is Henry Friedlander's "The Holocaust: Anti-Semitism and the Jewish Catastrophe," included in The Study of Judaism: Bibliographical Essays (New York: published for the Anti-Defamation League of B'nai B'rith by Ktav, 1972). This bibliography has the advantage of being annotated.

Journal articles have special value because they often contain the results of more recent scholarship than the monographs. For current articles appearing in journals, the following indexes should be consulted under the entries "Holocaust" or "Holocaust, Jewish (1939-1945)":

> Index to Jewish Periodicals.
> Reader's Guide to Periodical Literature.
> Religion Index One: Periodicals (formerly Index to Religious Periodical Literature).
> Social Sciences and Humanities Index (later just the Social Sciences Index).

The library catalog is, of course, always the most convenient and practical major resource to search. The first subject heading to check is HOLOCAUST, JEWISH (1939-1945). Books about specific subtopics in Holocaust literature appear in the catalog after the general books, and have a hyphenated addition to the basic subject heading. For example, personal accounts and memoirs, important eyewitness sources for the Holocaust, can be found under HOLOCAUST, JEWISH (1939-1945)--PERSONAL NARRATIVES. Accounts limited to one country can be found under HOLOCAUST, JEWISH (1939-1945)--(Name of Country). Since "Holocaust" is a relatively new term, cross-reference cards appear in the catalog directing the searcher to older books on the subject. Thus:

> HOLOCAUST, JEWISH (1939-1945)--see also
> WORLD WAR, (1939-1945)--JEWS

The names of concentration camps were formerly given in subject headings in their original languages. In such a case, the following cross-reference can be indispensable:

AUSCHWITZ (CONCENTRATION CAMP)--see also
OSWIECIM (CONCENTRATION CAMP)
The subject heading JEWS IN-- can be helpful in a more general
way. It can refer either to a country (JEWS IN POLAND),
a city (JEWS IN WARSAW), or even an entire continent
(JEWS IN EUROPE).

General non-Jewish background material can be found under
the name of a country itself, followed by the appropriate
subheading, like GERMANY-HISTORY--1939-1945. The searcher
should not forget movements, NATIONAL SOCIALISM, and ideas,
RACISM, ANTI-SEMITISM. Besides the names of individual concentration camps, one can look under a general heading covering
the entire subject, like CONCENTRATION CAMPS. For biographies of individuals active in the "Final Solution" and other
aspects, look under their names: HITLER, ADOLF or EICH-
MANN, ADOLF. Occasionally, a single outstanding event during
the Holocaust has its own subject heading, such as WARSAW-
HISTORY-UPRISING 1943. Other relevant subject headings
that might not be readily apparent are GENOCIDE, WORLD
WAR, 1939-1945--UNDERGROUND MOVEMENTS, JEWISH (the
latter for general works on Jewish armed resistance to the Nazis),
WAR CRIMINALS, and WAR CRIME TRIALS.

For libraries using the Library of Congress classification
system, these are the call numbers to browse in: D810J4 for books
on Jews in World War II (i.e., the Holocaust). DS135 is the
number for the history of the Jews in Europe, country by country.
D804 is the number for concentration camps. DD247-DD251 covers
Germany under Nazi rule. This includes general histories of the
Third Reich, biographies of Nazi party leaders, etc. Appropriate
Dewey call numbers are the 940.5s.

REFERENCE WORKS

Cargas, Harry James. The Holocaust: An Annotated Bibliography. Haverford, Pa.: Catholic Library Assn., 1977.
86p.

Containing short descriptions of 425 books and articles on
the Holocaust, this bibliography served as the forerunner to the
work in hand. Most of the books listed in the earlier compilation
are treated in greater detail here. The initial collection may
still be found useful for the articles mentioned, however. The
breakdown is somewhat different, as well, using twelve categories:
History; Hitler and Associates; Regional Events; Resistance;
Camps and Ghettos; Eyewitness Accounts; Samaritans; Justice;
Theological, Philosophical and Psychological Reflections
and Interpretations; The Arts: Fiction, Poetry, Drama, Art
and Interpretative Works; Children's Literature; Miscellaneous.

Friedlander, Henry. "The Holocaust: Anti-Semitism and the Jewish Catastrophe." In The Study of Judaism: Bibliographical Essays. New York: Ktav for Anti-Defamation League, 1972.
This is a good survey of basic sources on the Holocaust. More general and less comprehensive than the Robinson work, this might be a less overwhelming introduction to the subject. Also, since this is a bibliographical essay, helpful comments are included after most entries.

Friedman, Philip. "Problems of Research on the European Jewish Catastrophe." In The Catastrophe of European Jewry: Antecedents, History, Reflections. Jerusalem: Yad Vashem, 1976.
An illuminating essay by a veteran historian, this book discusses varying approaches taken by Jewish scholars researching the Holocaust. Some interesting archival sources are listed. In addition, Leni Yahil's "The Holocaust in Jewish Historiography," found in the same volume, deals with philosophical and ideological differences among Jewish historians on the subject of the Holocaust.

Gilbert, Martin. The Macmillan Atlas of the Holocaust. New York: Macmillan, 1982. 265p.
Some 316 maps and 60 photographs make up this study of the Nazi massacre of European Jews. All are arranged chronologically, so that this book can serve as a unique text on the Holocaust. The murder of non-Jews, including Gypsies, Spanish republicans, Jehovah's Witnesses, and Russian war prisoners is also chronicled. All of Gilbert's maps were drawn specifically for this atlas and are not found elsewhere. These include maps of slave labor camps, death march routes, deportations, and invasions as well as liberation maps and one showing the final numbers of murdered Jews by nation: Poland, 3,000,000; Greece, 65,000; Denmark, 77, for example.

Index of Articles on Jewish Studies. Jerusalem: Magnes Pr., Hebrew Univ., 1969.
Remarks for the Index to Jewish Periodicals generally apply here, except that this index covers more British periodical literature. It is also more scholarly, and includes works in other languages. Look up the "Jewish History" section in each volume.

Index to Jewish Periodicals. Cleveland Heights, Ohio: 1963.
The title is self-explanatory. Only English-language periodicals are indexed, mostly American, with one or two British journals included. Look up "Holocaust" in each volume. This continues where the Robinson bibliography stops, at least for periodical literature.

Muffs, Judith Hershlag. The Holocaust in Books and Films. New York: Anti-Defamation League, 1982. 67p.

A selected and annotated list, this is a handy resource bibliography giving brief descriptions of the books and films under useful headings. Other resources are also noted here, including the addresses of Holocaust centers throughout America, as well as Anti-Defamation League regional offices.

Robinson, Jacob. The Holocaust and After: Sources and Literature in English. Jerusalem: Israel Univ. Pr., 1973.

An excellent book-length bibliography on the subject, this work is divided into sections dealing with general background, the Holocaust itself, the reaction of the outside world (both Jewish and non-Jewish), and post-Holocaust developments. Both books and periodicals are noted.

Snyder, Louis. Enclyopedia of the Third Reich. New York: McGraw-Hill, 1976. 410p.

A very valuable one-volume reference work for the nonscholar interested in the facts of World War II and the Holocaust, this work is filled not only with basic facts but also with important, little known data as well. For instance, there is a chronology of every important date in the history of the Third Reich, as well as an entry on "Anti-Semit," a roll-your-own tobacco introduced by the Nazis in 1920. Hitler, the Nuremberg Laws, Martin Niemoeller, and other major topics are presented, as are less expected ones like films in the Third Reich, the Rublee Plan (unsuccessful proposal for the rescue of Jews from Nazi Germany), religion in the Third Reich, Halder Plot (to remove Hitler from power), Adolf Reichwein (professor executed for opposition to Hitler), and much more.

Wistrich, Robert. Who's Who in Nazi Germany. New York: Macmillan, 1982. 359p.

About 350 men and women prominent in the Third Reich receive entries here--averaging some 300 words each. There is an enormous amount of information presented. The compiler has attempted to link the careers of those represented here "to form an intricate web reflecting the multitude of cross-connections that made up Hitler's Germany." A particularly valuable aspect of this volume is that, where possible, Wistrich outlines the careers of individuals after the war. He indicates the war criminals who received lenient sentences, and documents those who were able to continue their lives relatively undisturbed. Another feature is the inclusion of women and men forced to leave their homeland because they were Jews (Einstein, for example) or for political reasons (Thomas Mann).

PERIODICALS AND ANNUAL PUBLICATIONS

Two periodicals devoted specifically to Holocaust studies are important:

Holocaust and Genocide Studies: An International Journal
Webster University
St. Louis, Mo. 63119
(U.S. address)

SHOAH
250 West 57th Street
New York, N.Y. 10107

Two single issues of scholarly periodicals that have been devoted to the Holocaust are the following:

"The Holocaust"
Centerpoint
Vol. 4 No. 1, July, 1980
The Graduate School and University Center
City University of New York
33 West 42nd Street
New York, N.Y. 10036

"Reflections on the Holocaust"
The Annals (of the American Academy of Political and Social Science)
Vol. 450, July, 1980
3937 Chestnut Street
Philadelphia, Pa. 19104

The Simon Wiesenthal Annual is published by Rossel Books for the Los Angeles Center. The first volume, edited by Alex Grobman, was published in 1984. It contains articles by, among others, Henry Friedlander, Sybil Milton, John Conway, Yisrael Gutman, and Christopher Browning, and covers women and the Holocaust, the Vilna Ghetto, the camera as a documentary weapon, etc.

RESOURCE CENTERS

Resource centers are available to those who wish further information on the Holocaust. Among them are the following:

Center for Studies on the Holocaust
Anti-Defamation League of B'nai B'rith

823 United Nations Plaza
New York, N.Y. 10017

The Delaware Holocaust Education Committee
Jewish Federation of Delaware
101 Garden of Eden Rd.
Wilmington, Del. 19803

Greater Orlando Holocaust Resource and Education Center
851 North Maitland Ave.
P.O. Box 1508
Maitland, Fla. 32751

Holocaust Awareness Institute Center for Judaic Studies
University of Denver
University Park
Denver, Colo. 80208

Holocaust Center of Greater Pittsburgh
315 S. Bellefield Ave.
Pittsburgh, Pa. 15213

The Holocaust Library and Research Center of San Francisco
639-14th Ave.
San Francisco, Calif. 94118

Holocaust Survivors Memorial Foundation
350 Fifth Ave.
New York, N.Y. 10001

Martyrs Memorial and Museum of the Holocaust
6506 Wilshire Blvd.
Los Angeles, Calif. 90048

National Institute on the Holocaust
P.O. Box 2147
Philadelphia, Pa. 19103

National Jewish Resource Center
250 West 57th St.
Suite 216
New York, N.Y. 10019

St. Louis Holocaust Center
611 Olive St.
Suite 1778
St. Louis, Mo. 63101

Simon Wiesenthal Center of Holocaust Studies
9760 West Pico Blvd.
Los Angeles, Calif. 90035

Southeastern Florida Holocaust Memorial Center, Inc.
Bay Vista Campus
Florida International University
151st Street and Biscayne Blvd.
Miami, Fla. 33181

United States Holocaust Memorial Council
Suite 832
425 13th St. NW
Washington, D.C. 20004

Zachor Institute for Holocaust Studies
4200 Biscayne Blvd.
Miami, Fla. 33137

REGIONAL INDEXES

By Nation

Books about specific countries or cities are listed by author under the name of the country or city (Vilna in Lithuania and Lodz and Warsaw in Poland).

By Concentration Camp

Books about specific concentration camps are listed by author.

AUTHOR-TITLE INDEX

Harry James Cargas is a professor of Literature and Language, and of Religion, at Webster University in St. Louis, Missouri. He serves on the Executive Committee of the United States Holocaust Memorial Council. Cargas has written 22 books and numerous articles on the Holocaust and topics in religion and philosophy.